Who Owns Academic Work?

Thomas J. Wilson Prize

The Board of Syndics of Harvard University Press
has awarded this book the thirty-first annual
Thomas J. Wilson Prize, honoring the late director
of the Press. The Prize is awarded to the book
chosen by the Syndics as the best first book
accepted by the Press during the calendar year.

CORYNNE McSHERRY

Who Owns Academic Work

BATTLING FOR CONTROL
OF INTELLECTUAL PROPERTY

Harvard University Press

Cambridge, Massachusetts, and London, England · 2001

Library of Congress Cataloging-in-Publication Data

McSherry, Corynne, 1969–
  Who owns academic work? : battling for control of intellectual property / Corynne McSherry.
    p. cm.
  Includes bibliographical references and index.
  ISBN 0-674-00629-1 (alk. paper)
  1. Intellectual property—United States. 2. Copyright—United States. 3. Public domain (Copyright law)—United States. 4. Scholarly publishing—United States. 5. Academic freedom—United States. I. Title.

KF2979 .M37 2001
346.7304′8—dc21   2001024463

To my mother

CONTENTS

AAUP   American Association of University Professors

AUTM   Association of University Technology Managers

COI   Conflict of Interest (Committee)

CP   Cognitive Property

IP   Intellectual Property

NSF   National Science Foundation

TTA   Technology Transfer Associate

TTO   Technology Transfer Office

UW   University of the West

Who Owns Academic Work?

Introduction

On May 5, 1993, Dr. Joseph Kraut, a senior biochemist at the University of California, San Diego (UCSD), received a disturbing phone call. Kraut's collaborator, Dr. Sam Wilson of the National Institutes of Health (NIH), had just learned that Agouron Pharmaceuticals was quietly working on the same project that had occupied Kraut and Wilson's attention for several years. Wilson feared that, given its substantial financial and intellectual resources, Agouron might obtain and publish results ahead of the NIH-UCSD team. Kraut shared that fear, but he wasn't especially alarmed on his own behalf. He was reaching the end of a successful career, and being "first" was no longer as crucial to his professional life as it once had been. But he had long since handed over the project—the growth of a three-dimensional crystal of a protein, polymerase beta (pol ß), that had been linked to cell repair of DNA—to a young postdoctoral researcher, Huguette Pelletier, and pol ß was supposed to be her ticket to scientific success.

Kraut grew more alarmed when he learned that Agouron's research was being managed by Jay Davies, who was married to one of Kraut's former graduate students, Michele McTigue. Pelletier, McTigue, and Davies had all received their doctorates in Kraut's lab. McTigue had a key to the lab, access to the pol ß data, and an open dislike for Pelletier. Certain that McTigue was channeling information to her husband, Kraut and Pelletier took McTigue's key away and filed protests with the UCSD

Academic Senate and the chief executive officer of Agouron. With all cards now on the table, the game was on.

Ten months later Agouron's researchers published a paper reporting substantial results in *Cell,* the leading journal in the field. Pelletier had been scooped. She could still publish her results—and did, in *Science*—but she would never be "first." Pelletier's only logical course, it seemed, was to cut her losses, start a new research project, and hope for better luck next time. She chose instead to sue Agouron for misappropriation of trade secrets.

Misappropriation of trade secrets? A trade secret is "a process or device for continuous use in the operation of business," the dissemination of which is carefully guarded by that business.[1] The formula for Coca-Cola is a trade secret, as are aspects of the construction of a Colt M-16 rifle. But surely there is a difference between scientific data produced in a public university and the formula for Coca-Cola? If so, that distinction was not clear to the San Diego jury that heard the case. In 1998, much to Agouron's surprise, Pelletier won her lawsuit.

The jury's inability to discern a qualitative difference between academic biochemical research and commercial recipes is emblematic of the rapidly changing configuration of the production of academic knowledge. In 1967 the many theorists concerned with the research university gave short shrift to issues of intellectual property (IP) (Barzun, 1968; Stadtman, 1970; Kerr, 1963/1995). In 1997 a former Stanford University president identified ethical management of intellectual property—patents, copyrights, trademarks, publicity rights, and perhaps even trade secrets—as one of the principal duties of the academy (Kennedy, 1997). The university's traditional service mission, once construed as an obligation to provide tools for public decisionmaking, has been substantially redefined to mean the transfer of university research from academia to the market via patenting and licensing.

This redefinition has not gone unquestioned. As university-industry partnerships proliferate, naturalizing metaphors for those partnerships such as "ecosystems," "incubators," and "infant technologies" are being met by fervent invocations of professorial autonomy and academic freedom. Ironically, though, academic freedom is increasingly treated as commensurate with ownership of intellectual property.[2] For example, faculty members, administrators, librarians, and students are mobilizing on several fronts in a war over control of academic copyrights, a war that is, in essence, a struggle over which knowledge workers can continue to position themselves as autonomous knowledge owners.

In this book I investigate the social production of academic intellectual property, or the bundle of rights the academy asserts with respect to intangible things. I explore how this property is formed and deployed, where, with what consequences, and for whom, and the border skirmishes attendant upon that productive process. In particular, I assess the stakes, for the law and the academy, of using intellectual property regimes to define and defend academic work. It is no longer surprising that a wronged postdoc would turn to intellectual property law to protect her investment of time and training. But the Pelletier case also bespeaks the cultural gyrations involved in using intellectual property categories as shields. To make her experience "count" in legal terms, Pelletier had to reconstruct the techniques and products of technoscience—experimental procedures, charts, data—as proprietary.[3] Indeed, she had to persuade the court that the entire pol ß project was "hers"—that her mentor had "given" it to her when he (or, more precisely, the University of California) hired her to work on it. She had to argue that the data were not simply facts but also the products of her "creative inspiration." She had to convince a jury that the labor, inspiration, and financial investment of assistants, a scientific community, her mentor, her university, and funding agencies did not make those entities joint proprietors of those products. Finally, she had to present scientific work as a trade, the practice of which involved secrecy, intrigue, confidentiality, and verbal contract. Accurate or not, this vision of scientific work is a far cry from the open, ethical community of scholarship in which many scholars prefer to imagine they participate. And nothing less than this vision would suffice if Pelletier wanted the courts to recognize that a wrong had been done.

In short, Pelletier had to tell a persuasive "property story," a term the legal theorist Carol Rose (1994) uses to describe narratives that offer to explain the origins of property institutions.[4] Property tales, Rose suggests, both speak to and constitute moral communities by setting up shared principles and assumptions that make origin stories seem like common sense. For this common sense to be maintained, property stories must be continually retold, and that retelling must assume and construct an audience. Further, ownership is a communicative act. To stake a proprietary claim, one must be skilled in the use of codes meaningful to an audience of persons interested in the object in question.[5] Property, then, depends on and continually re-creates a shared discursive field, a formation of statements, terms, categories, and beliefs.

More accurately, as the Pelletier case demonstrates, property depends on and re-creates *multiple* discursive fields, for heterogeneous discourses "appeal to one another's 'truths' for authority and legitimation" (Scott, 1988, 35). For example, Pelletier called on, even as she arguably subverted, the discourse of academic freedom to justify her property claim. By university tradition and policy, researchers are assigned most property rights in unpatentable works of scholarship in order to ensure that they are "free to publish" without interference from the administration. Pelletier argued that this policy extended to research results as well. Thus, following her university's own conflation of freedom with property rights, Pelletier was able to portray the propertization of scientific facts as consonant with academic tradition.[6] At the same time, the discursive fields of academic freedom and private property must remain distinct for scientific facts to retain their cultural weight. The discourse of academic freedom, after all, is based on the assumption that the university is a special site of disinterested inquiry, not a market for the exchange of intellectual property. Indeed, even as she analogized academic science with industrial production, Pelletier was careful to position herself as a scholar and a professional who had been cruelly misused by greedy commercial entities.

Because it involves the judicious and often complicated retelling of multiple narratives, property formation requires the simultaneous delineation of borderlines between those narratives. Legal theorists have long since observed that property marks, instantiates, and traverses borders, especially the "troubled boundary between individual man and the state" (Reich, 1964/1978, 179). I am interested in a slightly different set of troubled boundaries: between academic and legal discourses, between gift and market economies, and between public and private domains of knowledge. Borrowing an analytical tool from science and technology studies, I track the production of "boundary objects," concepts that carry different meanings for different audiences but are imbued with enough shared meaning to establish a common discursive territory (Star and Griesemer, 1989; Fujimura, 1992). I draw on legal, historical, and qualitative research to explore the cultural work involved in making and containing boundary objects at the intersection of legal, corporate, scientific, and technological discourses, and the consequences of that work for the subjects and objects of academic knowledge production. What decisions go into turning academic intellectual products into legal property, and what is the history of that process in university settings? What are the conditions that make it possible for the fruits of academic research, which are often understood by their producers as well as those who fund that production as fundamentally "public," to be treated as private property? What contests for meaning arise when academics position themselves as knowledge owners, and how are these contests resolved?

The stakes of these interrogatories seem particularly high in a society rapidly reorganizing around an informational mode of development (Castells, 1996; 1998). While an exploration of the nature of information and the information society as such lies far beyond the scope of this book, these shifting categories inform the epistemic regime with which we will be concerned. Information is crucial to the operation of any society, but it is now placed front and center as a political, economic, and ontological category. "I think," declares the sociologist Manuel Castells, "therefore I produce" (1998, 379). "Information society" designates a system of social relations oriented—economically, politically, legally, and culturally—toward the production, commodification, circulation, and manipulation of information (Boyle, 1997). Today, popular and academic literatures divide countries and communities into the "information-rich" and the "information-poor." The global labor force is also divided, between a generic, eminently replaceable, class of unskilled workers and a highly individualized class of educated and self-educable skilled "professionals." The "invisible goods" these workers and professionals produce are overtaking physical goods as a proportion of world trade and manufacture. It is not surprising, in this context, that intellectual property disputes have become central forums for debates over freedom of speech and the meaning of personhood (Barber, 1997; Coombe, 1996; Rabinow, 1996). If, as Castells argues, the action of knowledge upon knowledge (as opposed to the action of knowledge on machine) has become the main source of productivity, it follows that the ownership of knowledge denotes control of a central means of production. And that control depends, in large part, on both the circulation of property stories and the ongoing boundary work those stories occasion.

I seek to deepen our understanding of that boundary work by critically examining one set of property narratives on the much touted "knowledge frontier" (Faulkner and Senker, 1995). Taking as a starting point the curious fact that both IP law and the university currently are represented as "in crisis," in Chapter 1 I consider whether and how the "crises" of these two systems of knowledge management might be related. Tracing the historical emergence of IP law and the modern research university reveals that intellectual property is defined in contradistinction to a conceptual space—namely, the public domain—largely if not exclusively governed in the United States by the university. Put simply, intellectual property law polices the knowledge that can be owned, the realm of artifact, while the university polices the knowledge that cannot be owned, the realm of fact and universal truth.

In subsequent chapters I explore the controversies and negotiations that are shaping the articulation of academic intellectual property and the operation of boundary objects to manage the destabilizing effects of that articulation. In Chapter 5 I return to the Pelletier case and the propertization of scientific facts. In this case, special characteristics and norms of the university—rooted in principles of disinterested rationality, communal obligations, and trust—secure and are secured by individual property rights. Considered against the background of cases and activities described in earlier chapters, *Pelletier* suggests that the academy's own foundational terms—autonomy, freedom, integrity, collaboration, trust—implicate a discourse in which "the claim to describe man becomes the practice of the owner" (Edelman, 1979, 25). As in other arenas, property rights discourse offers to preserve and protect a "balance" between private property and the commons, even as the invocation of that discourse assists in a fundamental reconfiguration of that balance.

The production of IP is an ongoing process of enlistment and subversion that involves users as well as producers, and academics are involved in every stage of that activity. My focus here, however, is on problems of ownership by a particular set of creators, not on an analysis of the productive work of academics as "consumers" of IP. Fortunately, others have taken up various aspects of that analysis (see, for example, Crews, 1993; Coombe, 1994; 1996; Okerson, 1996).

My goal is to map the processes in and through which university research is reconfigured as property and scholars are repositioned as owners. Knowledge workers and knowledge owners are engaged, willing or unwilling, in a complex political battle fought on uncertain terrain. This battle is too often framed in utopic/dystopic terms that obscure the cultural, historical, and social dimensions of what has been called a "second academic revolution" (Etzkowitz, 1997). By making the many facets and tensions of academic property stories explicit, I hope to bring some of those dimensions into sharper relief, and thereby lay the groundwork for an empirically engaged politics of intellectual property.

In this book I demonstrate how IP is produced in the university and offer a snapshot of the university and IP law in a moment of dramatic change. I hope I also do rather more. With due respect to the many thoughtful critiques of "academic capitalism," my central concern is not whether it is good or bad to think of academic knowledge as intellectual property, but rather what it means to conceptualize academic knowledge that way and how that conceptualization is accomplished. If we look closely at property formation in the university, the very activity that would seem to be the most direct vehicle of privatization, we see a massive effort of boundary marking, the object of which is to ensure that the academy can continue to be represented as the realm of truth, of the gift, of nonproperty. How and where is that boundary continually redrawn, and what cultural work is performed in the process?

The concept of boundary objects provides a useful way into these questions because it places contingency front and center. Joan Fujimura (1992) observes that while boundary objects may indeed assist in "getting the work done," one has always to inquire "whose work?" and "which work?" In the case at hand, the work is the ongoing reinstantiation of the discursive fields of law and academic science, a process that affirms the central productive tensions of an epistemic regime. Because boundary objects are, as Fujimura notes, "often ill-structured, that is, inconsistent, ambiguous, and even 'illogical,'" they are well suited to this layered work. Boundary markers promote translation, but because their efficacy rests on the multiple meanings ascribed to them, they also "allow others to resist translation and to construct other facts" (175). Their openness to a range of interpretations supports collective action and tends to work against the long-term enlistment of allies behind a coherent set of facts and beliefs. The continuing force of the epistemic regime that intellectual property law and the university jointly compose relies precisely on the maintenance of ambiguity—it is crucial, in other words, that multiple social worlds be able to construct "other facts" and treat the propertization of academic work as impermanent and contingent. Indeed, it was this very ambiguity that allowed Huguette Pelletier to use a persuasive property story to defend her claim to status in the putative realm of nonproperty.

METHODS

This project brings into conversation three bodies of cultural studies: of law, of science, and of the university. Cultural studies, Michael Menser and Stanley Aronowitz (1996) argue, "begins in the middle [as] an intercession interfering with the relations among persons, places, and things," in order to obtain "an intimate experience of boundaries" (17–18). Each of these literatures raises questions, explicitly or implicitly, about boundaries, and border disputes, and the kinds of property stories it is possible to tell in the borderland of knowledge production.

The Law

"The law wishes to have a formal existence," observes Stanley Fish, meaning that the law does not wish to be "about" something else, such as politics, interpretation, or even morality (1991, 159). The law usually succeeds in this task, Fish argues, by resorting to formalism. Resolution depends upon putting the question at hand into its proper form, and thereby generating its solution. Thorny legal problems can be answered through invoking the correct precedent, examining the intentions of lawmakers, and determining how a given case fits into a legal tradition. As Robin West puts it, most jurists treat "law itself . . . [as] the basis for judgment" (1991, 123). Yet law's success is always a political and rhetorical achievement, a product of the cultural and political common sense law is supposed to reject in favor of "reason." This activity, Fish maintains, can be characterized as the articulation of a "persuasively told story" (1991, 172).

The persuasiveness of this story rests on the law's privileged claim to objectivity, a claim the Critical Legal Studies (CLS) movement has been at pains to debunk. For CLS scholars such as Gerald Frug, the law is a political strategy for the enforcement and naturalization of liberalism.[7] By organizing its analyses around liberal binaries (public/private, state/individual, rational/irrational, market/family) and treating the results of that analytical strategy as "common sense," law helps legitimate those dualities. "Whenever the legal process is adopted as the mode of analysis," comments Frug, "it fuels the notion that the results of application are natural, apolitical, and deductive" (1980, 1077).[8] In much of the work in this critical tradition, law is represented as following the real action. Its role under capitalism is to legitimate particular social and economic relations, and as those relations change, so too does the law.[9]

In contrast to mainstream CLS, poststructural critical legal scholars represent law as productive. They start by looking at the languages people use to conceive the world around them and situate themselves within it, paying close attention to how meanings change over time. The study of language offers a point of entry, in turn, for understanding the operation of discourses, or "historically, socially, and institutionally specific structures of statements, terms, categories and beliefs," as Joan Scott has usefully defined the term (1988, 35). Because from this perspective law, or, more precisely, legal discourse, is part of the real action, its analysis can help us understand how social relations are produced and reproduced over time. That understanding requires as well the study of the multiple strategies and apparatuses that shape and are shaped by the elaboration of legal discourse, including organizations, institutions, and social relationships. By attending to these strategies and locating them within specific cultural and temporal conditions, Scott argues, poststructural legal scholars can try to avoid "imposing simplified models . . . foreclosing new interpretive possibilities in favor of conventional understandings" (35).

Scott, like other poststructural legal scholars in a range of disciplines, is influenced by the work of Michel Foucault, who sees law as "an instrument of power which is at once complex and partial" (Foucault, 1980, 141). Legal discourses serve to fix the legitimacy of power, he suggests, by grounding the discourse of legal rights in a "grid of disciplinary coercions" (106). Poststructuralist legal scholarship endeavors to deconstruct the discursive terms that operate to maintain this grid and to expose the political contingency of foundational claims. So, for example, rather than asking how law is a form of domination which supports other forms of domination, poststructuralist approaches to law begin by asking what social bodies and relations legal apparatuses produce and normalize.

Scholars attached to "law and cultural studies" take up one thread of this poststructural project by tracing the construction of the "author-subject" in legal and cultural discourse (Gaines, 1991; Jaszi, 1994; Woodmansee, 1994a, 1994b). In this array of critical work, law is figured as both "a generative condition and prohibitive boundary" (Coombe, 1993, 412). Much of the investigation into this double figure will be elaborated in the following chapters; at this point I want only to introduce some of its major themes.

Cultural scholars' interest in intellectual property law has often focused on law's failure to attend to the "death of the author." Here, too, Foucault's work has been pivotal. In his seminal essay "What Is an author?" Foucault (1977) suggests the study of the individuated author-function as a fruitful starting point for a larger interrogation of the historical conditions for the appearance of discourses and subjectivities. The author anchors and confirms Western models of creativity and, by extension, understandings of the nature of meaning. Attentive observation of the space left empty by the author's disappearance, Foucault insists, can tell us a great deal about the "modes of circulation, valorization, attribution, and appropriation" of discourse (137). It can also expose potential strategies of intervention, beginning with the replacement of the question "Who is speaking?" with "What matter who's speaking?"

In law, however, the author, or at least the author-function, has not disappeared; indeed, copyright law begins with an investigation of "who is speaking?" (Waldron, 1993; Boyle, 1996; Rotstein, 1993). Bernard Edelman's (1979) work on photography and film production under French law, for example, suggests the author-function has not disappeared so much as it has been refigured. In theory, intellectual property law has historically emphasized the work of individual persons—"creative" individuals who invest of themselves in the making of the product. But within cultural industries, Edelman reasons, cultural production of a single work involves the labor of hundreds of individuals, who are often necessarily interchangeable. Artists create works for hire, thereby alienating their labor and becoming subsumed into capital. Confronted by multiple authors, the courts search for an individual who can occupy the place of the author. Who has invested the most in a given work? The answer to this question, Edelman notes, will inevitably be understood solely in terms of capital.[10] Capital becomes the sole essential element of the work, the "true creative subject." Thus, "capital assumes the mask of the subject, it is animated, it speaks and signs contracts" (1979, 57).

Jane Gaines (1991) and Thomas Streeter (1996) take up Edelman's project in the American context. Gaines unpacks a series of legal cases that helped configure monopolies in mass-mediated expressive technologies: photography, television, advertising, even comic book characters. Intellectual property doctrine, she argues, helps secure and enforce hegemonic cultural expression by treating oppositional reinterpretations as piracy and appropriation. Its success in this regard depends, however, on the ongoing location of a singular author-originator for products—films, television shows, celebrities—that are created by the work of many individuals appropriating from many sources. For Gaines, the author *is* disappearing in law, in the sense that the place that entity occupied is now being held by corporate entities. Streeter, for his part, has traced the propertization of broadcasting in and through regulatory practice. Crucial to his analysis—and useful to my own—is his critique of corporate liberalism, which joined traditional liberal principles to a profound faith in the ability of experts, systems, and the scientific method to address social problems. In the case of broadcasting, Streeter contends, "the discourse of the corporate individual allow[ed] a simulation of the individual author-owner," a simulation which justified, in turn, the treatment of television as commodity rather than public medium (Streeter, 1994, 325). Both of these scholars, in different ways, show how intellectual property law's overt commitment to rewarding the authenticity and originality of human persons becomes a vehicle for the assertion of cultural monopolies by artificial persons—corporations.

As Streeter's analysis of corporate liberalism would suggest, the individual author not only retains its force in copyright discourse but is being invoked in a range of legal doctrines. James Boyle has traced the appearance of the author-function in legal treatments of insider trading, blackmail, and, less surprisingly, invention. The author-function is comforting. Encapsulating as it does a vision of moral desert based on solitary creativity, it promises to resolve contests for the meaning of several classic liberal dualisms—labor and creativity, public and private, property and identity. But the price of resolution, Boyle notes, is the devaluation of the activities of sources and audiences, as well as the conferral of too many rights on those entities which can be positioned as authors. In other words, the concept of the individual author permits property rights to be assigned to the wrong persons, for the wrong reasons, in support of the accelerating privatization of the public domain (see also Gaines, 1991; Streeter, 1996; Bettig, 1996).

Investigations into the historical development of the author as a legal and cultural concept have helped push cultural studies of intellectual property law in new directions. Mark Rose (1993), in a study of the formation of copyright in England, traces the role of law in the emergence of the modern conception of authorship, with special attention to the articulation of key productive binaries—idea/expression, public/private—upon which copyright still rests. Martha Woodmansee (1994a) examines the emergence of copyright reasoning in the German states, demonstrating how economic need motivated German writers to embrace a representation of the author as originary genius. Well into the eighteenth century, Germans understood the writer to be one of many contributors to the creation of books, whose task it was to convey God-given knowledge. Influenced by the English, German writers began to rethink the author, an effort that would culminate in the recognition of literary property in German civil codes. Both Rose and Woodmansee draw our attention to the interplay of legal and cultural discourse—as well as the multi-layered boundary work that interplay has always called forth.

I situate my own project in the critical tradition of Boyle, Edelman, Gaines, Streeter, Rose, and Woodmansee, but I seek to expand its methodological boundaries. Cultural analysis of law was born in English and Literature departments, and its insights tend to emerge from close textual analysis of legal cases and the images, writings, and sounds IP law polices. Missing from this work, as from other critical legal approaches, is a substantive account of how IP law "works" in complex social settings. If, as Carol Rose (1994) suggests, property stories speak to and constitute moral communities, what precisely does this constitutive activity look like when those stories are told outside of courtrooms? How are law and its foundational dichotomies enacted and/or resisted in specific contexts? In her aptly titled piece "Copyright as Myth," Jessica Litman (1991) observes that professional authors and lawyers frequently have very different understandings of "authorship"—how are those understandings reconciled? If we think of law as a story, how does that story change in the retelling, and how does it speak to and help articulate other powerful tales in different social worlds?

These questions indicate the value of legal anthropology. Intellectual property law has only recently become an object of anthropological study, but work by Rosemary Coombe (1998) has done much to demonstrate the value of an ethnographic approach to intellectual property law. Coombe examines "the cultural life of intellectual properties," or how signifying practices are legally authorized, appropriated, concealed, and/or rendered subversive. As it identifies and protects some forms of cultural proprietorship, she suggests, intellectual property law "freezes the play" of practices of meaning-making but also creates new tactics of signification. One distinctive example of these new tactics is an enormous billboard of the legendary pioneer Paul Bunyan being assaulted with a walleye fish by Nanbouzho (a Native American trickster figure). Paul Bunyan is the trademark of the Red River Lumber Company of Minnesota, but his image has been appropriated by the Chippewa to mark their own national persona. The billboard, Coombe notes, looms above a highway in a Native American territory, proclaiming a rejection of both the American frontier myth and local logging interests—the walleye is a symbol of economic autonomy. Coombe's ethnographic approach to law, one that pays attention to the social uses of legal authority outside of courtrooms and the pages of official reporters, vividly illustrates how law occasions, disrupts, and responds to a dynamic cultural politics of possession.

Coombe's project is complemented by the work of Marilyn Strathern (1997; 1996), Paul Rabinow (1996), and Georgina Born (1996). Strathern takes up the multiple concepts of ownership attached to "products of professional commitment" such as publications, and suggests that those concepts help constitute particular collectivities, including universities, disciplines, and groups of authors. Rabinow uses a combination of qualitative research and textual analysis to present an ethnography of Western reason in which intellectual property emerges as a central organizing principle. Born, for her part, has explored the dynamics of intellectual property formation in software research, showing how systems of gift and commodity exchange interact to shape negotiations over intellectual property in that arena. In contrast to a model of legal anthropology as the investigation of law's insertion into social settings, and/or the law as a social setting (a courtroom, for example) these scholars investigate how different social settings construct intellectual property law and vice versa.

Surprisingly, inventorship has been of relatively little interest to law and cultural studies. Despite intense and growing interest by critical cultural scholars in copyright, trademark, and even the right of publicity, patent law has been virtually ignored. Rabinow and Boyle are notable exceptions; they both offer provocative analyses, for example, of the reconstruction of the human body as patentable raw material. Rabinow, in particular, has shown how debates over the patentability of human blood and tissues have challenged, reinforced, and refigured ancient conceptions of embodiment, the soul, and the nature of personhood. Patent law may strike cultural scholars as rather dry and technical and more properly the concern of engineers and lawyers. As we will see in Chapter 4, this perception is inaccurate. Patent law is riddled with anxieties about language and the nature of argument, and is thus ripe for cultural analysis. Such an analysis must be informed, however, by another body of scholarship that takes the work of technoscience as its object.

The Community of Science™

Academic intellectual property, especially the subcategory of patents, is often (though not exclusively) derived from research in the arena of technoscience. To better understand this arena, I turned to a body of interdisciplinary sociological, historical, and ethnographic work that falls under the heading of Science and Technology Studies (STS). STS, and especially the ethnographic subset sometimes called "laboratory studies," can be understood as a kind of counterpart to cultural studies of law, for the two share the conviction that knowledge and all knowledge claims are necessarily socially constructed.

While intellectual property has only recently become central to STS, a few pioneering studies inform my own research, while others have contributed important navigational tools. Though she does not address intellectual property specifically, Sheila Jasanoff's (1995) analysis of the mutually constitutive relationship between the cultures of legal and scientific inquiry traces some of the key shared premises of legal and scientific modes of reasoning. Dorothy Nelkin's (1984) review of science as intellectual property was one of the first books to call attention to changes in the ownership and control of scientific information. Alberto Cambrosio and Peter Keating's (1995) study of battles over patent rights in biotechnologies also indicates how scientific and legal discourses can work together to create new "fields of action," and highlights patent law's interest in processes of production rather than scientific facts. Stephen Hilgartner and Sherry Brandt-Rauf (Hilgartner and Brandt-Rauf, 1994; Hilgartner, 1998) explore IP law's imbrication of data access practices in genome research communities. Andrew Webster and Kathryn Packer's qualitative analyses of patenting experiences in British scientific communities were invaluable to the development of my own qualitative methodology (Packer and Webster, 1996; Webster and Packer, 1997).

Finally, work from S. Leigh Star and James Griesemer (1989), Geoffrey Bowker and S. Leigh Star (1999), and Joan Fujimura (1992) on the articulation of boundary objects has been crucial to my understanding of how legal categories are deployed and reshaped in academic contexts. The concept of boundary objects was initially developed as part of an "ecological approach" to the production of scientific facts and systems of classification. In contrast to, for example, Bruno Latour's actor-network analysis of laboratory practices (which has been criticized as overly "Machiavellian" in its emphasis on the highly strategic management of fact production across networks by scientist-entrepreneurs), an ecological approach investigates the production and management of meaning through collective action (Fujimura, 1992). Scientific knowledge, on this account, develops in complex and ongoing processes of translation, and its study demands attention to the cooperative relationships between multiple actors located in multiple social worlds (Bowker and Star, 1999).

Boundary objects facilitate cooperation across social worlds without requiring agreement. Thus, to take an example from Star and Griesemer's examination of the founding of the Museum of Vertebrate Zoology, bird specimens might carry very different meanings for bird watchers and professional biologists, but nevertheless be recognizable by each group and, as such, work as mechanisms for building highly provisional common territories. As this example suggests, boundary objects emerge only through use in a set of activities and relations. Once articulated, they shape as well as mediate subsequent relations and, by extension, the social worlds that provide their context. As we will see, the boundary objects that have emerged in and through communication across legal and academic discourses act in precisely this way, which is one reason their identification is crucial to understanding the sources and implications of academic intellectual property.

STS scholars directly concerned with IP have tended to focus on practices of invention and inventorship. Equally important to the concerns of this book, though, have been the insights of Latour and Steve Woolgar into the broader problem of scientific authorship. Latour and Woolgar take issue with Warren Hagstrom's (1965) portrait of scientific communities as gift economies. I join with them in being suspicious of the "gift" model of scientific authorship, and in taking seriously the proliferation of terms like "investment," "credit," and "return" in scientific discourse. I am also concerned to show how authorship and inventorship are hybrids in Latour's (1993) sense of concepts that intermediate mutually constitutive oppositions, such as gift and market. Latour's theory of hybridity complements Star and Griesemer's conception of "boundary objects" by indicating that boundary objects translate across both social worlds and central binary oppositions and, as such, are themselves foundational mechanisms.

But as Chandra Mukerji (1989) has noted, STS has been less concerned with the social role of science. I argue that, with regard to IP law in particular, academic science has had a distinct role to play as one of the primary arbiters of that body of knowledge which is understood to define and inhabit the public domain. IP law, in turn, is playing an increasingly visible role in defining science, or at least academic science. Patent law has long since infiltrated many arenas of scientific work, but copyright, trademark, and trade secret law are rapidly becoming important tools in the technoscientific kit as well. When the very phrase "community of science" is subject to trademark "protection," IP law is no longer a mere sidelight of academic scientific work (if indeed it ever was).[11] Rather it helps create the conditions of possibility for academic science just as surely as academic science generates much of the "raw material" of intellectual property.

The Academy

STS provides an important resource for this book, and many of the stories I tell are about and by scientists. My focus, however, is on academic intellectual property, and the social context of that category is provided not by communities of technoscience as such but by one of the primary conceptual and institutional homes of technoscience in the United States: the research university. To study the production of academic intellectual property, I could have attended to the rhetorics of literature professors, visual artists, or historians. I chose instead to talk to academic scientists and engineers, for three reasons. First, I was following the basic ethnographic adage to "go somewhere strange [to you]." I found the worlds of technoscience strange indeed, and sought to make my own discomfort a starting point for critical insight. Second, I wanted to speak with people I felt would be more informed by their own experience with some of the pressure points of academic intellectual property, such as patenting, multiple authorship, and the use of scientific databases. My initial review of legal disputes involving academics suggested these issues were sources of enduring controversy. While I did not try to adhere to strict disciplinary boundaries, I wanted to ensure that the backgrounds and practices of my respondents would be at least roughly comparable to those of the major players in the groundbreaking cases I planned to discuss. Finally, I was interested in a specifically modern, research-oriented incarnation of the university, an entity that is historically defined by its embrace of natural and social sciences.

Yet while the liberal arts receive relatively short shrift in the following pages, much of what is said here about scientific authorship, inventorship, and ownership applies equally well to all kinds of academic creators, for scholars of all disciplines share an overt commitment to a distinct property story. This property story actually tells a tale of "nonproperty," a narrative in which independent scholars pursue knowledge for its own sake and share it with one another. In this "ethic of sharing," the progress of knowledge is furthered and, not incidentally, glory bestowed on institutions and academics themselves. Because it underscores the idea that professors should and do seek recognition in lieu of high salaries and are therefore relatively immune to the influence of politicians and/or corporate executives, the scholar's property story also forms the historic basis for direct and indirect public support of the university. I will have much more to say about this, but for now I'll simply quote Walter Metzger's observation that "the professor can only be of use . . . if his conclusions are disinterested and his own" (Hofstadter and Metzger, 1955, 408–409).

My account of the "rarefied world" of the university is indebted to a wealth of historical research tracing the emergence of the research university and the professoriate in Europe and in the United States.[12] However, my understanding of this history as well as of contemporary deformations of the university is derived primarily from a body of cultural scholarship that takes up Immanuel Kant's originary formulation of the university in *The Conflict of the Faculties* in order to reconsider the uses of the modern university in postmodernity (Derrida, 1980, 1983, 1992; Kamuf, 1992; Young, 1992; Readings, 1996). While much of this work was developed in response to the "culture wars" of the 1980s, the account offered therein of a more basic contest for the meaning of the university is salient to today's "property wars" as well. By foregrounding "reason" as the essence of the university (or, more specifically, a mode of scientific normativity that currently inhabits the category of reason), these cultural scholars point to the shared premises of legal and academic discourses and indirectly suggest how the university and IP law might be caught up in a mutually constitutive relationship.

Jacques Derrida (1983) puts the question thus: "Does the university, today, have . . . a raison d'être?" (3). In a series of articles and lectures (1980, 1983, 1992, 1999), Derrida examines the first principles offered by Kant in *Conflict of the Faculties,* principles taken up by the German universities and adapted in the formation of modern research universities throughout the West. Derrida reminds us that the traditional *raison d'être* of the university (by which he means the modern research university invented in the nineteenth century) *is* reason, or, more directly, the exercise of noninstrumental, disinterested reason. Kant and his successors advocated a "theoretico-political hierarchy," as Derrida puts it, headed by a faculty of philosophy that, because it was the lowest and most useless order, was "free to evaluate everything," could serve as the final arbiter of value (Derrida, 1983, 18; Kant, 1794/1979, 27). Paradoxically, universities founded on this hierarchy were presented as "useful" to the nation-state because they could produce both the objective information upon which rational social policies could be developed and citizens skilled in rational inquiry to develop, enforce, and support those policies.

The ground upon which this vision of the university is built, never especially solid, has been rapidly eroded as academic work is revealed and actively reconstructed as "interested." In this respect, the cultural critic Allen Bloom was correct to suggest that the interrogations of reason mounted by critics in several disciplines in the past few decades might help produce a "lack of belief in the university's vocation" (Bloom, 1987, 312).[13]

That vocation, argues Bill Readings, has been replaced by a kind of placeholder concept: the "idea of excellence." Readings shows how the Kantian ideal was joined to the nation-state via a discourse of national culture and suggests that the decline of that geopolitical entity has resulted in the evisceration of the university's reason for being. That legitimating space, Readings continues, is occupied, though not filled, by the idea of "excellence." Excellence is a kind of common term, infinitely malleable to circumstance, that promises quality but frees it from any particular definition. Its very vagueness makes the term effective, for it forestalls the dangerous political contests that specific definitions of value often engender. Where specific components of excellence are identified, their selection can seem almost arbitrary. For example, a Research Assessment Exercise conducted by the United Kingdom Higher Education Funding Council measured departmental "excellence" in research by the number of faculty publications (see Strathern, 1996). In the United States, these assessments are supplemented by measurements of the number of research products transferred to "the public" as commodities. And so on: the point is, excellence is an almost infinitely amorphous term that excludes only "questions about what excellence in the university might *be*" (Readings, 1996, 27). The embrace of excellence as a common standard, therefore, ironically reveals a "ruined institution" whose foundational category (reason) appears "a broken and lifeless tradition" (170).

From different standpoints, Readings and Derrida encourage academics to refuse to rebuild the university, and to choose instead to dwell in its ruins. By this they mean that academics must take responsibility for enacting a community of thought that, because it does not pretend to be either disinterested or secluded from society, will no longer work to legitimate particular inquiries, policies, and property claims. As we shall see, many scholars are adopting a different strategy, choosing instead to invoke the alternative rational tradition embodied in legal discourse, specifically IP law, to guard and rebuild the university. This strategy involves more than simply engaging in "market-like behaviors," as Sheila Slaughter and Lawrence Leslie (1997) put it, for its object is not the privatization of the university but rather the protection of academic freedom. The concomitant entanglement of academic freedom with property rights (as occurred in *Pelletier*) suggests that the community of scholarship is already constructing itself as "interested," though perhaps not in quite the way Derrida and Readings have in mind.

To understand the broader context of contemporary refigurations of the academy and its inhabitants, I turn to a group of sociological and economic studies of dynamic information practices in a global knowledge economy. Manuel Castells' seminal trilogy on "the information age" exhaustively documents the emergence and spread of an information technology paradigm (1996, 1997, 1998). This paradigm has five essential characteristics. First, information itself is the raw material of production: new technologies are intended to act on information, rather than the other way around. Second, new technologies have pervasive effects because information is integral to all human activities. Third, new information technologies facilitate and respond to complex *networks* as opposed to more linear or corporatist forms of organization. Fourth, because these networks can be continually reconfigured, the information technology paradigm demands flexibility from the systemic to the local level. Finally, this new paradigm is distinguished by a high level of technological convergence: information systems integrate telecommunication, microelectronic, computing, and manufacturing technologies. As this paradigm takes hold, Castells contends, our modes of mental discipline are transforming as well: the integration of ideas is now less important than the management of complexity.

Castells pays rather little attention to the university as such, and gives equally short shrift to law. He pays very close attention, however, to labor, and education access, and the academic research that has helped fuel the emergence of the paradigm he identifies. Work, he argues, is becoming individuated, disaggregated, and stratified in new ways, even as capital is increasingly globalized and concentrated. As we will see, professors may merely occupy the leading edge of a broader trend toward the hyper-individualization of the capacities, conditions, and projects of labor.

The specific position of the university in the global knowledge economy is more directly taken up by Michael Gibbons and his colleagues' (1994) analysis of new and old modes of knowledge production. The authors suggest that the "familiar" mode of knowledge generation (Mode 1) in disciplinary contexts is being replaced by a system in which knowledge is produced in broader transdisciplinary contexts (Mode 2). Mode 2 knowledge is developed in the context of application by persons with heterogeneous skills and experience who are socially and ethically accountable for that knowledge. This emphasis on transdisciplinarity and social (or at least socioeconomic) accountability is present as well in the "triple helix" model of knowledge production offered by contributors to Henry Etzkowitz and Loet Leydesdorff's (1997) collection (see Chapter 1 for more on this model). The premise of the collection is the idea that the university, the government, and private industry are the three essential elements of a "triple helix," and, as this metaphor suggests, that their interaction promises to be an "evolutionary" step in knowledge-based socioeconomic development.

The characterization of this interaction as evolutionary is called into question in critical studies by Slaughter and Leslie (1997), Philip Altbach (1980), and Walter Metzger (1987) on the changing conditions of academic labor and the (re)production of the professoriate. Slaughter and Leslie's cross-national study of the construction and operations of professorial markets is especially useful. Their documentation of market and market-like behaviors on the part of universities and faculty provides a political economic counterpart to Pierre Bourdieu's (1988) and Latour and Woolgar's (1979) analyses of the buildup and management of "academic capital" and "cycles of credit" in academic cultures.

MATERIALS

IP is constructed in multiple sites, through the operation of a constellation of discourses, activities, and social worlds, and it was their very interaction I was hoping to trace. Thus some traditional approaches—an ethnographic study of a laboratory, a cultural analysis of case law, a historical interpretation of academic IP policy—would not do. I also had to recognize that linear, continuous relationships between the discursive spaces of IP production would be difficult to identify at best. Emily Martin's (1996) discussion of the coproduction of the immune system by scientists and laypersons offers a helpful illustration of this problem. Borrowing from Gilles Deleuze and Felix Guattari (1987), Martin imagines the relationships between science and culture as rhizomatic: "A rhizome as a subterranean stem is absolutely different from roots and radicals. Bulbs and tubers are rhizomes. Rats are rhizomes. Burrows are too, in all their functions of shelter, supply, movement, evasion, and breakout. The rhizome itself assumes very diverse forms, from ramified surface extensions in all directions to concretion into bulbs . . . A rhizome may be broken, shattered at a given spot, but it will start up again on one of its old lines, or on new lines" (Deleuze and Guattari, quoted in Martin, 1996, 103). Academic intellectual property is also rhizomatic, and it was therefore necessary to look at a range of "sites," some of which were not located in space so much as in time, to understand its construction. Legal inventorship, for example, is articulated in and through scribbled writings in laboratory notebooks, the recollections of scientists and technicians, drafts of patent applications, disclosure forms, telephone calls, and so on. These markers intersect, in turn, with legal principles and judicial decisions handed down decades ago, the meaning of which must be constantly redefined in response to new technologies of knowledge production.

The qualitative portion of my effort to map the complex relationships within which academic property is produced was organized around open-ended interviews with a panel of informants who could help me better understand how problems of authorship, inventorship, and ownership were raised and "resolved" in academic research settings. My object was to study a process—the construction of IP—and at each stage of the research I sought to identify and speak with persons intimately involved in that process.

Most of the interviews took place on or near the University of the West at Collingwood, one of several campuses of the University of the West (UW) system.[14] Collingwood is a Cold War school, born of the national anxieties about America's technoscientific competitiveness that followed the launching of Sputnik. Famous for its founders' commitment to building "from the top down" by hiring academic stars to anchor fledgling departments, the university is equally dedicated to "excellence" in science and engineering. Only 14 percent of its undergraduates (and 10 percent of its doctoral students) take degrees in the arts or humanities. Collingwood also prides itself on excellence in technology transfer: officials have been leading national promoters of university-industry partnerships, and the campus ranked high among all the UW campuses in net income from technology licensing when I conducted my field research. Collingwood's promotional literature emphasizes that it is "no ivory tower" but rather an institution actively concerned with the needs of private industry. Not coincidentally, the campus looks rather like a commercial research park.

I used snowball sampling to generate a list of staff, students, and researchers who work in two Collingwood computing research units.[15] I chose to focus initially on the field of electrical engineering, an applied science with a tradition of relatively close ties to private industry and concomitant anxiety about its status as "science," whose investment in boundary maintenance is therefore particularly visible (see Noble, 1977). Several of the professors I interviewed had worked in private industry before being recruited by the university; all held Ph.D.'s, all had numerous publications, and most were "senior" (tenured) researchers. The students were all current or very recent doctoral candidates in electrical engineering or computer science with one or more publications. In interviews lasting one to two hours, I asked respondents to tell me about the preparation of research articles and conference papers, how they decided who should be named as authors in a given publication, in what order, and who was and was not included in that decisionmaking process. In most but not all of the interviews, we also discussed experiences with secrecy and plagiarism. Finally, we talked about inventions and patenting. Several respondents had come up with inventions in the course of their research, and some had pursued patents on those inventions.

These conversations yielded wonderful stories about authorship, plagiarism, secrecy, technology transfer, and university-industry relations. To improve my understanding of the context of these stories, I consulted with research administrators, lobbyists, and faculty members actively involved in IP discussions at the local campus and university-wide level. I also spoke with senior administrators. And I participated in a systemwide committee on copyright policy, which proved an invaluable source of background material and an interesting case study in struggles to use copyright to defend academic labor.

A second strand of my inquiry involved close analysis of legal discourse. Some of this work required investigation of the legislative and doctrinal framework of academic intellectual property. Study of state and federal legislative debates about such diverse issues as technology transfer and the powers of university corporations gave me insight into the relationship between university and national identities and how that relationship has changed over time. Examination of the statutes that define and regulate intellectual property drew my attention to similarities and differences in the assumptions about creative production that inform patent, trade secret, and copyright regimes, and helped me understand how scientific and legal discourses of invention could be reconciled.

The bulk of this research track, however, was focused on case law. Legal cases often come into being when there is a rift in the "common sense," or the shared beliefs and assumptions that regulate most behavior (Gabel and Feinman, 1982). Thus, as Gaines observes, legal disputes "pinpoint cultural trouble spots" that can be used to orient oneself in a cultural landscape (1991, 14). To investigate these disruptions, and the work necessary to "make sense" of them, I looked at judicial decisions, arguments filed by disputants, and coverage of the cases by the news media. Disputes over academic intellectual property have, until recently, been treated as mere footnotes to the respective histories of the university, patents, and copyrights, but they are taking on new prominence as IP becomes a crucial source and guarantor of title on the elusive "knowledge frontier." The increasing importance of these cases indicates a need to expose the assumptions about power, knowledge, property, and identity that were challenged, circumscribed, and enforced in their resolution, and the stakes of that operation in a fluctuating epistemic regime. Some of that need, I hope, is met in the following pages.

CHAPTER ONE

Building an Epistemic Regime

The terms "intellectual property" and "the modern university" resist easy definition. At least, so it would seem from the multiple and contradictory usages that percolate through scholarly, legal, and popular literatures. These terms are clearly in flux at this historical moment, a turmoil that is emblematic of wider political, economic, legal, and ideological struggles over the meaning of knowledge and knowledge work. As I attempted to wade through this confusion of meaning, though, I discovered one place where these contests converged. Players in these struggles disagree on many things, but on one point they are unanimous: intellectual property law (IP) and the university are both "in crisis."

"Crisis" is not the most promising point of commonality. Let's say a crisis is under way. Where does this observation take us? Sheldon Wolin's comment that "the word 'crisis' fairly oozes with banality" is as salient here as in other sociopolitical arenas (1981, 7). As we will see, crisis rhetoric is omnipresent in the history of both the academy and intellectual property law. In fact, it is difficult to find an extended period in the past two hundred years when a crisis *hasn't* been going on in the university, and the same can be said of intellectual property law in the past hundred years.

The very familiarity of crisis, and the fact that it provides a common reference point for highly disparate groups, should make us uncomfortable. It suggests a need to think about the work performed by crisis rhetoric, and what is—and is not—called into question when this rhetoric appears. Crises, argues Wolin, are commonly portrayed as "events," discrete moments of anxiety with beginnings, middles, and eventual ends. Because these events, like "the drug war," or "Y2K," are also portrayed as huge and complex, their resolution depends on the action of experts. Incapable of intervening, nonexperts can only watch, and worry, and wait for the next crisis to come along, as it inevitably will. Crisis, Wolin concludes, is therefore a technique of social control and dependence rather than a moment of possibility and opportunity.

In this view, crisis rhetoric emerges as a strategy of mobilization that allows an identified problem to be "fixed" or at least managed, but leaves underlying issues unexamined. Consider, for example, one of the most visible "crises" in copyright law—the problem of the Internet. It has become a commonplace among legislators, academics, lawyers, and businesspeople that a copyright regime rooted in the paradigms of print culture does not easily apply to virtual culture, itself ill defined. When documents can be copied and circulated worldwide with a few clicks of a mouse, and multiple forms of media (textual, visual, musical) can be digitized and recombined such that all traces of "originary" sources are practically dissolved, it is genuinely difficult to ensure that persons (corporate and "natural") are compensated for their investments. Hence the development of legislation, legal doctrines, and technologies designed to track and limit the circulation of digitized information and thereby to contain the "crisis." All of this activity figures the "problem" as essentially technical and therefore answerable by technical means, an approach that leaves untouched the basic assumption, itself a product of an earlier "crisis," that the natural compensation for creative effort is property ownership. So long as this assumption remains in place, the "crisis" can be described as a matter of "preserving the existing balance" between private and public spheres of the marketplace of ideas, and "intellectual property" can continue to be construed as a solution rather than a problem.

In this light, it would seem that, far from being a common ground, the term "crisis" is a dead end, one that is likely to hinder an effort to discover the meanings of "intellectual property" and "the university." Perhaps we can avoid this cul-de-sac and make crisis a condition of possibility if we follow Wolin and recall one of the oldest meanings of the term. According to Greek healers, a *krisis* was a turning point in a "developing general condition of the body" rather than a temporary ailment. A genuine crisis, Wolin argues, raises questions about fundamental structures of power and "what kind of people and society are supposed to be nurtured over the long pull" (7–8). A "true crisis" cannot be answered by experts because it is not a matter of policy but of *polis*.

Let me put the point a slightly different way in order to bring the problem of definition into relief. The cultural identification of a "crisis" could be seen to demand exploration of the set of values, aims, and justifications that provide its context and maybe its cause. Such an inquiry could begin precisely where the crisis managers leave off—with an examination of definitions. Borrowing from Paula Treichler, I understand a definition not as the "set of necessary and sufficient conditions that constitute a known, fixed starting point for political, economic and ideological struggles" but rather as the product and embodiment of those struggles (1990, 133). Treichler represents crises as battles over the standards by which some stories are selected to "constitute an official definition of reality" (116).[1] The recognition of a "crisis" correlates with the moment when definitions, or the premises of existing social arrangements, are called into question at multiple and highly visible points.

Treichler's formulation of crisis offers a powerful way into Wolin's *krisis*. Indirectly picking up on Wolin's concern for the condition of the body politic, Treichler refers to definitions as "cultural prescriptions." At the risk of overloading this metaphor, I would suggest that an investigation of what has been prescribed, when, and in what circumstances to cure whose "body politic," could take us a long way toward discerning whether a "general developing condition" exists.

I believe that the identification of IP law and the university as "in crisis" at the same time is not coincidence. In what follows, I delineate a mutually constitutive relationship between IP and the modern research university and the consequences of that relationship for the social construction of knowledge and knowledge work. And I want to start by observing that problems of definition themselves are symptomatic and constitutive of those moments of visible controversy scholars and politicians like to call "crises." In what follows, I will look closely at processes in and through which particular definitions of the university and intellectual property have been prescribed. We will see that intellectual property is defined in contradistinction to a conceptual space, namely, the public domain, that is anchored in the United States by the research university. Put simply, intellectual property law polices the knowledge that can be owned—the realm of artifact—while the university polices the knowledge that cannot be owned—the realm of fact. Borrowing a phrase from Björn Wittrock (1993), I understand this relationship to embody an *epistemic regime*. Wittrock uses this phrase to refer to the overlapping cognitive, social, and institutional strategies central to the (re)production of the Germanic research university. The term *epistemic regime* stresses that discursive fields penetrate, compete with, and authorize one another (Scott, 1988). We will find that intellectual property law and the university do indeed appeal to each other for authority, which is why the rearticulation of one correlates with the transformation of the other.

ORIGINATION ANXIETY

Although lawyers, jurists, and scholars disagree over the basic premises, reasoning, and even utility of intellectual property law, there is a general agreement that IP law faces unprecedented challenges (Boyle, 1996). This crisis is hardly recent, but what does seem to be new is the visibility of the contest, as evidenced by the multiple accounts promulgated in popular and academic forums. One common model for the crisis is a technological determinist one. This account points to the emergence of digital technologies, biotechnologies, and complex information networks as the locus of change because "fixed expression," one of the key elements of copyrightability, is difficult to locate when texts, images, and sound may be broken down and/or resituated with ease (Cook, 1996; Cleveland, 1989). The Internet, in particular, is seen to demand a fundamental reconsideration of the limits of copyright to ensure that educational uses, for example, do not undermine the value of commercial goods.[2]

Others emphasize the globalization of information markets, pointing to the national economic stakes in information control and seemingly perennial subversion of that control by "piracy" and other forms of seepage across political, economic, and legal boundaries (Gordon, 1993; Nerona, 2000; Declet, 1997). Proponents of this "piracy" model also worry that new technologies of reproduction in themselves facilitate unauthorized uses. As "invisible exports" steadily overtake "physical exports" as a proportion of world trade—resulting in what one analyst has called the "knowledge-value revolution"—information-rich countries have grown intensely interested in enforcing international IP agreements (Sakaiya, 1991, cited in Boyle, 1997). In this frame, "immature" nations that resist enforcing international intellectual property norms are the culprits. The United States finds itself in an awkward position in this regard, for it, too, has often resisted major international IP regulations; it did not ratify the prevailing international copyright treaty, the Berne Convention, until 1989—more than a century after most Western countries. Fortunately, pundits claim, "America's attitude toward intellectual property matured." Today's juvenile delinquents (among them China and Israel), they predict, will also "come of age" (Siskind, 1998).

Critical scholars, for their part, worry that intellectual property law is promoting the "propertization" of all forms of information. Jane Gaines, for example, characterizes intellectual property law as a site of profound contradiction. Despite their commitment to the discourse of originary genius, Gaines suggests, the courts are not genuinely "interested in asking questions about who is 'really' producing the sound or image" (1991, 105). If the courts were genuinely interested in that issue, they would discover that large entertainment corporations use the image of the individual human author to justify corporate control of information production. The academic critics find their counterparts in activists such as the "free" software developer Richard Stallman and the Electronic Frontier Foundation co-founder Mitch Kapor, who foresees an imminent "Bhopal" of patent claims on software once considered part of the public domain (quoted in Shulman, 1999, 70). Summarizing arguments by Stallman, Kapor, and others, the science journalist Seth Shulman argues that "without thoughtful intervention the current trajectory promises nothing less than an uncontrolled stampede to auction off our technological and cultural heritage, a future of increasing conflict and dissension, and the specter of an ominous descent into a new Dark Age" (1999, 3). Shulman trots out a parade of horribles, from a cancer patient denied treatment because the procedure he needed was the subject of an intellectual property dispute to a 1997 patent on Kirchoff's Law, a scientific model of electrical current flow dating to 1845.

These models of crisis share a concern that one of the organizing dichotomies of intellectual property law—that between monopoly and freedom—is being destabilized. The basic rationale and contradiction of intellectual property law is that limited monopolies on information are permitted, even encouraged, in the name of making information widely available. Patents, for example, grant a strong but short-term monopoly on inventions in order to encourage inventors to make the details of their creations available to the public. In copyright law, meanwhile, a "delicate balance" between the needs of authors and the claims of the public is nominally resolved through the idea/expression binary, which locates ideas and expressions in public and private domains respectively (Goldstein, 1992a, 86).[3] As an author, I am granted exclusive rights in my expression on the assumption that my ideas can be freely used by the public, and that even my expression will be eventually "released" for public use. A similar rationale is evident in trademark law. Thus the monopoly of intellectual property rights is justified by the idea that those rights are always limited by a larger arena of shared cultural resources. The essential task of IP law is to ensure that monopoly rights (the private) do not erode the space of freedom (the public).

It appears the law is failing in this task, and that failure looks very like a problem of definition: a contest for the meaning of the public domain. To begin with, as the legal scholar Jessica Litman notes, the contents of the "public domain" have historically been unclear, and "the task of distinguishing ideas from expression in order to explain why private ownership is inappropriate for one but desirable for the other . . . remains elusive" (1990, 999). Part of the problem is that we tend to assume that "the public" and "the common" are "synonyms for 'what is political'" (Wolin, 1978, 9, in Pateman, 1989). In reality, "public interests" and what might be construed as "private interests," that is, the interests of advertisers and sponsors, are conflated with relative ease. For example, state doctrines permitting celebrities to control the use of their personas for commercial purposes have been attacked as an impermissible encroachment on the free speech of advertisers. As Litman (1990) and Gaines (1993) have observed, it is not clear how we should think about the "public domain," when "public" means "available for unfettered commercial use."

It does not help that common intellectual resources are increasingly likely to be defined in negative terms, as "uncopyrightable" or "unprotectible" expression rather than public domain material (Litman, 1990, 995). In trademark discourse, symbols that have "fallen" into the public domain are often characterized as "abandoned." One of the consequences of treating "private" and "public" as equivalent to "property" and "no-property," argues Gaines, is that the public domain comes to look "more a junkyard . . . than a popular, shared, 'live' space" (1995,

146). Mark Lemley takes these observations one step further, noting that "the very *idea* of the public domain as an intrinsic part of intellectual property law" is under attack (1997, 902).

IP law needs that idea, for at least two reasons. I have already alluded to the first: the public domain helps combat the aversion to even limited monopolies expressed by judges and legislators from Thomas Jefferson forward (Burchfiel, 1989). Second, the public domain also allows us to avoid some (not all) of the difficult questions about the limits of originality. Focusing on copyright law, Litman has shown how the concept of the commons means plaintiffs and defendants do not have to prove or disprove "actual" originality, or "ineffable creation from nothing" (1990, 1023). The public domain acknowledges and partially conceals the disturbing likelihood that original ideas usually aren't. Concepts, facts, themes, languages, and expressions in a given work are most often encountered by the named creators through the work of others. That is why, Litman argues, a legal system really committed to granting copyright in truly original creations alone would require that authors acknowledge and obtain permissions from a multitude of sources. "Originality is an apparition," but the public domain allows us to pretend otherwise, and thereby to reconcile principle with practicality (1023).

The crisis-management response to the "shrinking" public domain is to restore balance by shoring up that public territory. But this approach misses more interesting questions, such as why it is so difficult to produce a public domain in this historical moment. The almost universal answer to that question, that the intense profit potential of information pushes economic interest to simply override public interest, does not completely satisfy. It is true that in a knowledge economy the appetite for ideas, expressions, and other information technologies is as voracious as the appetite for profit, and that these two appetites are easier to satisfy when information is propertized. Yet the production of IP is dependent on the production of a public domain, as are the returns IP generates. Moreover, information-based industries, from entertainment to biotechnology, are aware, perhaps now more than ever, of the economic benefit of a "knowledge commons." The "commons" not only legitimates their activities, it is also a source of new, "propertizable" ideas and expression. Thus economic interest, while deeply influential, does not, by itself, explain the visible instability of the public domain.

So I ask again, What is occurring to upset the "no-property" term of the intellectual property equation? Part of the answer may have to do with developments in the very entity that is supposed to be most fully invested in producing a common stock of intellectual resources—the research university.

THE "SECOND ACADEMIC REVOLUTION"

The university is "in crisis," and this, too, is nothing new.[4] The contours of the present crisis look like this: The research university is being rapidly repositioned as a site of commodity production in an information economy. With the end of the Cold War and the emergence of a knowledge-based global economy, commentators suggest, a "new social contract" is being negotiated between the university and the public (Etzkowitz and Leydesdorff, 1997, 1). Under the terms of this contract, (1) the transfer of knowledge from the academic to the "productive sector" is being accomplished through direct rather than indirect means; and (2) that transfer process is becoming a central part of the university's *raison d'être* and the professoriate's self-definition.

In this "second academic revolution," contends the sociologist Henry Etzkowitz, the university's traditional interest in the "advancement of knowledge" is matched by its interest in the "capitalization of knowledge" (1997, 141).[5] Through consulting arrangements, patenting of "fortuitous by-products of research," and, in some places, the formation of "incubators" for new technology companies, entrepreneurial professors and their universities have become active rather than passive actors in the information economy. Industrial corporations, meanwhile, are sponsoring scientific conferences and setting up in-house "universities" to train and improve their stock of human capital. This activity, Etzkowitz contends, generates a "triple helix" of knowledge production, in which the three institutional spheres of liberal capitalism (public, private, and academic) are intertwined rather than distanced.

As Etzkowitz notes, this revolution is facilitated by the academy's own practices. Drawing on Bruno Latour and Steve Woolgar's (1979) work on credit and credibility (which I will discuss in Chapter 2), Etzkowitz suggests that "entrepreneurial" universities are an outgrowth of academic scientists' own efforts to translate reputation into financial support for further research. The ever-present pressure to find research funds, exacerbated by perceived and real declines in federal and state spending on research, socializes faculty to "capitalize knowledge," or find ways for research to generate income as well as more knowledge (Collins and Tillman, 1988). Federal funding of non-defense university research, once adjusted for inflation, leveled off or began to decrease by 1988, with similar trends evident in defense-related projects by the early 1990s. State support of public research universities is also declining (Slaughter and Leslie, 1997). Small wonder, then, that many scientists are more willing to pursue industrial support for their research, including funding derived from the licensing of patents, consulting, and sponsored research projects. In 1996, royalties paid to 131 universities on licensed inventions alone reached $336 million (Blumenstyk, 1998b).

These activities are validated, in turn, by universities' own rhetoric, particularly the increasingly common definition of higher education's traditional public service mission as "support for economic growth." The stated premise of this argument is that the academy's survival depends upon its ability to move from a "reactive" to a "proactive" approach to society's problems (Leydesdorff and Etzkowitz, 1997; Collins and Tillman, 1988). The sociologist and university administrator Mary Walshok (1995) has characterized this challenge as a "crisis of relevance." Walshok seeks to make the university "relevant" by promoting social as well as economic initiatives, but for many analysts of the new social contract between university and society, social impact means economic impact. University presidents, for example, point to a series of studies by "new growth theorists" showing that university research has been responsible for 50 percent of new economic growth since 1945 and use those studies to promote the idea that "the university means business" (Atkinson, 1996a, 1996b). This justificatory rhetoric, combined with industrial pressures on the federal government, gives sense to research policies that reward institutions for "transferring" research to the private sector.

Sheila Slaughter and Lawrence Leslie (1997) present a less sanguine view of the triple helix, arguing that new practices of "academic capitalism" threaten the autonomy that sets professors apart from other information workers. Academic capitalism, they suggest, involves more than "entrepreneurial activity," for this phrase implies that a researcher's primary motive is still finding support for "curiosity-driven" research. In reality, they argue, profit itself has become a significant imperative within the professoriate. In the 1980s, moreover, as federal and state science policy began to emphasize technology transfer and applied research, the ability of the professoriate to define research agendas that responded to "pure" as opposed to economic imperatives was curtailed. For Slaughter and Leslie, the academy does indeed face a "crisis," but the problem is not relevance. Rather, the problem is the decline of academic freedom.

Yet it is not clear just what is new about the "new social contract" that Slaughter and Leslie, Etzkowitz, Walshok, and others identify. The land grants that helped found many public universities in the late nineteenth century were justified in large part by the idea that universities would produce research for the agricultural sector. Both the University of California and the Massachusetts Institute of Technology, among others, had small but viable patenting programs in the 1920s, encouraged faculty to consult with industry, and relied on private industry for research support (Matkin, 1990). Further, if academic researchers were ever truly free to ignore political and economic imperatives, they have not been so for several decades (see Mukerji, 1989; Lowen, 1996). Scientists' dependence on state and federal funding agencies for support helped clear a space, in fact, for the practices of academic capitalism that Slaughter and Leslie document. Even scientists doing research that still counts as "basic" serve government interests by helping to ratify political decisions about what constitutes "quality research" (Mukerji, 1989). These historical and contemporary practices suggest, at least, the need for a closer examination of the "revolutionary" claims made by surveyors of the so-called knowledge frontier (Faulkner and Senker, 1995).

What is new, or at least newly visible, is the proliferation of contests for the meaning of intellectual work. Slaughter and Leslie offer a telling description of such a contest. Focusing specifically on the introduction of new management practices in the university, such as the use of standardized evaluation mechanisms across disciplines, they note that "as decisions about professors' performance of academic work were moved outside the purview of professional expertise, professors became more like all other information workers and less like a community of scholars" (60). The linkage of professional autonomy to peer review dates to the medieval university, and in this sense Slaughter and Leslie are correct that the deployment of administrative technocratic practices to define high-quality research directly challenges the traditional prerogatives of the professoriate. The result? A blurred boundary between academic and other information workers.

Autonomy, Freedom, and Property

This blurred boundary is nominally defended by the discourse of academic freedom. The starting premise of this defense is that scholars are defined by their ability to disseminate the results of their research. At UW, for example, the freedom to publish, or to refuse to do so, may not be contractually rescinded (though it may be informally abandoned) in research agreements. Ironically, perhaps, this starting premise is invoked repeatedly by proponents of technology transfer, who can legitimately claim that the capitalization of university research does not prevent (though it may delay) publication of results. A related argument emphasizes protection of faculty autonomy, defined as the ability to set one's own research and teaching agenda and manage one's own time. Under these criteria, which set faculty apart from knowledge workers in private industry, academics are the true liberal individuals: freely choosing, radically autonomous, hampered only by voluntary obligations.

What seems strange, however, is that academic "freedom" and "autonomy" are invoked to defend opposite positions. Thus, for example, critics of university-industry liaisons insist that research contracts with the private sector subordinate free inquiry to the interests of capital. Proponents of such liaisons reject this "ivory tower syndrome," arguing that diversity of inquiry should permit free choice of research partners—including industrial partners.[6] The right to manage one's own time and research interests includes the ability to market one's intellectual labor to private industry as a consultant.[7] Following this line of reasoning, new modes of knowledge production would seem to be perfectly consonant with "traditional academic values."

Which brings us to the final and strangest development in this "crisis": the use of intellectual property discourse to define and defend academic freedom. Simply put, professors are deciding that they would rather be knowledge owners than knowledge workers. In overlapping debates over academic intellectual property—including rights in written materials, software, lecture materials, research data, and useful inventions—academic autonomy, equality, and freedom are increasingly treated as commensurate with individual property rights. Lecturers and administrators square off in a battle for control of ownership of courses and "the classroom," a struggle that turns on the real difficulty of delineating "the class" and its legal author. Scientists are asked by their administrators to retain copyrights in their articles rather than assigning them to the journals in which they are published (in order to ensure educational access to those works), yet are pitted against those same administrators in disputes over licensing arrangements. Further down on the food chain, graduate students scheme to avoid their contractual obligation to share intellectual property rights with the university—keeping in mind perhaps that a student was once sent to a prison camp for "stealing" intellectual property from his university.[8] Participants on all sides of these debates insist that they are struggling to preserve academic freedom.

In this context, the only question really worth asking, indeed the question most often asked by "revolutionaries" and critics alike, seems to be, Who will own the properties in question and on what terms? The trouble is, the more faculty look like property owners, the more their work looks like a potential commodity and their institution looks like the knowledge factory Clark Kerr once was accused of celebrating.[9] As an engineering professor declared at a UW retreat on university-industry relations, "It really does change the nature of the place when you can look around and see someone, not very much older than you *or better than you,* driving around in expensive cars" (italics mine). The nested claims that (1) professors do not labor for money (or expensive cars) but for recognition; (2) academic knowledge is not proprietary; and (3) academia rewards brilliance rather than luck and/or marketing acumen remain crucial pillars of the professoriate and the academy itself, for they ground the university's claim to the space of disinterested reason. Former Stanford president Donald Kennedy has argued that the spectacle of a wealthy professor "just gets under people's skin" (1997, 261). I would go further and suggest that the "spectacle" directly challenges the university's theoretico-political hierarchy based on the superiority of impractical knowledge—a hierarchy the university simultaneously defends through its repeated characterization of intellectual properties as accidental "by-products" of research. As we shall see, the stakes of the university's struggle to retain its status are very high, for the institution and for the information economy.

Subjects and Objects of Knowledge

We can now begin to see how the crisis in the university overlaps with that of IP law. Even as the professoriate turns to the law to rescue and redefine its central categories and the conditions of intellectual work, intellectual property law is facing its own "crisis," within which those same categories (autonomy, freedom, public domain, and private interest) seem to be up for grabs. In particular, the space of the commons is becoming ever more elusive, making it more difficult to justify its complement, the space of property. Part of the reason the public domain is being redefined is that one of its major policing mechanisms—the university—is itself refiguring the "public" as a space of private property. As Mario Biagioli observes, an identifiable public domain "legitimizes private property defined as the result of specific 'deviations' from public, 'universal' knowledge" (1998, 5). Because the research university is one of the anchors of that public space, a second academic revolution that threatens to reconfigure the means of production of "universal" knowledge raises questions about the definition of "specific" (private) knowledge. Those questions were difficult to answer at the birth of modern IP and are equally troublesome now.

The research university's own legitimacy, meanwhile, is rooted in its location at the neutral site of universal scientific truth, outside of politics and the money economy (Biagioli, 1998). That the university has never been a truly neutral institution is a given. The point is that it has been *situated* as the space of disinterested intellectual production, in contrast to a commercial space of "interested" intellectual production. The drama of identity crisis and uncertainty being played out at major research institutions across the country, therefore, responds to and helps create a broader juridical struggle for the meaning of knowledge ownership and production in an information society.

To understand this drama, it is necessary to historicize the unstable shared assumptions of current jurisdictions of private and public domains of knowledge. In the next section I draw on the work of Mark Rose, Ronald Bettig, Christine MacLeod, Harold Dutton, and others to examine the emergence of two of the principal forms of intellectual property—copyrights and patents—in seventeenth and eighteenth century Anglo-American law. In the following section I pick up the story of the public domain by looking at the history of its leading protagonist, the university, tracing the reconfigurations of the higher learning in the nineteenth and twentieth centuries that left its institutions uniquely positioned to police the knowledge that cannot be owned.

FROM REGIMES OF REGULATION TO REGIMES OF PROPERTY

The modern concepts of patents and copyrights did not fully emerge until the fifteenth and seventeenth centuries, respectively, and the term "intellectual property" did not gain currency until the middle of the twentieth century. The *idea* of intellectual property, however, has a much older pedigree. The historian Pamela Long (1991) suggests that a robust concept of intellectual property in Europe dates to the thirteenth-century craft guild. Venetian glassmakers, for example, built their industry on craft secrets and allied with the state to protect those secrets. Export of craft knowledge (such as formulas) was forbidden by the guild, and the commune of Venice imposed heavy fines on those who flouted the rule. The transmission of this knowledge within the guild, through apprenticeship and family tradition, was strictly regulated as well.

Guild practices indicate two elements of intellectual property important to our concerns here. First, intellectual property was already located at the boundary of public and private, though the content of those terms was fundamentally different from their modern conceptualization. Guild knowledge was owned by the glassmakers (the private) for the benefit of Venice (the public). Second, the property in question confirmed and was confirmed by its owner—ownership of craft knowledge was integral to the identity of the guild corporation and to individual members—thus property was closely tied to corporate and human personhood.

Yet this early form of intellectual property did not embrace a notion of individual proprietary rights. In the medieval period, a claim to knowledge as one's own possession was a denial of God as the ultimate source of enlightenment and authority. In this period, observes Marlon Ross, "for an individual alone to possess . . . knowledge would make it . . . purely private truth, a blatant self-contradiction" (1994, 235). Even guild ownership reflected an order of truth under which knowledge was attached to authority and shared according to how persons were situated within that authority. The guarding of craft knowledge signified protection for the commune of Venice and the birthright of its members, rather than a form of individuated possession. Even the secret glassmaking formulas were usually claimed by families rather than individuals (Long, 1991).

The transformation of this communal precursor of intellectual property into its modern form would require a dramatic rearticulation of the relationship between persons and creative works. Because the features of this transformation were different for copyright and patent law, I will trace the emergence of each of these doctrines separately. I conclude this section with a discussion of a shared legitimating premise of copyright and patent law, namely, the existence of a public domain.

Copyright

In the primarily oral culture of medieval and even early modern Europe, writing was still conceived as a collaborative process, wherein the writer was a craftsman working with papermakers, proofreaders, and booksellers to reproduce knowledge. By the sixteenth century, though, the creative process was already being reorganized around the persona of the individual genius (Long, 1991). The construction of the author as originary genius accelerated during the eighteenth century and came to fruition in the Romantic movement's promulgation of the idea that the value and "truth" of writing should depend upon its "new" and unique qualities (Woodmansee, 1994b). By the early nineteenth century, originality was firmly entrenched as the essence of authorial practice. Indeed, in 1815, the poet William Wordsworth could declare, "Of genius the only proof is, the act of doing well what is worthy to be done, and what was never done before" (quoted in Woodmansee, 1994b, 16).

Behind the flowery rhetoric of creative genius lay a set of economic, political, and legal imperatives that were to shape the status of that genius. The first modern form of copyright found in Britain, the seventeenth-century monopoly on printing granted to the British Stationers' Company, protected the economic interests of printers rather than authors. In the second half of the seventeenth century, the position of the author began to shift, as printers began to pay writers for the right to reproduce their works and some writers began to view writing as a full-time profession.[10] As the Stationer's monopoly reached its expiration date, printers saw the value of supporting an author's property right in the reproduction of her work, a right which could then be assigned to printers to reestablish the privilege of exclusive publication (Bettig, 1992).

Two problems had to be resolved at this early moment in the formation of modern literary property. First, the author had to be discursively separated from the work but remain sufficiently bound up in it to legitimate a claim to property. Second, the boundaries of the property in question had to be drawn. Opponents of copyright insisted that ideas were too ephemeral to be claimed as property. Then, as now, critics of exclusive literary property argued that once ideas were expressed they were common property (Rose, 1993; Patterson, 1968).

The idea/expression dichotomy presented an answer to both of these problems. In response to the charge that ideas were ephemeral, proponents of authorial rights argued that ideas were embodied in the process of expression. Language, they maintained, gave substance to the idea, or what would later be called the "tangible means of expression." The work, as a whole, was the embodiment of the author, "the objectification of a writer's self" (Rose, 1993, 121). This object could be copied, of course, and the ideas within it circulated, but the author's expression remained as "personal" as her very self. Thus the author and the work were represented as both intimately linked and autonomous. Authenticity was located in originality, which was "underwritten" in turn by the authorial personality. In a feat of circular reasoning, the radically autonomous individual author-genius was confirmed by the work's uniqueness, while the uniqueness of the work was confirmed by the individuality of the author.

As the boundary between person and property was secured, the author's position "at the center of [an] entire galaxy of literary commodities" was established (Rose, 1993, 123). The institutionalization of the author/work unit also helped stabilize relations of production that had been challenged by the rise of mechanical reproduction (Lury, 1993). Mechanical reproduction allowed the cultural work to be separated from the context of its production, thereby rendering it more vulnerable to resignification and appropriation. Linked to a "tangible means of expression" and an authorial self, however, even widely reproduced cultural works could be represented as inextricably tied to an originary sign, at once commodities and highly circumscribed works of genius.

The logical progression from idea to expression to property depended upon the characterization of the author as a liberal subject (Rose, 1993). In liberal theory, particularly as articulated by John Locke, individuals exist as subjects in law, bearers and possessors of rights, to the extent that they can own themselves and their labor (Edelman, 1979). One owns one's person, and this sense of the self as something one both "is" and "has" supports a second claim to property in one's actions and those objects to which one's actions are joined.

As free and autonomous owners of their actions, and especially their labor, copyright advocates reasoned, authors had a natural right in the products of those actions. Literary property was treated as "imprinting . . . the author's personality" on a thing; a process verified by the thing's "originality" (Rose, 1993, 114). This process of imprinting involved individual mental labor, carried on "separated . . . from the rest of Mankind" (Daniel Defoe, quoted in Rose, 36). Labor, argued William Enfield in 1774, gave "a man a natural right of property in that which he produces: literary compositions are the effect of labour; authors have therefore a natural right of property in their works" (quoted in Rose, 85). At the same time, just as property marked full liberal personhood, copyright ownership confirmed authorial status. "Property alone," claimed Edward Young in his influential *Conjectures on Original Composition*, could "confer the noble title of an author" (in Woodmansee, 1994a, 39). To be an author, then, was to be an owner.

As Michel Foucault (1977) argued in "What Is an Author?" the installation of the author as sovereign subject and owner refigured the relationship between authors and discourse. According to Foucault, the author, or "author-function," located some discourses as "authored" and excluded others. It also marked texts as objects of appropriation rather than acts. Discourse was not originally seen as a thing, an object of property, but as an action. Writings were seen as political performances, statements of loyalty, faith, or sedition, rather than objects of legal ownership, and the Stationers' monopoly facilitated the management of these statements. Printers were legally obliged to gain an author's consent to any publication, and to identify the author on the title page, so that any unlawful "actions" might be punished. Printers who failed to do so would be considered the authors themselves, and therefore responsible for any libelous or seditious content (see Rose, 1993). Thus texts began to have authors, in the modern sense of individual human creators, "when authors became subject to punishment" (Foucault, 1977, 124). In this sense, copyright was born at an intersection between censorship and the regulation of piracy (Goldstein, 1992a; Kaplan, 1967).

The shift from "speech as performance" to "speech as commodity" liberated authors from the control of the state and located authors within the "vibrant workings of the marketplace" (Goldstein, 1992b, 82). But the "liberation" of the author came at a price. With the removal of copyright claims to the private realm, a new form of information control was authorized and enforced. The now autonomous author-subject could function as "a principle of thrift" in the private sphere, a way of channeling and organizing discourse, while ostensibly promoting the relatively free circulation of ideas in the public sphere, now characterized as "the commons" (Foucault, 1977).

I will return to the problem of the commons in a moment. First I want to consider the parallel emergence of the "inventor-subject" in patent law. Much of the copyright debate focused on the need to distinguish it from the stronger rights over ideas found in patent law (Rose, 1993). Ironically enough, and responding to similar forces, patent law would soon be engaged in its own "liberalization," as patents for invention, like copyrights, were reconfigured in terms of property rather than privilege. This reconfiguration, too, depended on and reinforced one of the foundational premises of liberalism: the binary opposition of nature and culture.

Patents

In many respects, patents antedate copyrights as a form of intellectual property. Seeking to encourage the importation of knowledge to their communities (even as they sought to contain its exportation), the fifteenth-century Italian city-states began to award limited monopolies to individuals for novel and/or innovative techniques and machines.[11] Noting the success of the practice, other European countries and England followed suit in the sixteenth century.

These early patents usually lasted at least fourteen years, and most were specifically designed to enhance the ability of a geopolitical entity to compete in the international market. According to the historians Christine MacLeod (1988) and Harold Dutton (1984), in England as elsewhere originality, novelty, and utility were often spatially and politically defined. "A new invention" said Sir Edmund Coke in 1624, "is that which brings to the commonwealth [what] they had not before" (quoted in MacLeod, 1988, 13). What was novel in England, therefore, might be an old but fiercely protected trade secret in Venice.

Like early copyrights, patents were initially characterized as explicit privileges or rewards rather than rights, and were often refused where they might interfere with state tax revenues (MacLeod, 1988).[12] Patent holders, for their part, were not obligated to publish the details of their invention in exchange for those monopolies they did obtain, but only to train others in its use. Thus the early patent system, like the copyright system, was located in a discourse of authority and privilege as opposed to a discourse of rights. To represent patents for inventions as property rather than privilege, it was necessary to refigure the inventor and that inventor's relationship to society and the invention itself.

Patents for invention were caught between a liberalizing political economy and the communal guild system, for guilds, jurists, and the press viewed patents for invention with intense suspicion. This suspicion was justified, for as patents began to be used to identify product authenticity (and, by implication, superiority) with specific individuals, they undermined both the fiercely defended guild trademarks and what remained of the ethic of sharing within the guilds. Yet while early patent grants were assigned to individuals, they were not understood to reward individual creative genius. Until the seventeenth century it was widely believed that only "providence" determined the kind of inventiveness that could support patent claims (MacLeod, 1988; Dutton, 1984). Some effort might be expended in developing inventions, certainly, but discovery was not equivalent to individual creativity.

By the late seventeenth century, however, inventors were being represented as heroic figures who wrestled with material nature to dislodge its secrets, and legal theorists were suggesting that patents could be claimed as the "natural rights of genius" (Kenrick, 1774, quoted in MacLeod, 1988, 199). John Locke provided the conceptual infrastructure for this approach, as he had for copyright. God, he argued, had provided nature for man's cultivation, and through labor His creation could be transformed into human creations. Once God became a source of raw material that only human genius could fashion into new inventions, it was relatively easy to see patent claims as natural rights, conceptually equivalent to a property claim to a plot of land in which one had also "invested" one's labor (MacLeod, 1988). Indeed, patent rights could even be construed as the least the state could do to recognize such heroic investment.

That recognition became tied to a kind of early industrial nationalism, for victory in the battle with nature was seen as a source of national pride as well as economic wealth. Mechanical invention itself was treated as a new and potentially infinite resource, the exploitation of which should be rationalized. As John Chitty put it, patents were necessary to spur the "production of genius" (quoted in Dutton, 1984, 21). In 1774 Alexander Gerard emphasized the need to systematize inventive genius lest "useful discoveries . . . continue to be made, as they have generally been made hitherto, merely by chance" (quoted in Gleick, 1993, 314). Even critics implicitly recognized this function when they argued that the patent system did not encourage "the real inventor," a claim that assumed and invoked just such an inventor and indicated the state's obligation to help produce that being (Dutton, 1984, 27).

Yet that obligation was tempered by a continuing public suspicion of the patent monopoly. As with copyright, efforts to mitigate that suspicion by delimiting the "metes and bounds" of the property right were linked to a reformulation of the connection between the creator and the work. In the case of patents, that reformulation was informed by a new understanding of the relationship between man and nature. The early modern period saw the conceptual establishment of man as the patriarchal ruler of the natural world, a position that depended, in the first instance, upon the location of humanity "outside" of nature (Fox Keller, 1985, 54). Patent law was thoroughly engaged in the project of isolating some forms of creation as distinctly human activities. The 1694 Statute of Monopolies defined patentable material as "new manufactures," meaning "made by the hands of man"[13] Laws of nature—mathematical principles, for example—were God's creation and therefore His property.[14] Paralleling copyright's circular reasoning, the investment of an individual mortal genius made an invention patentable, while the patentability of the work affirmed the originality, hence the individuality, of its maker. Proof of manufacture was manifested, in turn, in the ability to visibly manipulate nature—to physically embody the abstract idea in a tangible machine. This commitment to materiality persisted through the nineteenth century and was eventually encoded in the requirement that inventions encompass both "conception" and "reduction to practice."[15]

The "reduction to practice" rule and the "law of nature" exception established some limits on patents for invention, but they still represented an extraordinary private monopoly. Furthermore, the limits of a given patent remained unclear. Improvements on a patented invention, for example, might or might not be included in the original patent, depending on how much money the patent holder was prepared to spend on litigation.

In 1778 *Liardet v. Johnson* solved this problem by codifying the specification requirement.[16] As noted, prior to the eighteenth century most patentees were required only to train native craftsmen in the manufacture of their invention. By midcentury, patent grants often included clauses demanding the submission of a written description, but these descriptions might be as vague as the inventor desired. In *Liardet,* Lord Mansfield ended this evasive activity by requiring the "specification" to be detailed enough that any person skilled in the art might be able to reproduce the invention. A "quid pro quo" was established: limited private ownership in exchange for disclosure to the public (see MacLeod, 1988).

This quid pro quo, like the idea/expression dichotomy in copyright, depended on—and would subsequently work to enforce—a set of binary oppositions. As inventors became owners they also became guarantors for several foundational dualisms: monopoly/freedom, creator/work, and, especially, public/private. Once patented and bounded by the process of specification, patents, like copyrighted texts, could circulate in the private sphere as commodities and in the public sphere as a form of speech. The state, again, guaranteed this property—but, as with copyright, the state no longer directly regulated it.

Too, patent law mirrored copyright doctrine in assuming and invoking an autonomous liberal subject, in the persona of the heroic author or inventor, with a property claim to the product of his or her inventive effort. Thus both copyright and patent law replicated a larger discursive shift whereby, as the legal theorist Bernard Edelman puts it, "the claim to describe man [became] the practice of the owner" (1979, 25). In

IP law, that practice depended on (1) the specification of a "work" that both guaranteed and was guaranteed by its owner and (2) the division of creative work into public and private elements. Invention, in its literary and mechanical forms, was liberated from the state and "permitted" to circulate freely in the private sphere. The liberation of the creator/work unit, however, was legitimated by recourse to an equally novel concept: a public domain of knowledge.

Public and Private Domains

The concept of the public domain was imported from tangible property law, and, in the seventeenth and eighteenth centuries as now, it was most often construed negatively, as that space of expression which could not be owned. Copyright law was organized around a three-tiered separation of public and private discourse: (1) between protectible and unprotectible works; (2) between "idea" and "expressive" elements of protected works; and, eventually, (3) between public and private uses of the work (Rose, 1993). Copyright was constructed as an intermediary between public and private, a channel that both secured private rights and ensured the continued availability of literature to the public.[17] The battle over copyright could then turn on the terms of this mediation—such as the length of time an expression was permitted to remain private (subject to copyright)—while the incommensurability of these two poles went unquestioned. In patent law, practical ideas were susceptible to ownership, but ideas coded as "philosophical" or as "laws of nature" still eluded patentability. The latter form of knowledge, plus ideas on which patents had expired, constituted a public commons from which the private domain of patented mechanical inventions could be derived.

The conceptual organization of creative work around the public/private split lay at the heart of what Mark Rose calls the shift from a "regime of regulation" to a "regime of property" (15). As we have seen, under the regime of regulation the state was directly involved in policing, or regulating, the circulation of ideas and expression. This regulation meant, among other things, that the creation and expression of knowledge were seen as explicitly political and potentially dangerous activities. Property claims could still be construed as contingent privileges rather than natural rights. As the law became concerned with the preservation of an individual's property rather than with the state, however, the basic premises of property claims were no longer seen as sites of political contestation. As Paul Goldstein notes, copyright was "about enabling an individual to craft [works] out of thin air and intense devouring labor" (1992b, 80). Patents, in turn, rewarded the crafting of mechanical things out of the raw material of nature. Both doctrines firmly located creators and their works in the private sphere, where cultural production continually referred back to owners and disputes over the circulation of meaning could continually be recoded as struggles for property rights.

Karl Marx (1843/1972) developed the ramifications of the public/private opposition for liberal theories of property and subjectivity, and his observations hold for the subcategory of creative owner-subjects as well. In *On the Jewish Question,* Marx characterizes the liberal subject as a natural, authentic, sensuous, and "real" but also nonpolitical individual. In contrast to the autonomous, disembodied, rational persons who assert political rights in the public sphere, the private individual's rights are seen as natural rights, with which the state should only minimally interfere. Secluded in a private sphere, individuals may look solely to their own self-interest. In this context, Marx argues, "the only bond between men, is natural necessity, need and private interest, the preservation of their property and their egoistic persons" (43). Indeed, the pursuit of self-interest is seen as the natural activity of man. Socioeconomic relations are thereby naturalized and individuals figured as sources of power rather than effects (Brown, 1995).

Having relegated various characteristics to the nonpolitical realm (the private), the state could then treat all its subjects as equal in the political realm (the public). That "nonpolitical" distinctions continue to work in the "private" sphere to produce most subjects as unequal is not, in this definition, an acceptable political question. Thus, as Wendy Brown puts it, "the subject [was] *ideally emancipated* through its anointing as an abstract person, . . . and is *practically resubordinated* through this idealist disavowal of the material constituents of personhood, which constrain and contain our freedom" (1995, 106).

This observation is as relevant to IP law as it is to other arenas of political struggle, and it brings into sharp relief one source of IP law's instability. Consider, for example, the political consequences of the line between idea and expression. The legal scholar James Boyle suggests that the idea/expression split requires and helps conceal the tension between "private" authors and "the public as audience": "Information is [both] the lifeblood of the noble disinterested citizens of the public world and a commodity in the private sphere to which we must attach property rights if we wish our self-interested producers to continue to produce. By disaggregating the book into 'idea' and 'expression,' we can give the idea . . . to the public world and the expression to the writer, thus apparently mediating the contradiction between public good and private need" (1996, 57–58). In the late twentieth century, "free expression" is often treated as expression that is protected from state regulation, while private regulation of information is not only a lesser concern but considered one of the necessary preconditions for creativity (Goldstein, 1992b; Gordon, 1993). Because "free speech" in the United States is usually understood to require protection from the power of the state, the law ignores how property rights discourse may be deployed to limit the information commons (see Boyle, 1996). A copyright suit may be brought for the sole purpose of obtaining a preliminary injunction against a publication. A patent on a method of golf putting can be used to prevent golf instructors from teaching the latest innovations in the sport.[18] A trademark action can be brought to prevent use of the word "olympics" to refer to a national sports competition involving gays and lesbians.[19] And so on.

Yet the force of the idea/expression—or, in the case of patents, the nature/culture—dichotomy depends on the construction of a public domain. And if the only bond between persons is a mutual interest in the defense of property, who is left to preserve the commons? It is no wonder that this arena has been so frequently treated as a kind of conceptual placeholder, a barely discernible realm of unprotectible, and therefore unprotected, expression (Gaines, 1995; Litman, 1990).

If we look more carefully at the history of patents, however, it appears that the task of preserving the commons was *not* left unassigned. The public domain was neither entirely empty nor entirely uncultivated in the seventeenth and eighteenth centuries. In fact, as the laws of nature shifted from God's hands to those of the scientist, nurturing the public domain became his special obligation as well. Scientists were the self-proclaimed "ingenious heads" from which inventions were most likely to spring, at least according to the natural philosophers Robert Boyle and Thomas Sprat, because they were skilled in the use of reason (MacLeod,

1988). For followers of Francis Bacon, those ingenious heads were also the least likely to claim property in invention. The force of science relied on its claim to facts about nature, and the status of those facts as "true" depended upon their location outside of the realm of artifact, or manufactures—the realm of human invention. In other words, as readers of the Book of Nature, scientists had no business claiming its expression as their personal property (Shapin, 1996). This attitude was also inherited, in part, from Plato and Aristotle, who argued that any scientific claim had to be publicly justified and openly shared (McMullin, 1985).[20]

Robert Hooke, among others, did advocate rewards for invention, but in the form of pensions, awards, or monuments "proportionable to the worth of the invention and the merits of the person" (quoted in MacLeod, 1988, 191). Honor and a lump sum reward, he suggested, were compensation enough for ingenious persons.[21] In the seventeenth and eighteenth centuries members of scientific societies tried to develop alternatives to patents. Scotland's Society of Arts, for example, offered cash prizes in exchange for submitting new inventions to the Society, thereby making them, in effect, public property. Legal scholars also saw a bright line between patent holders and scientists. William Blackstone was explicit on this point in 1760, declaring in *Tonson v. Collins:* "Mechanical inventions tend to the improvement of the arts and manufactures, which employ the bulk of the people . . . but as to science, the case is different. That can and should be the employment of a few" (quoted in Rose, 1993, 119). The creator of patentable (that is, commercially useful) inventions, then, was very clearly not a scientist.

Thus, just as patent-holders were establishing a special relationship to commodified knowledge, scientific societies and some individual scientists were busily laying claim to "public knowledge." This claim was not universally endorsed: many scientists did seek to gain financially from their inventions and worried about "practical" problems (Etzkowitz, 1997). Nevertheless, the construction of the laws of nature, facts, and rational knowledge was the principal activity of science, and that activity was defined as not only "public" but specifically in tension with the interested realm of private property. Ironically enough, then, disinterested science both provided the conceptual justification for patent rights by underscoring the domination of man over nature and helped legitimate the private ownership of knowledge by building a contrasting space of communal ownership. Meanwhile, intellectual property law helped affirm the credibility of science—the refusal to patent supported scientists' claim that their creative work was a matter of fact rather than artifact.

Recognizing this ironic operation, we can begin to trace the outlines of an epistemic regime comprising two mutually constitutive economies of creation. To fill in those outlines, however, we need to investigate the "public" economy of knowledge. More precisely, we need to know more about the emergence of the institutional home of truth and reason: the modern research university.

THE MODERN UNIVERSITY

It is not surprising that the university has not been seen as a significant player in the development of intellectual property. Most of the prominent authors and inventors of the early modern period were not attached to universities, and universities resisted many of the political and social changes that helped make possible the new regime of private property in knowledge. Nevertheless, attention to the history of science can help us see that the university actually has played a crucial role in the development of intellectual property rights. In particular, the university's nineteenth-century incarnation was crucial to the production of "the commons," the background against which intellectual property could be discerned. Once positioned as the guarantor of the public domain, moreover, the university became a guarantor of value as well, producing and certifying new knowledge that could be developed into intellectual property and/or incorporated into the "cognitive property" of the professions.

Others have provided detailed accounts of the "first academic revolution" in America, and I commend the reader to their work.[22] My own objective is to sketch the contours of this first revolution and thereby establish a context for understanding current cultural gyrations. Because my focus is on the formation of the university as a modern research institution, and especially its reconstruction as the home of technoscience, I will pay less attention to the specific history of the liberal arts college. In making this choice, I do not intend to discount the continuing role of the liberal arts tradition in the university, and I will have a few things to say about how this tradition was at least partially reconciled with the scientific research model. The university did not take its place in the modern epistemic regime until it had remade itself in the German tradition, and to focus on the story of that positioning I must bracket some important trends in the humanities.

The Medieval University

Intellectual property in its premodern sense was as evident in the university as in the medieval guildhall. Just as craft guilds claimed a kind of intellectual property in craft knowledge, so too did university guilds establish a kind of monopoly over the four faculties: law, medicine, theology, and philosophy. The contours of this monopoly varied widely in different universities—in Bologna, for example, student guilds influenced many of the terms of university education, including teacher appointments, while University of Paris students had rather less control (Rudy, 1984). The master's guild in both universities, however, controlled the production of professionals by controlling the granting of degrees. This power was found in most of the medieval European universities and gave the guilds considerable control over the production and circulation of the knowledge of Christendom.

In the twelfth to fourteenth centuries, most of the university corporations were chartered by the state but derived their real power from the Church (Rudy, 1984; Ross, 1994). Their autonomy from local government control, in other words, depended upon their subordination to the community of God. Academic work was organized around the four faculties, with the three "higher" faculties available only to the student who had first mastered the "lower" *artes liberales*. The definition of the liberal arts varied across universities, but certain characteristics of the *artes liberales* ideal can be identified (Kimball, 1986). A liberal education was supposed to train active, competent, and virtuous citizens, committed to a set of prescribed values encapsulated in classic Greek and Latin texts. Mastery of these texts was considered an end in itself, rather than a starting point for further inquiry, and it also positioned one as a member of an elite.[23] In keeping with the Christian order of truth, knowledge was constructed as eternal and scholarship as a matter of interpretation, imitation, and cultivation.[24]

During the Reformation, many universities were "freed" from the direct control of the Church and refigured as objects of secular state supervision. In the process, they lost their monopoly over knowledge and science (Ridder-Symoens, 1996). As authority was vested in individual genius and the scientific method, "true knowledge" moved from the academy to scientific societies. The academy still had the power to license professionals, but it could no longer claim to license "knowledge" in the sense of "that which is worth knowing" (Ross, 1994, 236). What it licensed, instead, was professional skill in specific areas and mastery of a program of culture appropriate to a gentleman. The return of the broader mantle of truth and nature to the university would take two centuries and would require a fundamental reformulation of that institution.[25]

The Rational University

According to Bruno Latour, the task of the seventeenth century was "the conjoined invention of scientific facts and citizens" (1993, 33). Two hundred years later the reproduction of this conjoined invention became the task of the modern research university. Between 1830 and 1920 the university would be thoroughly enlisted in the central modernist project: the scientific construction of, to borrow from Sheldon Rothblatt, a "character who [could] transcend himself," meaning a sovereign subject who could abstract himself from particular circumstance through the use of disinterested reason (Rothblatt, 1993, 30).

Rather than attempting to survey the multiple antecedents of this revolution, I will follow Bill Readings (1996), Max Weber (1911/1974), and Jacques Derrida (1983, 1992) in focusing on one of its most cogent articulations: Immanuel Kant's *Conflict of the Faculties* (1794/1979). Kant positioned the university as the embodiment of "thought as action toward an ideal"—the ideal being the production of a national culture and a reasoning subject to serve as its vehicle. As adapted by Wilhelm Humboldt to resurrect the university in the service of the Prussian state, this basic formula would provide the blueprint for the modern research university.

Kant argued that the higher faculties (theology, law, and medicine) of the university should examine and guide the "inmost thoughts," the "secret intentions," the conduct, and the health of the citizenry (31). But the "truth" of the higher faculties and their concomitant right to examine the citizenry could only be confirmed by the lowest faculty, namely philosophy, the site of pure rational disinterested reason. Reason was self-justifying; no one had to confirm it. The principle of reason, in turn, could be deployed to produce subjects trained in a *method* of knowledge production (the scientific method) rather than a specific body of knowledge. "Educated properly, the subject learns the rules of thought . . . so that thought and knowledge acquisition become a freely autonomous activity, part of the subject" (Readings, 1996, 67). The resulting hierarchy encapsulated the central premise of the German university: to be useful, the university had to be useless, in the sense that it should not exist to produce objects of practical utility.[26]

For this contradictory mission of producing the autonomous liberal citizen to be accomplished, the university itself had to be positioned as an autonomous, freely reasoning entity.[27] In taking on this task (later conceived by Humboldt as *Bildung*, or formation), the university rejected the medieval conceptualization of autonomy built on the notion of the contemplative life (Wittrock, 1993). Its autonomy was founded instead upon reason, the faculty that justifies itself. Only reason can critique reason, so no outside body, including the state, could possibly judge the university. "It is absolutely essential that the learned community contain a faculty that . . . having no commands to give, is free to evaluate everything" (Kant, 1794/1979, 27). Kant invoked the medieval guild rights of the university masters in this regard: only the university, he noted, had the right to "create doctors," that is, to certify scholarship.

Largely absent from this model was an account of the relationship between the university and the market, for Kant was more concerned with ties to the state than to the world of commerce. Nevertheless, the university's relationship to the market can be inferred. The Kantian university, by definition, was not concerned with knowledge commodities, or knowledge useful to capital. Indeed, the power of reason was precisely that it had no market use-value.[28] Further, Kant wrote in a period when the pursuit of knowledge "could still be accorded a status independent of material concerns" (Salomon, 1985, 78).[29]

Thus reconceived, the university was uniquely positioned as the home for, and producer of, "basic" research ostensibly shielded from the operations of power (Derrida, 1983). As it became possible to say that "the concept of being scientific . . . [gave] the university its internal intellectual coherence," moreover, the university could at last take its place as the central institution of the public domain (Schmidt-Biggeman, 1996,

489). It was not the only such institution, of course, since intellectual and cultural resources were not confined to the university sphere. However, the university was a space where the public domain was supposed to be actively and continuously *produced*. Art, music, and literature, by contrast, transformed common resources into privately owned expression, moving signs and symbols from the public to the private and, once terms of protection had expired, back again to the public domain. University research was similarly engaged in transformation of the common (nature) into the specific (facts about nature), but academic expression was figured as permanently public by definition. If that expression was to claim the status of fact it could not be anything else (see Biagioli, 1998).

Yet the university was located in a rather peculiar position with respect to the public/private divide. The philosophy faculty, Kant argued, had to be free from government control with regard to its content if it was to be a space where reason was "authorized to speak out publicly" (1794/1979, 29). Endowed with academic freedom and corporate liberty, the university was a kind of corporate person with specific rights as against the state. Philosophers also had to be free from the private sphere, for pure rational knowledge could not be beholden to the realm of self-interest. The university founded on reason was thus conceptually autonomous from both state and capital. At the same time, the university was the servant of the state, earning its protection by encouraging "the rule of reason in public life" (Readings, 1996, 58).[30]

Further, the university was the servant of capital, legitimating the commodification of knowledge through the construction of the uncommodifiable. Indeed, the status that the university gained from its position in the public domain was precisely what would ultimately make it useful to capital. A permanent space of nonproperty was created, a "knowledge commons" that could legitimate private property in expression and invention—remembering that the (re)creation of a private domain of intangibles was and is justified by the existence of a public domain—and provide new exploitable resources (Biagioli, 1998).

The American Turn

An examination of the American university brings into relief a second position for the university with respect to intellectual property formation: its role in the production of value and, more directly, cognitive property. Readings has argued persuasively that the German vision of the university, in particular its mission of building national culture and a national subject, has been eviscerated in recent decades. As the identity of the nation-state has been destabilized, and with it the concept of a stable rational subject, the ideal of culture has been emptied of content and replaced with an object that serves primarily to mark an absence: the ideal of excellence.[31] For Readings, this absence is particularly notable in American universities, and his survey of academic administrative discourse supports the claim. Yet the extension of the academic revolution to the United States incorporated a distinct nationalist vision that was tied as closely to economic prosperity as to culture-building. The usefully useless American university was asked to produce both rational subjects and the rational knowledge those subjects would need to make political and economic decisions. To understand what is at stake in the contemporary "academic revolution," therefore, we need to consider the specific genealogy of the modern American university.

The First Academic Revolution   The American research university that emerged in the nineteenth century united the Germanic principles of reason and autonomy with a commitment to empirical social inquiry drawn from English liberalism (Shils, 1989). This union was facilitated by the emergence of a new vision of liberal education, which Kimball (1986) characterizes as the "liberal-free ideal." Prior to the nineteenth century, the higher learning in the United States was confined to the liberal arts college, itself modeled on Oxford and Cambridge universities. As in Europe, American educators largely rejected scientific study in favor of the "gentlemanly" contemplation of the *artes liberales*. By the late eighteenth century, however, a more rationalist liberal educational ideal had taken root, one that emphasized "liberty," "equality," and "freedom" rather than virtue and classical study. This ideal was taken up in the early nineteenth century by an incipient nationalist movement looking to promote American science and culture. It was supported as well by the U.S. Congress, which looked to the college as a vehicle for political and economic progress.

   The "liberal-free ideal" helped clear the way for a larger transformation in which educational institutions "took custody of the technical apparatus of modern science, the questing spirit of German scholarship, and the pick of the nation's scientists and scholars" (Metzger, 1987, 135).[32] Between 1870 and 1920 more and more American scholars went abroad for advanced study in German universities and returned with plans to remodel the higher learning at home. Natural sciences, modern languages, and even such "applied" disciplines as engineering were embraced by the academies.

Yet changes were not merely additive. Across disciplines old and new, academic work became secularized, specialized, and research oriented. The classical tradition defined by Matthew Arnold's phrase as the study of "the best that has been thought and known in the world" did not disappear but it began to lose its organizing force (1869/1993, 79). While tensions between humanist and scientific studies remained, a sign of the times may be found in the 1892 suggestion, from President Daniel Coit Gilman of Johns Hopkins University, that the only distinguishing characteristic of liberal studies was that they were not "technical" (in Kimball, 1986, 182).

Like the German university, at century's end the American academy was being rapidly reorganized around a theoretico-political hierarchy within which practical utility was often derided in favor of basic research. But the American university had fewer aspirations to purity. Scientific research was seen as a tool of national progress (Kimball, 1986; Mukerji, 1989). The land-grant universities, founded to take advantage of the Morrill Act of 1862, were instructed to promote agribusiness by developing agricultural science and the mechanical arts. Prior to the Civil War most advocates of "practical" higher education were found outside the university, but by 1900 several (such as President David Starr Jordan of Stanford) had been embraced by the institution (Veysey, 1965). By the early twentieth century, the new social sciences, too, were building on the German useful uselessness paradox. Their objective, notes the historian Edward Shils, was not only the building of a character that could transcend itself but the "infusion of ordered knowledge in society" (1989, 432). At the University of Chicago, for example, John Dewey endorsed an experimental approach to learning in direct opposition to the lingering *artes liberales* ideal of education as the contemplation of received knowledge (Kimball, 1986). As institutions of reason, universities could produce and disperse knowledge that permitted individuals to make appropriate market and political decisions.[33] "We should seek to withdraw as many questions of statesmanship and social science as we can from the sphere of party politics," a Lafayette College professor had argued in 1869, "and hand them over to the investigation and experiments of our scholars" (quoted in Veysey, 1965, 72). By the 1920s this argument had been widely adopted as a guiding principle for the new university.

Meanwhile, American academic leaders developed close ties to industrial elites and adopted management styles patterned on the corporate world. While the same general tension between direct and indirect utility held for both German and American universities, in the latter the line between academy and capital was less a binary opposition than a vexed point of intersection. Yet the value of the academy's intellectual products still derived from its positioning outside the market: free from the short-term profit needs of capital, the university was free to serve capital's long-term needs, including its need for basic research.

The university was also free to serve the nation's cultural needs (Readings, 1996). The nationalist vision was represented as a universal project in the United States: one did not seek to study and teach national culture but rather the best that had been thought and said in the world, a canon. And that universal project, too, began to be reformulated along rational lines at the end of the "first academic revolution," as a specific kind of objectivity was introduced as a value to the study of literature.

American New Criticism, which flourished from the late 1920s through the 1950s, epitomized this reformulation (Readings, 1996; Eagleton, 1983). New Critics argued that social and historical context and even authorial intent were irrelevant to the study of literature. The transcendental power of the text, then, was increasingly understood to derive less from the work's position within a specific tradition than from the rationally determined characteristics of the text itself. According to this logic, comments Eagleton, "meaning was public and objective, inscribed in the very language of the literary text," discernible through equally "objective" analysis, and therefore available to any reader who could be taught to approach the text correctly (48). Specialized historical knowledge was unnecessary; indeed, the text was to be "plucked free of the wreckage of history and hoisted into a sublime space above it" (48). New Criticism offered disinterested, humble contemplation, through the exercise of which the reader could connect to the "world's body" (46).

The medieval university had been the keeper of the common culture of Christendom (Ross, 1994). The modern university was the guardian of a "universal" culture, now contained in a technique as much as a specific body of literature, and therefore the protector of a reformulated public domain of literature as well as of science. The products of critical contemplation could not be other than "public," if meaning itself was public and objective. Thus New Critics, like scientists, offered merely to assist in the discernment of an objective reality: they were no subjective Romantic geniuses but rather humble and rigorous investigators. Not coincidentally, they were also professionals, for American New Criticism took hold in U.S. universities just as literary criticism was establishing itself as an academic discipline.

Professors and Owners Crucial to these transformations in American higher learning was the concomitant rise of professionalism, beginning with the professionalization of science. As we have seen, the university, like IP law, was invested in the construction of a liberal subject. But it was also invested in the production of its own specific creative subject: the professional. As science became an "institutionalized quest for knowledge," the "scientific researcher" began to displace the "man of letters" as the model of a scientist (Rothblatt, 1985, 45). Institutionalized scientific discourse, in turn, offered a strategy for the reformulation of skilled work as "cognitive [professional] property."

The market for professional work, argues Magali Larson (1977), was organized around the supply and demand for services, or intangible goods. Because these services, or "cognitive property," were inextricably bound to the personality of their provider, their value was dependent upon the "production of the producers" themselves, including the standardization and control of the means of production. The production of cognitive exclusiveness depended on control of objectively rigorous, "scientific" mechanisms of certification, such as standards of licensing and examinations. Further, a historic obligation to train and license the classic professions as well as to govern the public domain made the university the logical guarantor of a peculiar form of intellectual property—professional knowledge—just as many trades and crafts were struggling to refigure themselves as owners of that property. Professionalizing occupations sought to develop recognizably "scientific" bases for their work. In the field of engineering, for example, shop-trained craftsmen waged an unsuccessful campaign against university-trained professionals in the 1870s and 1880s over the practical need for extensive mathematical education (Larson, 1977; Noble, 1977). As Larson puts it, "The understandably heated argument of the shop-men . . . [could not] hide that they had already lost the battle" (34). In 1880, 226 academic degrees in engineering were awarded in the United States. By 1930 the number had grown to 11,000 (Carlson, 1988/1991).

Larson draws a telling analogy between cognitive property and intellectual property. Just as patents permitted the monopolization of new technologies, she suggests, so too could protective boundaries be erected around new professional knowledge. The modern research university provided an institutional basis for that monopolization, and thereby became the "central hinge" in the professional as well as the national project. The link between research and training offered a means of controlling the cognitive base and hence the value of the professoriate in particular and the professions in general. In addition to defining and providing a standard body of content, university educators trained aspiring professionals in common methodologies. United at least in their commitment to specialized research and critical study, moreover, professors in science, engineering, and even the liberal arts were themselves standardized both within and across disciplines. By the late nineteenth century, the importance of university-based education to the creation of monopolies of competence had been secured.[34]

The defense of those monopolies was tied, in turn, to the principle of academic freedom. Like the research university itself, the idea of academic freedom was imported to America from Germany, but American universities were less interested in political freedom than in the production of dignity, the latter being deemed to provide a more solid basis for social influence (Veysey, 1965). In the aftermath of the Ross case of 1900 (in which one Stanford professor was fired for his political views and seven others resigned in protest), however, a distinctly American vision of academic freedom took root: one that included protection for faculty political activities as well as freedom to do research and teach without government interference. In 1915 the landmark Report of the Committee on Academic Freedom and Tenure of the American Association of University Professors characterized academic freedom as "breath in the nostrils of all scientific activity" and a basic prerequisite to the fulfillment of the university's mission of research, teaching, and the development of experts (AAUP, 1915, 28; Hofstadter and Metzger, 1955). That prerequisite could not be met, the committee argued, without the establishment of a system to prevent the dismissal of professors because of their opinions, including due process, tenure, and disciplinary standards of competence against which performance could be measured objectively. Only these mechanisms could protect the professoriate from the influence of big business and government. Though its recommendations would not be embraced until the 1920s and 1930s, the Report laid a foundation for the invocation of a professorial ideal of autonomy in support of the status of faculty within the university institution. As Lawrence Veysey puts it, "Liberty, even in an academic context, became inextricably linked with matters of security, status, salary, and power" (1965, 387).

By the 1920s the American research university had been thoroughly reorganized around the principle of reason and was able to occupy and monitor a significant portion of the public domain as surely as did its European counterparts. Just as IP law constructed authors and inventors, the university too built a particular subjectivity that could traverse and construct the public/private boundary: the professional. The American university's distinct notion of academic freedom and its incorporation of both economic and political benefit into its service mission, however, placed it in a more obviously vexed and unstable position with respect to public and private boundaries. This instability is evidenced, for example, in the periodic alliances formed through 1945 between humanists and scientists to resist the perennial threat of "utility" to professorial autonomy (see Veysey, 1965; Kimball, 1986).[35]

The Cold War and Academic Science   The modern research university that emerged from the first "academic revolution" has gone through major changes in subsequent decades, the most dramatic being those associated with the emergence of "big science" in the context of the Cold War. As we will see, the discourse of academic science that emerged in this period refigured and solidified the university's position as an arbiter of the public domain.

University research was enlisted in war efforts during World War I, but that enlistment was temporary, organized by individual scientists rather than by institutions (Leslie, 1993; Lowen, 1996). After the Great War, academic science relied heavily on business and philanthropic foundations to supplement limited governmental support. For some applied disciplines, such as engineering, industrial alliances meant relatively easy funds but also significant vulnerability to the concerns of businessmen.[36]

Continuing the nineteenth-century tradition of support for research of practical significance, other scientific and social scientific fields managed to enlist federal support for their research where social utility could be identified.

"Big science," and especially the vision of the "endless frontier" offered by Vannevar Bush in 1945, did much to rescue university research from the clutches of "utility" and install it more firmly as the imagined site of free and rational inquiry. Bush was largely responsible for weapons research and development during World War II, but he is most famous for his development of a comprehensive plan for the postwar exploitation of the "largely unexplored hinterland" of science (Bush, 1945/1960, 2). Without basic research (meaning research "performed without thought of practical ends"), Bush argued, industrial development would stagnate and the nation would fall behind in economic and military competition. Mechanical ingenuity would not suffice. And basic research could only be carried out in universities and research institutes, where scientists could "work in an atmosphere which is relatively free from the adverse pressure of convention, prejudice, or commercial necessity [and be provided with] a strong sense of solidarity and security, as well as a substantial degree of personal intellectual freedom" (19). With this argument Bush articulated the U.S. version of the old Kantian ideal: industry and the government would benefit from a "useless" university. Despite its focus on research, however, the Kantian university was committed to pedagogy as well—part of the object, after all, was the production of reasoning subjects. Bush's vision detached the university research from all but graduate-level teaching, for no scientist could possibly teach a full load of classes and simultaneously devote herself to intellectual inquiry.

Private industry was unlikely to directly promote such beneficial research, Bush argued further, but the federal government could and should. Bush proposed that millions of dollars be immediately invested in science via a new national research foundation (later dubbed the National Science Foundation, or NSF) organized around two key principles: basic research and peer review. Successful research contracts, he emphasized, should be evaluated solely on their contribution to knowledge, and that evaluation could only be conducted by men of competence and experience who were not motivated by self-interest, that is, other scientists. This "peer review" approach was not novel—it harked back to the medieval notion that only masters could certify the quality of research—

but it directly rejected a once-powerful "democratic" approach to research funding which tied support to demographics (Veysey, 1965; Guralnick, 1991).

Once committed to exploiting the resources of the "endless frontier," the state was fully enlisted in support of the "usefully useless" university. According to Chandra Mukerji (1989), this enlistment was successful because two world wars had taught the federal government the importance of maintaining a "reserve labor force" of scientific experts for consultation on policy issues. The value and legitimacy of that expertise, and by extension the legitimacy of policy decisions it justified, depended in turn on a system of apparently independent "quality control." The government could count on "basic" researchers to define high-quality research through the system of peer review and endorse that definition with funding.

Private industry, for its part, could look to the basic research produced by universities as a "fund" from which practical applications could be drawn (Bush, 1945/1960, 19). Despite its commitment to basic research in the Germanic tradition, the university that emerged in the first academic revolution was never fully divorced from the realm of commercial utility. The Cold War university, in contrast, could claim to be more thoroughly financially and conceptually detached from the commercial sector. The irony was that the academy's reconceptualization left it more thoroughly committed to national economic projects than ever, tasked to build a reserve and active labor force, a system of quality control, and a fund of basic research as useful to industry as to the state.

Though initial funding did not match Bush's hopes, research appropriations would keep pace with escalations in the Cold War. By 1960 NSF appropriations had skyrocketed to $159 million per year in contracts and grants (up from $16 million in 1956). Nor was the NSF the only source of government funds: multiple federal agencies, most notably the Department of Defense, took an interest in "basic" research. As a result of this funding, the academic wing of the military-industrial-university complex grew very rapidly, changing the face of academic science. Scientists became active grant-seekers looking to fund long-term research projects, building or working in huge laboratories, and using expensive, complex, and sometimes just plain massive apparatus. Research of interest to various government agencies was promoted and, as Mukerji observes, scientists "became clever at designing research agendas that would yield solid scientific gains . . . while also touching on issues vital to the state" (1989, 51). Less obviously, scientists came to provide the "authoritative voice of scientific dispassion as an instrument for politicians in shaping policy" (21).

It is this last effect that matters most for our concerns here, for its appearance marks the completed installation of the epistemic regime currently in flux. The dispassion of academic science (including social science), and specifically academia's ostensible detachment from "politics," worked both to confirm the correctness of policy decisions based on academic research and to construct politics itself as a contrasting realm of "passion" or irrationality. It also helped legitimate the propertization of knowledge by creating a comforting space of nonproperty. According to Daniel Kevles (1977/1991), postwar research policy was quite deliberately designed in contradistinction to the patent system. A U.S. Senate committee on patents had suggested in 1941 that giant private corporations were using the patent system to suppress competition and "inventiveness." Further, extensive media coverage of the licensing of patented strategic technologies to German cartels prior to the war (technologies often developed as part of government research contracts) had led to what Bush called "extravagantly critical attacks which tend to discredit a basically sound system" (1945/1960, 21). Dispersed government investment in research, arbitrated by peer review, offered a way to rescue the patent system by re-creating a distinct public domain of knowledge. Active support for a primary space of disinterest—pure research—could set clear limits on and thus legitimate the realm of commercial interest. Giant corporations might still engage in anti-competitive activities, but "inventiveness" would be protected.

To sum up: the "first academic revolution" culminated in a new epistemic regime, which was itself partially reformulated in the United States during the Cold War. This regime depended on the rationalization and professionalization of science and, less obviously, the liberal arts; the production of the category of "pure" science; and the construction of new institutions for scientific production. Wittrock implies that this regime is the counterpart of the simultaneous intensification of interest in "propertized" knowledge. I would extend Wittrock's concept to *include* the realm of propertized knowledge. The modern research university, resurrected in the nineteenth century as a semi-autonomous producer of knowledge and cognitive property, was installed as well as the primary anchor and defender of "public" knowledge. As we have seen, the modern university's relationship to the commons was hardly unproblematic: the point here is that it was identified as the center of a powerful communal resource. Thus resurrected, it represented a necessary if not sufficient condition for assertions of property rights in "private" knowledge: a space of freedom which could "balance" the space of monopoly. But this regime was built on a double paradox: to be useful, the university must be useless; in the name of vibrant public expression, some information must be privatized. It is this double paradox that occasions the perpetual boundary work of both the university and intellectual property law and, in turn, their perennial, overlapping crises.

KNOWLEDGE OWNERS AND KNOWLEDGE WORKERS

I began this chapter by telling a story of "crisis" in intellectual property law and the academy. I want to revisit this story and reassess its possible meanings and stakes. Thorstein Veblen insisted in 1918 that the higher learning "is the only end in life that indubitably justifies itself" (1918/1965, 10–11). In fact, the higher learning helps justify a great deal more than itself. Truths generated by the university are, by definition, universal truths, assigned to the public domain. Thus the university's *raison d'être* situates it, in principle, as a primary arbiter of the public domain that balances a "real world" defined by utility and self-interest.

At a minimum, the academy, and especially academic science, certifies knowledge and knowledge workers (Larson, 1977). Modern universities are crucial "knowledge resources" precisely because of their "reputations for neutrality" (Walshok, 1995, 191). Clinical trials of new drugs, for example, are partially validated by the scientific integrity of the laboratories conducting the trials. Investment decisions are based in large part upon faith in the results of those trials. Universities acknowledge that faith by carefully policing the use of their names for advertising purposes. Even industrial partners, though they grumble mightily about the "bureaucratic red tape" that limits their access to university research and researchers, recognize their interest in maintaining the fiction of university neutrality. As a senior executive of a major corporation noted at a UW conference on university-industry relations, "the university shouldn't be afraid to say no." Why not? Because if it says yes too often the university loses the basis of its credibility, and the products it certifies lose value. Indeed, the stakes are higher still. The university works to guarantee the intellectual property system as well by assuming and defending a public domain of knowledge to balance the private realm of knowledge commodities (Young, 1992; Biagioli, 1998).

In sum, the university's reason for being is inextricably tied to that of the intellectual property system. The relationship between IP law and academia is not a simple one, and IP law, by itself, no more defines the "crisis" in the university than academia, by itself, defines the public domain. But the emergence of IP discourse in the university does challenge the constitutive boundaries of a shared epistemic regime. As with the fundamental dualisms upon which academic and legal discourses rest (public/private, idea/expression, fact/artifacts, nature/culture, science/utility), the rearticulation of one demands the reconstitution of the other. Hence the enormous political, social, and economic stakes of maintaining and policing the boundary between these discursive formations.

Parallel border skirmishes are happening all over the world, from Uruguay to Britain to China (Webster and Packer, 1997; Turpin and Garrett-Jones, 1997; Sutz, 1997). The features of these battles vary considerably, but they reflect a common struggle by universities, industrialists, governments, and judiciaries to intermediate but maintain the boundaries between their respective domains. These struggles are sometimes international in scope. For example, the Digital Millennium Copyright Act— which required, among other provisions, that universities more actively police use of intellectual property by students, faculty, and staff—was ostensibly passed to bring the United States into line with international rules concerning intellectual property. The Copyright Term Extension Act that lengthened the duration of copyright by twenty years was voted in and signed on the same rationale. In addition, the needs of transnational corporations are pushing the development of a for-profit learning industry in which traditional U.S. colleges and universities are active players (Schiller, 1999). This industry relies heavily on proprietary distance-learning programs to deliver instruction around the world, and the production of these programs necessarily involves the commodification of professorial skills and training.

Thus the IP disputes arising in the context of "the second academic revolution," though they often seem local, in fact respond directly and indirectly to the emergence of a global information market and mode of development. At the same time, in the United States at least, debates over specific issues such as technology transfer are framed by distinctly nationalist rhetoric. Legislation facilitating the patenting of federally funded research was promoted as a strategy for ensuring that U.S. companies and consumers benefited from U.S.-taxpayer-funded inventions (see Chapter 4). U.S. universities have also been subject to periodic public criticism for assigning to foreign-based companies patent rights in research partially funded by taxpayers (Hilts, 1993b, 1993c; Rosenblatt, 1993). In short, the production of academic IP involves the subversion and reconstruction of multiple political borders.

One commonly noted effect of these subversions is the diminution of cultural resources for creative works, including new commodifiable products (Lange, 1981; Gaines, 1991; Boyle, 1996). Critics of this effect often argue for reestablishing a balance by sharply limiting the reach of intellectual property claims and/or investing in public creative resources. While I am sympathetic with these arguments, the proposed strategy ultimately reinstalls a public/private binary, thereby restabilizing an epistemic regime in which we might be strategically intervening. To take a concrete example, the logical extension of a limit-based argument is that conflict-of-interest offices should more actively police university-industry relationships, ensuring that the public/private divide is maintained rather than taking advantage of the blurring of that divide to rethink its underlying premises.

Equally conservative but more tactically interesting are efforts of university inhabitants to claim property rights. These efforts, too, leave virtually unexamined the central categories upon which the intellectual property system relies. Yet these property claims are also a powerful destabilizing maneuver, for they call attention to the multiple investments in locating intellectual labor in the public rather than private domain. Not surprisingly, these claims make jurists uncomfortable. Note, for example, a 1987 comment by the Seventh Circuit in a legal dispute between three academics regarding the ranking of names on a scientific publication: "Many disputes may be compromised by converting the stakes to a common denominator such as money and splitting the difference. Few commercial disputes end up in court, because the disputants may readily compromise and move on. Other disputes are harder to resolve because they seem to involve principles for which no compromise is readily apparent. The result may be a private war. A dispute that would be resolved quickly in the commercial world may fester."[37] The academy, the court suggests, is the site of "principles," and it would do well to handle its disputes itself. The fact that the academy is unable (or unwilling) to do so suggests that a battle over the standards by which particular meanings will be accepted as official definitions is under way. At stake in this contest are the truth claims of law and the academy and, by extension, the epistemic regime those claims assume and produce.

In the following chapters I take up a series of legal cases and academic practices that challenge the constituent dualisms of the system of knowledge production outlined here and the subject positions that serve as its vehicles and guarantors. These moments of contest expose the cultural work involved in resolving and concealing the inherent instability of this regime. I begin with one of its most powerful legitimating mechanisms: the gift/market binary.

CHAPTER TWO

An Uncommon Controversy

Authorship is an at once profoundly mundane and deeply vexing category in the university. It is mundane because every member of the academy must by definition be an author, and because authorship is not necessarily valued in and of itself. Particularly in technoscientific arenas, authorship is primarily a matter of marking the really important actions: the research, the discovery, the experiment, the credit, and the responsibility. Because it is such a matter, however, authorship is also a very uncomfortable issue. It is embarrassing to discuss, particularly with one's collaborators, a frequently necessary but awkward topic, often decided by inference when the "real work" is done. It is the subject of scandal, so much so that scientific societies have taken to promulgating elaborate authorship policies in a desperate attempt to make sure that responsibility, at least, can be assigned to a name (Biagioli, 1998).

One of the most vexing and most useful features of academic authorship is its ability to instantiate and traverse competing visions of scholarly exchange and thereby work as a "boundary object." According to one vision, scientific authors participate in a gift economy, a system of exchange premised on reciprocity, reputation, and responsibility in which the commodification of scholarship is, quite directly, immoral (Hyde, 1983; Hagstrom, 1965). A competing account argues that the academic knowledge economy can be better understood not as a web of moral obligations but as a system of capital accumulation and investment. In Pierre Bourdieu's (1988) view, for example, the value of publications depends on the continuing ability of the academy to define and guarantee a market for those publications.[1] Taking the laboratory rather than the university as their unit of analysis, Bruno Latour and Steve Woolgar (1979) portray authorship as the cornerstone of this market, or, more directly, of a "cycle of credit" wherein data are made available in exchange for credit and that credit is then reinvested toward producing more data. These models of authorship are at once opposed and interwoven. Plagiarism, for example, is figured as both a betrayal of the gift community of scholarship and a theft of the fruits of an investment.

The concept of "boundary objects" provides a way into this vexing category. As noted in the Introduction, I use "boundary object" to denote a concept that holds different meanings in different social worlds, yet is imbued with enough shared meaning to facilitate translation across those worlds. Boundary objects are constructed through the collective activity of multiple groups—they are not imposed as preconstituted definitions but rather built in processes of translation (Fujimura, 1992). Because particular meanings, definitions, and boundaries are stabilized, albeit temporarily, in the process of mediation, those "translation" activities are also modes of production. Geoffrey Bowker and S. Leigh Star (1999) provide a useful historical illustration of this point. In the nineteenth century, they note, the category "hysteria" became a medium of communication across medical, sociological, and literary communities, a common object for discussions about the pain, anxiety, and status of women. Through use in the service of multiple activities, "hysteria" became a bridge that, once "built," influenced public and private debates about the category of "woman." Authorship, we will discover, similarly bridges, mediates, and reproduces gift and market knowledge economies.

This kind of productive work is also, very often, a mode of betrayal. Indeed, the Spanish verb for translation, *traducir,* is closely related to the tort of *traducement,* meaning to expose to shame by misrepresentation. In what follows, I want to raise questions about what is being betrayed in some of the multiple boundary crossings that seem to be necessary in this millennial moment, how that betrayal is accomplished, and what is considered immune to betrayal.

To ground this inquiry, I offer several true stories. The first concerns a copyright dispute between a junior professor and her mentor, the resolution of which would require the mobilization and concealment of a set of assumptions about the nature of academic authorship and, most remarkably, the reconstruction of scholars as celebrities. This legal tale is supplemented by narratives of authorship told by researchers, students, and staff at University of the West–Collingwood. Using these stories as a compass, I will map the movement of boundary objects across multiple social worlds and track the cultural work involved in restabilizing the boundaries their crossing creates and disrupts. Boundary objects do not merely cross borders; rather, they make them, for object production is also a way of forming common boundaries between disparate economies. As law reconstructs its foundational categories to apply to the university—categories rooted in a market economy, yet imbued with values and rhetorics associated with a gift economy—it helps rebuild and reconfigure common territories between competing models of knowledge work and knowledge ownership.

GIFTS AND MARKETS

The leading protagonist of our first property story, Heidi Weissmann, was something of a wunderkind. A college graduate at nineteen, she completed medical school at twenty-three. At thirty she was a rising star in radiological medicine, working as an associate professor at Albert Einstein College of Medicine and an attending physician at Montefiore Medical Center. Leonard Freeman, chief of nuclear medicine at Montefiore and professor of radiology and nuclear medicine at Einstein, was Weissmann's mentor and co-author. Under Freeman's guidance, Weissmann pursued research in the application of derivatives of a radionuclide, iminodiacetic acid (IDA), to the diagnosis of liver and biliary disorders and published several well-received papers. The research was funded by Merck-Frosst, a Canadian manufacturer that had obtained approval from the Food and Drug Administration (FDA) to study an IDA analog known as HIDA. Merck-Frosst had contracted with Freeman for the study.[2]

In 1980 Weissmann and Freeman created a syllabus reviewing topics in nuclear medicine and IDA-related diagnostic techniques for use in a course they would co-teach at Harvard Medical School. "Syllabus," in this context, means a paper reviewing the recent literature in a given field, rather than simply a listing of topics to be covered in a course. This kind of syllabus accompanies lectures given in a course and is used by students to study for medical board exams. A few weeks before the first of the Harvard lectures, Weissmann used a slightly revised version of the syllabus for a course at another institution. The syllabus was subsequently assigned for the Harvard course and then revised several times by both parties for review courses at various schools.

In 1985 Weissmann published a version of the syllabus under her name alone. This version reorganized the original material and added new illustrations and captions, references to four recent research reports, and some new text. Unbeknownst to Weissmann, Freeman reproduced this version for his 1987 review course, listing himself as its sole author. When Weissmann learned of the reproduction, she demanded that the syllabus be withdrawn from the course materials. Freeman complied, but not before the work had been circulated to a few people. Weissmann promptly filed suit for copyright infringement, arguing that her revisions had been significant enough to grant her individual copyright in the syllabus as a derivative work (one that modifies a preexisting work such that the new product represents an original work of authorship). Freeman counterargued that the piece was jointly authored, a product of their collaborative research relationship. He further argued that, even if the revised syllabus was not the product of that collaboration, his use was a "fair use." Who was right?

According to the *Chicago Tribune,* the answer to this question mattered less than the fact that the case, along with several others like it, had been brought to the courts at all (Grossman 1997). In a lengthy article, the newspaper suggested that the "human architecture of higher education" was being dismantled. The agents of change were resentful graduate students and junior researchers, who were turning to the legal system to resist the appropriation of their research by their mentors—takings prompted, in turn, by increasing anxiety about publication rates and productivity. In a world of shrinking research budgets, the *Tribune* contended, professors and graduate students had become rivals rather than collaborators. It was perfectly logical, therefore, for students to try to gain competitive advantage by asserting property rights. If the trend continued, the report concluded, the "medieval" guild structure of academia might at last be dragged into modernity.

If the university is no longer a guild, does it look more like a factory or a limited partnership? Or perhaps a temp agency? These are questions worth keeping in mind, for they point to the stakes of *Weissmann v. Freeman.* Those stakes are brought into sharper relief by Weissmann's simultaneous pursuit of a sex-discrimination case against Montefiore and Einstein. Weissmann argued that she had been denied promotions and received negative performance reviews because of her gender. As I see it, both suits represent an effort to claim a space of equality in a hierarchical institution. And, to the extent that property rights were deployed to create that space, this effort directly challenged and exposed basic premises of the academy and the information economy. The gift model of academic exchange grounds the university's enviable and strategic position as producer and guarantor of valuable information at a time when information is increasingly coveted in the market. As we saw in the previous chapter, modern universities are crucial "knowledge resources" precisely because of their "reputations for neutrality," reputations based on their location "outside" of the realm of economic interest (Walshok, 1995, 191). At the same time, the university and its inhabitants must ultimately operate in the market and assert themselves as property owners if they are to reap the benefits of this position. Scholars may "reach beyond the walls," as the former Stanford president Donald Kennedy (1997, 241) puts it, but their feet had better stay firmly planted within those walls if the academy is to retain its position outside the messiness of "society" and its products are to retain the value generated from that location. By bringing the case, Heidi Weissmann positioned herself as an autonomous individual property owner rather than an aspiring member of an academic gift community. She pulled "society," specifically the market-based model of authorship found in intellectual property law, right into the walls of academia, thereby exposing the unstable foundations of the walls themselves. And like many academics before and since, she paid a price for it: Montefiore fired Weissmann shortly after she filed the initial complaints that led to the two suits.

Without Foundations

Montefiore's actions were not enough to shore up those foundations. That task was left to the courts, or so it would seem from the reasoning advanced by the district and appellate court justices who heard the copyright case. As far as the District Court for the Southern District of New York was concerned, the dispute was a simple matter of misguided ego on Weissmann's part, a view that was given sense by the court's own misguided effort to ignore basic premises of copyright law and treat the matter as a problem of credibility.[3] The Court of Appeals for the Second Circuit would sharply rebuke the lower court on this point, but, as we shall see, the appellate court offered a strange and contradictory rhetorical strategy of its own.[4]

To parse these interpretations we need to know something about joint authorship doctrine, a body of law that is itself fraught with contradiction. On its face, the notion of joint authorship seems to contradict copyright law's individualized model of creative production. U.S. copyright law acknowledges that some works are collaborative, such as a song that emerges from a partnership between a lyricist and a musician. In such cases, all identifiable contributors are considered equal authors and owners of a joint work, with an undivided right of ownership in that work. In principle, then, joint authorship seems to carve out room for sociality in copyright law. To be identified as a joint author, however, each individual must have contributed an independently copyrightable element.[5] In addition, each author is granted property rights in the work as if he or she were the sole author. Authorship, therefore, is only "shared" in an economic sense. For example, creators are not obliged to consult with other authors regarding subsequent use so long as they "share" the profits of that use. Thus an individualized system of rights is preserved where the law could support continuing mutuality (Jaszi, 1994).

Under this doctrine, two questions should have been asked in the Weissmann case: First, did both authors intend the piece to be a joint work? And second, were Weissmann's changes substantive and original enough to transform the syllabus into a derivative work? Strangely, these questions were not prominent in the first phase of the case. Instead, Judge Milton Pollack focused on Weissmann and Freeman's relationship and on their individual credibility.

Judge Pollack's analysis began and ended with the pair's history of research and publication. Joint authorship of early versions of the syllabus, he reasoned, automatically conferred joint authorship of the version in dispute. The work, he suggested, was an "evolutionary stock piece," a product of ongoing interaction and reciprocal obligation (1261).[6] Under copyright law, however, the appearance of an evolutionary process should have been less important than the question of whether Weissmann's revisions were original enough to render the specific work in question a new subspecies. Fortunately, Judge Pollack declared, the court was provided with the "best qualified expert opinion [on the matter], that of the defendant, the acknowledged outstanding expert in the field" (1257). Such an eminent scientist would, surely, be capable of forming an objective opinion on the originality of Weissmann's changes. Freeman had found those changes to be "trivial." Enough said.

Well, almost. Made uneasy, perhaps, by his own quick acceptance of the "objective" viewpoint of the defendant, Pollack was careful to emphasize Weissmann's lack of credibility as a witness and as a scientist. Weissmann had testified that Freeman had not contributed at all to the piece. "This is my words, my work, my expression," she said. "Dr. Freeman had no participation in it" (1258). This claim, combined with her "hostile" demeanor, fatally damaged Weissmann's credibility in the court's eyes. First, physical evidence of Freeman's contribution of visual material existed. Second, Freeman was listed as a co-author on previous versions of the syllabus. Besides, Judge Pollack stressed, Freeman *had* demonstrably contributed in another way: it was his name as principal investigator that made the research possible, and, as such, he was "the person with whom 'the buck stops'" (1259). Obviously, Weissmann had lied on the stand when she said Freeman had not participated in the creation of the work. Freeman's claim to joint authorship of the piece was affirmed.

Empirical studies of scientific authorship suggest that Weissmann's claim was not so incredible, and that Freeman's position as co-author might have been based on minimal or no written contribution to the work (Shapiro, Wenger, and Shapiro, 1994; Tarnow, 1999). I want to defer the issue of contribution, however, in order to address a different question, namely, what could justify Judge Pollack's preoccupation with the relationship between the authors, and their individual credibility, rather than the object of the dispute—the work? The answer is: a set of barely submerged beliefs about the exceptional nature of academic authorship and the economy of knowledge within which it is situated.

The Gift

Judge Pollack characterized the Weissmann case as an "uncommon controversy." The only thing really uncommon about it was the profession of the parties involved, a profession in which it is inappropriate to identify one's creations as private property. Copyright law in general assumes that authors need and deserve monetary profit, and fosters a market economy in intellectual commodities. Few bonds of trust exist in this market, and one of the principal objects of copyright law is to make up for that lack by defining and defending the respective economic interests of property owners.[7]

In contrast, academicians are supposed to write for honor, and the academic system of exchange is supposed to be based on the reciprocal and personalized exchange of gifts rather than the impersonal selling of private property (Hyde, 1983; Mauss, 1967). Jim Swan neatly summarizes this ideal—and its contradictions—in a comment on his own work on authorship and plagiarism: "This essay of mine, though it will be added to the inventory of my own intellectual capital, my curriculum vitae, and hopefully will count toward enhancing my academic status and income—it is still a gift, to be consumed and circulated in the gift culture of research and scholarship; no one will pay me for writing it and I will not sell it" (1994, 75n61). In a gift economy, social relationships are marked and contained by the exchange of gifts that instantiate more or less complex obligations. Market exchange is a mechanism for allocating labor and capital toward commodity production (Gibbons et al., 1994). Gift exchange, ideally, is a mechanism for allocating resources toward community reproduction. Through the quality and generosity of one's giving and receiving, one demonstrates authority, spiritual favor, and especially, honor and status. As Marcel Mauss observes, "men could pledge their honour long before they could sign their names" (1967, 36). Which is not to say that reputation is fully separated from more mundane forms of wealth. Reputation is invested in and guaranteed by things, and that investment guarantees, in turn, future prosperity in the form of more gifts.

By the same token, the gift is intimately and inextricably tied to the giver. Mauss is interested in the processes by which the "law of things remains bound up in the law of persons" (2). As a marker of obligation, he argues, gifts remain bound up with the giver, such that the giver's identity works to animate the gift: "The thing given is not inert. It is alive and often personified and strives to bring to its original clan and homeland some equivalent to take its place" (10). This close relationship between giver and gift reflects a prior obligation on the giver's part, for individuals owe themselves, as well as their possessions, to the community. Impelled by the same obligation, other community members must accept the gift and thereby create a channel to relieve themselves of their own obligation to give to others.

Searching for remnants of a gift economy in liberal societies, Mauss points to the "liberal professions," within which, he implies, "honor, disinterestedness and corporate solidarity" are most likely to be realized (1967, 67). Applied to the academic professions, "the gift" is most often invoked in the context of a boundary, as in Jim Swan's suggestion that university presidents stand on the "boundary . . . between the 'feminine' economy of a gift culture and the market economy of risk and competition, profit and exploitation" (1994, 77). A study by the Pew Higher Education Roundtable (1998) describes the "gift" side of the border as occupied by a "community of devotees bound by a common interest . . . [each hoping] to win the regard of other members" (3).

Objects that circulate within academic gift communities are imbued with the spirit of the donor, not least because donors are held responsible for those objects long after the objects leave their control. And, like all gifts, academic efforts are sent out into the world to bring equivalent gifts back to the donor.[8] Once accepted for publication, an article can garner recognition and status for the giver, and the more recognition the gift (and therefore the giver) receives, the greater the value of the original and subsequent gifts from that person (Hyde, 1983; Hagstrom, 1965). The community, in other words, determines value. Indeed, it is by instantiating mutual obligations (to truth, to persons) that the gift presumes and affirms a receptive community even as it marks the giver's status in that community. For the poet Lewis Hyde, this operation is made visible in the breach. Hyde argues that the production of knowledge as a commodity situates the producer as "less a part of the community" (1983, 81). "Community appears," he insists, only when "a part of the self [in the form of research] is given away" (92). Community ties are further affirmed through repayment in the form of reciprocal papers, citations to the work, and financial support (in the form of research funding) for the creation of new "gifts." At the same time, as the sociologist Warren Hagstrom (1965) notes, an academic scientist cannot publicly admit to any expectation of reciprocity, for the admission would signal a less than perfect devotion to the production of truth.

Remnants

To understand the conceptual disjunctures between the assumptions of market and gift models of authorship, it is helpful to compare copyright infringement with the category into which academics usually place unauthorized appropriation of expression: plagiarism. Both terms refer to the reproduction of all or part of a work without permission, but they differ with regard to the object of the violation. Copyright infringement cases tend to focus on "the work," and particularly the existence of substantial similarity between the "original" and the "infringing" work. Guilt depends on the fairly extensive borrowing of explicit expression, and it is not excused by attribution. The question is, has one person's property been copied and distributed without that person's permission, and the answer is found through examination of the work. Plagiarism, however, involves ideas as well as expression, explicit borrowing may be slight or nonexistent, and attribution will often resolve the issue. This last aspect is crucial, for it bespeaks a different valuation system with a much older pedigree. Condemnation of plagiarism in this sense was present in ancient Rome and Greece, where "literary theft" was viewed as an appropriation of another's honor and "immortal fame" (Long, 1991, 856). The term derives from *plagiarius,* to kidnap, and it signifies breaking a connection between the author's name and the work (Stearns, 1992; St. Onge, 1988). To sever this relation is to destroy the basic requirement of the gift: that it be imbued with the spirit of the giver and remain tied to that person. This link makes gifts risky to give and to receive, but it also helps make them valuable.

Yet the connection also marks a point of shared meaning between plagiarism and copyright, for a tight linkage between authorial identity and authorial property is also one of the pillars of modern copyright. Recall that seventeenth- and eighteenth-century copyright advocates constructed the work as the embodiment of the author, "the objectification of a writer's self" (Rose, 1993, 121). The object could be copied, of course, and the ideas within it circulated, but the author's expression remained her own. Thus copyright rules, like gift norms, recognize an intimate relationship between property and identity, or the law of persons and the law of things. It is not surprising, therefore, that Mauss identified a "remnant" of gift culture in intellectual property rights. This "remnant," the author-work connection, facilitates the operation of the concept of "authorship" as a boundary object across legal and scientific discourses, even where the academy's model of authorship appears directly opposed to the commodification of knowledge that intellectual property law works to guarantee.

Copyright infringement and plagiarism differ as well, however, with respect to the *nature* of the violation. Copyright law holds an infringer responsible whether or not there was any deliberate effort to deceive, because the copyright holder's economic interest has been damaged. Plagiarism, in contrast, is directly concerned with process and intent (Stearns, 1992). Money is not at issue, at least not overtly—what is at issue is truth. Plagiarism is an assault on the code of conduct in and through which rational discourse is produced, a crime against reason rather than an infringement of individual economic rights. Thus, demonstrably accidental copying is often excusable, for though it may still harm the original creator, it is less threatening to the imagined process of original creation.

The comments of the Collingwood researchers and graduate students with whom I spoke in 1998 illustrate the point. In unstructured interviews, most of these individuals expressed a profound reluctance to make plagiarism public. The majority of researchers reported at least one instance of suspected plagiarism of their work by a peer or a researcher of higher status. Of that majority, only three pursued the issue beyond expressing irritation to close colleagues. The observations of two scientists may help indicate why. One, who did in fact protest to an editor when he came across a book that blatantly reproduced whole pages of a then-unpublished manuscript he had sent to the book's author, described the plagiarism as an act of "intellectual rape." This description resonates with the language used by another senior researcher to describe his experience with plagiarism:

> I had submitted a grant proposal . . . [and] I got a review back that didn't match the quality of the science, it was much more negative than it should have been. The science was good and I rebutted it, the thing was ultimately funded. But then I got to review myself a grant from . . . a very prominent investigator, someone I knew, whom I compete with but I knew not to be a very honest broker, and in his proposal verbatim were sections from my proposal . . . and basically all I did, although I was pretty

animated about it at the time, was decide that you only end up smelling when you get in a fight with a skunk.

He didn't want to be "known" for that complaint, he said, but for his work. Several other researchers who felt they had been plagiarized expressed similar concerns. "My experience is that people who make a big stink about these things are considered to be hotheads," said an engineering professor.[9] Indeed, there is something unseemly about accusing another of plagiarizing your work, for it implies a degree of desperation. A really creative scientist does not need to control one idea—she has others. She can also rely, in theory, on an informal enforcement network: three researchers expressed the belief that plagiarizers eventually acquire a "bad reputation."[10]

Disciplining plagiarism stains the reputation of the victim as well as the perpetrator, but it also undermines the credibility of academic science itself by calling attention to flaws in a system for the production of truth. "The trust that society places in science," notes Marcel LaFollette, rests on "assurances of authenticity and accuracy," which rest in turn on the honor of the scientist (1992, 1). Note that plagiarism is not so much a matter of inaccurate *facts* as of inaccurate *sources*. The attachment of a true name to a set of facts is a way of locating responsibility and assigning credit for the actions that produced those facts, thereby guaranteeing that the scientific method can continue to be represented as the ultimate source of truth. Plagiarism voids the warranty, and, made public, may lead society to question the "trust" it puts in science. Much better, then, to resolve the issue informally, trusting that a plagiarizer's reputation will eventually suffer and/or that the creativity of one's own work will out. After all, as Hagstrom has observed on a related point, "Denying that norms have been violated is one way of maintaining them" (1965, 86).[11]

The boundary object of authorship offers an alternative strategy for maintaining norms. Star and Griesemer observe that boundary objects enlist participants in an endeavor by serving as "anchors or bridges, however temporary" to which multiple social worlds can be linked (1989, 414). The prioritization of economic rights over reputational claims promised by copyright infringement doctrine suggests a profound disjuncture between the legal vision of authorship and the gift-oriented model that informs plagiarism. Yet both copyright infringement and plagiarism offer to manage "the anxiety that authorship always embodies," as the legal scholar Rosemary Coombe puts it, that authors "might not be the exclusive and originary sources of meaning for those signifiers that circulate in their names or embody their personas in the public sphere" (1996, 206). Intellectual property law creates and maintains the exchange value of texts by policing and constructing producers and reproduction. As we saw in Chapter 1, this activity, and the economy of knowledge it engenders and secures, rests on the fiction of the singular creator. Codes forbidding plagiarism, coupled with unspoken pressure not to accuse suspected perpetrators, similarly work to maintain the value of academic gifts by producing those gifts as the "true" products of the givers. In short, at stake in the containment of both violations is the position of the authentic author as the anchor of value, a position that allows "authorship" to bridge as well as identify difference.

Sociality

Against this background we can begin to understand Judge Pollack's concern with credibility and relationships. In a gift economy, objects are meaningful in the context of relationships. Because Weissmann and Freeman had co-authored numerous written works, the judge seemed to suggest, they had established a system of mutual exchange as well as a position in the wider gift culture of research and scholarship. Weissmann's attempt to claim the revised syllabus as her own signaled a denial of that exchange relationship with Freeman.

Gift logic also explains the court's focus on reputation. In a gift economy, persons are bound to things. The court argued that Freeman had invested his reputation in the initial syllabus, and that that investment was as important as the actual writing. Having thereby imbued the syllabus with his spirit, Freeman remained tied to the product of his venture, and "trivial" modifications could not sever that connection.

Finally, a gift culture model explains the sense of moral outrage that infused Judge Pollack's opinion. Implicit in the court's reasoning was a claim that Freeman had given Weissmann several gifts—use of reputation, mentorship, access to the research, and by extension the prestige of publications based on the research. "It was the defendant," the judge insisted, "who opened the doors for Dr. Weissmann, making all of her research and writing possible and professionally recognized" (1258–59).

Gifts must be permitted to circulate; the gift cannot be withdrawn from circulation (transformed into capital) without losing its status as a gift. Weissmann's effort to treat the syllabus as property by claiming copyright ownership was, in a gift context, immoral. By claiming a sole property right in what the court saw as the product of that gift, she had transformed it into capital.

In the final paragraph of the opinion, Judge Pollack at last referred directly to the great sin of academic life. In claiming that she had written the entire piece, he argued, Weissmann was accusing Freeman of plagiarism: "Plainly the overbroad position she took resulted in a grave insult to her mentor and professional colleague. Dr. Freeman had neither motive nor need to plagiarize, considering his preeminent grasp of the subject" (1263). Weissmann's lawsuit, Judge Pollack suggested, was an attack on Freeman's reputation, and the judge's concern for that reputation marks a final invocation of the gift rhetoric to resolve a contest for private property. Faced with an outrageous transgression of the gift/market boundary, Judge Pollack deployed the language of the gift to resolve the dispute and thereby simultaneously restabilize and bridge that border. The work remained a gift in the eyes of the court, thoroughly imbued with the spirit of Dr. Freeman as well as Dr. Weissmann.

The importation of gift rhetoric into a body of law organized around the production and protection of commodities is not surprising, given that the reproduction of an author-work relation is as essential to the constitution of intellectual property law as it is to the gift economy (see Chapter 1). It is surely surprising, however, that this importation was used to reproduce as well a vision of scholarly creation as a space of sociality rather than of private property. There is a profound irony to Pollack's reasoning, for authorship at once is and is not permitted to inhabit two social worlds. At the end of the day the case *was* about property, and "gift" rhetoric was ultimately used to secure Freeman's market-based private property rights. In this regard, it would seem that this process of translation was also, as perhaps it had to be, a process of betrayal, and what was betrayed was the very "gift culture" Judge Pollack seemed to want to defend. The gift did not remain a gift but rather was conceptually transformed into a commodity.

Yet betrayal signifies "admission" as well as treachery, and we might want to ask what is admitted about gift and market knowledge economies in this border dispute. For critical legal scholars, joint authorship cases in general reveal the persistent commitment of intellectual property law to the individual creator. To the extent that Pollack's opinion set claims of sociality above those of the individual author-subject, it might be celebrated as a resistant approach to collaborative authorship. If so, it is also a cautionary tale. Indeed, the vision of "sociality" proffered in the district court opinion actually betrays a great deal about creation and credit in a "gift" economy.

Orders of Authorship

The case, for Judge Pollack, began and ended with status. The dispute, he declared, had to be understood in light of "the parties' relationship, the stature of the defendant . . . defendant's supervision, guidance and control [of Weissmann's career]" (1251) and Freeman's role as principal investigator on the joint project in the context of which the syllabus had been created. Discussing that relationship and the parties' respective backgrounds—"in order of seniority"—the court emphasized that Freeman alone was specifically authorized by Montefiore and the FDA to experiment with the investigational drugs that were the subject of the pair's primary research. Weissmann's task, as the "developing junior member of the association," was to conduct the experiments and write up the findings: the court apparently accepted Weissmann's testimony that "he [Freeman] was responsible for what I was saying, but I was really doing the primary research," and the opinion concedes that Weissmann did "almost all of the writing" as well (1254). Freeman's role was to supervise, review article drafts, and, above all, lend "credibility . . . by his standing, reputation, knowledge, perception and experience" to the project and its reported findings (1251). Interest on that loan was understood to take the form of authorship credit: the court noted Weissmann's testimony that Freeman expected to be named as co-author on any papers resulting from the project—including, presumably, the syllabus.

On the basis of this description, Freeman didn't look much like an author, or even a joint author, of other works produced from this collaborative relationship. Recall that every joint author must contribute an independently copyrightable element. Freeman did not conduct the primary research for the articles on which he placed his name, nor did he himself write up the research, yet he "expected" to be, and therefore was, named as a co-author. He may have contributed creatively in other ways, but if so, Judge Pollack was not interested in describing that contribution. The court instead argued that Freeman had donated his position within the scientific community, a position that had garnered the authorization to embark on the research in the first place. Authority, in this discursive formation, was the true ground of authorship.

Judge Pollack's reasoning acknowledged that while gift cultures may be communitarian in some respects, they are not egalitarian. In fact, gift giving is one of the principal strategies for re-creating hierarchy: gift-giving marks position, as does the ability to accept a gift. "Political and individual status . . . and rank of every kind, are determined by the war of property" (Mauss, 1967, 35). Chiefs exchange with other chiefs, family leaders with other family leaders, and with every exchange they risk losing status through inability to repay. Freeman, as Weissmann's "chief" [the court's term], was "responsible" for the gift, and the junior associate's effort to claim it as her own property signaled a denial of her obligation to repay her chief and, by extension, a denial of her proper rank.

The ability to "count" as even a potential author—a giver of gifts—is an often hidden marker of membership and status in the university community. Knowledge workers positioned as staff, for example, are usually not expected and/or permitted to claim the status of authors. Informally, the contributions of "invisible technicians" are rarely considered "original" enough to require naming them as authors (though their assistance may be acknowledged) (Shapin, 1994). The writers of policy reports, speeches, position papers disappear, for in academia as in the private sector most employee works are considered "works for hire" and therefore the intellectual property of the university. By tradition and law, however, professors are considered an "exception" to this rule, meaning that they can claim copyright ownership in most of the creative works they produce (see Chapter 3). Some staff members I interviewed were not disturbed by their exclusion from exceptional status. But others expressed anger. "Individual credit is one of the things that marks the difference between faculty and staff," said a senior staff member who had paid close attention to copyright issues on campus. "[Authorship credit] would get me a bigger sense of identity [because] this is an institution that rewards creativity." Denial of authorship credit, then, marked some individuals as lesser members of the academy: workers rather than owners.

For those who do count as authors, gifts to the community (research), and the community's acceptance of them, determine status. The worth of both gift and giver is constructed in and through repayment—an uncited work, for example, is less valuable and accrues little honor for its maker. The highest repayment comes via the scientific method—the testing and/or use of the work by others signals value. The risk, however, is that the repayment may impoverish the giver, as when another researcher takes published work and refutes or transcends it. The latter gift may trump the first, and the status of the maker of the "transcendent" gift will improve, while that of the first researcher will drop.

But there is a prior authorial hierarchy to be negotiated—that between collaborators seeking to determine order of authorship. Authorship is ranked in many fields, with the first person named in a publication, the "primary author," presumed to have contributed the most to the work.[12] Promotion committees pay attention to order of authorship—papers on which one is named as first author count more than papers on which one is a second or third author. According to Hagstrom (1965), this valuation is due to the association between first authorship and the distinctive exercise of critical reasoning in the formulation and analysis of a given problem. And indeed this association was embraced by scientific authorship policies promulgated in the 1990s (see, for example, Houk and Thacker, 1991). In practice, however, contribution is a highly contingent decision, involving explicit and implicit claims about labor, origination, and status. A closer look at these claims suggests just how scandalous Weissmann's lawsuit really was.

The researchers and students with whom I spoke indicated that in collaborative groups where co-authors were not listed in alphabetical order the highest-ranking member of a group had the power to determine authorship—both who should be included and in what order their contributions would be ranked. This decisionmaking power was most visible in collaborations involving professors and students. Both groups emphasized that authorship was primarily determined by who "did the work," especially the work of coming up with "the key idea" and doing the "actual writing" of the paper. Further, the "actual writer" of the paper usually composes the initial authorship list. But professors clearly establish the authorship policy. Said one senior researcher, "[It] is my judgment to make and I think that there has to be a boss in every institution." One faculty member said he assigned authorship credit according to his perception of the number of hours put in by the students. This professor prides himself on being fair, as indicated by his use of a seemingly neutral category—number of hours—to determine authorship. But in the end it is *his* perception that controls, and it is for others to be "surprised" by their recognition. Or to be annoyed by it, as one imagines the student referred to in the following story, told by a professor, may have been:

> I had been thinking about a problem . . . and I'd been suggesting to him that he work on this problem . . . I went into this thinking I'd be co-author with my student on this, this would be part of his thesis and going into it that was the mindset. But I was interested in the problem . . . so I wrote it up, actually wrote up the first draft. I put the student's name on it as the second author and in this particular case the student asked to be removed from the author list. And I felt this [was] unusual . . . so I asked the student, "are you sure?" [The student said] "I just don't feel it's right, you did 100 percent of the thing." I said, "Well, I have been talking to you about this . . . and you were doing some of the hard work. There's always a period where things don't work out [and] you were contributing by being there and listening to this and doing that" . . . It was a pretty close call. It could have gone either way. In the end I didn't take his name off.

In this layer of gift giving, the recognition of one's ability to give to the larger community (authorship credit) is itself a gift from one's advisor. And, as Mauss notes, some gifts cannot be refused.

Many professors take what they perceive to be the student's best interest seriously, and many consciously view their ranking decisions as signals to a larger community. One researcher with extensive experience in private industry noted that until coming to the university he had always listed authors in alphabetical order. After joining the university faculty, he learned that this practice could be "academically damaging" to his students because his last name began with one of the first several letters in the alphabet. "People will interpret that as I did most of the work, and the student was peripheral." A majority of professors said that they almost invariably put their students' names first, even when they felt they themselves had made a substantial contribution, not only because the students did most of "the work" but because "they need it more." And students recognize this attitude—as one doctoral candidate put it, "There's an idea of trying to give some status to the students."

Surprisingly, given that they "need it more," most students did not seem to resent their lack of control over assignment of credit. Respondents referred to their advisors' "generosity" with regard to authorship, often contrasting that generosity with the unfair practices they had "heard" went on in other labs. Underscoring the donative quality of authorial credit in this context, students repeatedly characterized authorship not as something claimed but as something they were given. "I just took whatever [my advisor] gave me," said one. "He's not going to leave anyone out," said another.[13] One student described an uncomfortable moment when he feared his name would be low on the authorship list despite his substantial contributions to the work. He did look on authorship credit as his just desert but was unsure about how to raise this issue. In the end his advisors and a fellow student raised the issue, to his benefit. He was pleased by the outcome, but he admitted he probably would not have challenged the authorship order on his own. Authorship depends on and helps create a trust relationship between advisor and advisee. To question it is to question that relationship and the advisor's authority.

No wonder the court was shocked at Heidi Weissmann's lawsuit. Indeed, the judge reemphasized in his evaluation of damages that the suit could only have been motivated by some kind of malice. The court discovered this after having taken the extraordinary step of stating, for the record, its desire to know why this "uncommon controversy" had come before it: "Judging by the hostility evident in Weissmann's demeanor and testimony, the answer appears to be that this action was brought for personal reasons—be they grievances . . . [against] Montefiore, or against Freeman himself for recommending her for reappointment on a probationary basis" (1258).

The case, the court concluded, was a matter of "misguided ego" on Weissmann's part, an "unfortunate lapse of judgment" (1258). But the case can also be read as a tactic of subversion. The lawsuit threatened the hierarchy embedded in mentorship: a decision in Weissmann's favor would have suggested that mentor and mentee were equal and autonomous individuals (property owners), thereby necessarily undermining a trust relationship based on dependence and obligation. In the face of the contest for the meaning of scholarly production this assertion engendered, Judge Pollack reconstructed the university as a site of collaboration—but also of hierarchy.

Taken as a whole, the district court's reasoning promised a reconciliation of academic and legal visions of authorship and ownership. To make the academic author "work" in a legal context, however, critical elements of its enactment had to be concealed or ignored. The accounts of authorship offered by students and professors alike suggest that Weissmann's claim that the piece was entirely her words and work is, in an academic context, quite plausible. Judge Pollack gave this claim considerable weight in determining Weissmann's credibility, and he relied on the fact that Freeman was listed as a co-author on some versions of the syllabus to support his conclusion that Freeman must have written some portion of the work. This fact was crucial, for, as noted above, the ability of "authorship" to traverse academic and legal contexts depends in part on a shared commitment to an identity-property relation formed when a "creative spark" is invested in a work. If Freeman did not actually contribute to the formulation of the expression, he could not look much like the creative genius assumed by both gift- and market-based discourses of authorship. As indeed he did not, according to the next court to hear the case.

OUT OF THE GUILD AND INTO MODERNITY?

In its report on the first phase of the Weissmann case, the *Chicago Tribune* referred to Pollack's opinion as a classic example of the "chilly reception" students, research assistants, and other junior scholars suing for copyright infringement could once expect from the courts. The same article pointed to the subsequent appellate opinion as the first step in a long-delayed institutional transition from feudalism to modernity. Summarizing several cases involving junior and senior academic authors, the *Tribune* declared that the "serfs" might at last be poised to "topple the lords" (Grossman, 1997).

Writing for the Second Circuit, Judge Richard Cardamone quickly dismissed Judge Pollack's evolutionary theory of authorship, noting that co-authorship of preexisting works did not confer authorship in subsequent works. "If such were the law" argued Judge Cardamone, "it would eviscerate the independent copyright protection that attaches to a derivative work" (1317). The issue, then, was the intention of the alleged authors and the content of the work. With regard to the former, the judge invoked Learned Hand's famous rule that all contributors must "plan an undivided whole [in which] their separate interests will be as inextricably involved, as are the threads out of which they have woven the seamless fabric of the work."[14] Weissmann clearly did not intend for this particular work to be jointly authored; she neither submitted the syllabus to Freeman for comments nor published the syllabus under both names. In addition, Judge Cardamone argued, the authors could not have intended for the work to remain "forever indivisible" given that scientific research "is a quest for new discoveries" (1319). Weissmann, as a scientist, had embarked on such a quest and left her mentor behind. In so doing, she had made the new product her own.

Having dispensed with intent, the court turned to originality to determine whether Weissmann's revisions were sufficient to make the piece a derivative work. He began by rejecting Judge Pollack's credibility analysis as irrelevant. Credibility does not determine originality under copyright law, he said. "Credibility might have been relevant . . . had the question of who actually authored the new material been contested. But it is scarcely pertinent to determining whether the newly-added matter satisfies the statutory requirements for protectability" (1322). To be protectible, the new matter merely had to be nontrivial. Weissmann's modifications fit firmly into that category. Indeed, Judge Cardamone observed, they *must* have been nontrivial, else Freeman would not have copied the syllabus but used an earlier version of the work.

In sum, the court treated academic authorship like any other joint authorship dispute. More directly, it treated the dispute as it would treat a commercial dispute, ignoring the "gift economy" model of the university and the status of the parties. Credibility, reputation, authority: all were overtly rejected as sources of authorship. Rejected as well was the respect for sociality embedded in the deployment of those categories. Judge Pollack had portrayed academic authorship as corollary to a web of relations and practices; the Second Circuit reestablished the primacy of the originary, radically autonomous author-subject. One would expect, therefore, that the decision marked a fundamental disconnect between legal and academic representations of authorship. A closer examination of the context of authorship suggests, however, that scientific authors do indeed look as much like atomized property owners as gift givers and that the knowledge economy looks as much like a market as a "community of devotees." To see why, I want to return to the problem of ordering authorship, paying special attention again to situations involving authors of unequal status.

Originality, Investment, Labor

Copyright law is often criticized for its refusal to acknowledge or accommodate collaborative practice, and the law's treatment of joint authorship is considered a case in point (Jaszi, 1994; Lunsford and Ede, 1994; Boyle, 1996). Yet there are important ways in which collaborative scientific knowledge production depends on an authorial discourse that reflects the individualist elements of joint authorship doctrine. In the academy as in legal arenas, collaborative ownership of an object of knowledge depends on the individuation of subjects of knowledge.

To begin with, gift systems of reciprocity, as conceived by Western social scientists such as Mauss and Hagstrom, include individualistic elements. "Pains are taken," Mauss notes, to "show one's freedom and autonomy as well as one's magnanimity" in gift giving, so that the gift can seem a product of individual free will rather than obligation (1967, 21). Picking up Mauss's lead, Hagstrom notes that "[academic] recognition is awarded to the individual who exercises the decisionmaking functions, who freely selects problems and methods, and who evaluates the results" (1965, 69). It is awarded, in other words, to the individual who looks most like a rational liberal subject. Biagioli puts the point rather differently. The production of scientific truth, he suggests, rests on the transformation of generic "nature" into a specific knowledge claim (1998, 5). It is necessary, then, to "mark" that claim to knowledge, to differentiate it by attaching it to an individual name.

That process of individuation, however, can be difficult to delineate. It is an "embarrassing" topic, an "intangible negotiation," according to my respondents, a subject that, said one senior researcher, "I don't discuss and I don't like to discuss." For this researcher, ranking authorship was a betrayal of a collaborative creative process—credit, he said, properly "belongs to the interaction." The unease attached to the individuation of authorship can result in rather elaborate exchanges, as this description of an "authorship conversation" by a senior researcher attests: "Everyone knows the problem of primary authorship will come up at some point. So someone says, 'I guess we have to figure out who should be first.' And then someone else says, 'Well, why don't you be first.' And you negotiate in a friendly way, 'No, you be first,' yada yada yada." This researcher stressed that the first concern was rewarding the most significant contribution or, as he put it, asking "Do you have an intellectual right to it?" But he conceded that the answer to that question is not always clear, which is why "it comes down to human relations." Echoing the senior researcher quoted above, he added, "I don't care to enter into those battles." This "collegial" image of authorship negotiation was contradicted, however, by the comments of a junior researcher. He agreed that the negotiations were usually friendly but also suggested that even friendly discussions about authorship were covertly if not overtly tense because "we all have strong egos, that's why we're in this business."

Problematic as it is, the negotiation must and does take place at some point in every collaboration leading to a publication. Where collaborators are nominal equals, this process of individuation (again bracketing instances of alphabetization) rests on a more robust version of the same principle found in law: originality. Max Weber neatly summarized this ideal: "There is a very widespread notion that science . . . is carried on by cool calculating reason, as if it were something produced in a factory. Such ideas reveal not the slightest understanding of what takes place in a factory or in a laboratory. In the former as well as the latter, a person must have an inspiration, an idea, if he is to accomplish something valuable" (1919/1974, 59). According to the researchers with whom I spoke, the position of first author is normally assigned to the person understood to have had the "inspiration" for a given paper, the "key idea" that made the work possible. Furthermore, anyone who can be identified as having lent a "creative spark" to the work may be included.

When identified contributors do not hold equal status, however, at least two senses of origination may come into play. One may be a recognized originator of an idea. Or one may be an origin point in the sense of providing the conditions of possibility for the idea's appearance. In the authorship hierarchy, the position of *last* author often marks its occupant as an originator in the latter sense, the source of the research if not the specific topic of the paper—the principal investigator. This is particularly true where professor and student are co-authors. One professor told me half-jokingly that it was somewhat embarrassing to be first, because readers might wonder why he was not delegating work to students.

Ironically, therefore, while first place marks principal authorship, last place may be a more significant marker of status. Several professors noted that last authorship signaled overall management of the investigation. In other words, the practice of listing advisors and/or principal investigators for a given project in last place results in a redefinition of that position as the site of productive power. Appropriately, this position couples originality with investment.

Investment

Scientists, argue Bruno Latour and Steve Woolgar (1979), are like corporations, and their curriculum vitae are like annual profit-loss statements. Authorship credit signifies credibility—recognition of an "ability to do science" rather than simply a "job well done." This credibility, or scientific capital, can be accumulated and reinvested in support of someone else's work, in research proposals, and/or in getting subsequent work accepted. If credit is invested wisely, it will garner a return in the form of, for example, research funding. Wise investments are those which respond most effectively to the laws of supply and demand. In this model, scientists are figured as both employers (corporations) and employees: their funding sources remain the ultimate power in this market, one over which they have limited control.

Successfully invested, scientific capital creates more capital, such as authorship credit on publications to which one has, as the district court put it in *Weissmann*, "lent authority." Students and professors often describe this investment in nonfinancial terms—as a matter of time spent discussing research directions, editorial feedback, problem formulation, even writing. Nevertheless, intellectual and financial investments are closely linked. One professor (I'll call him Professor Richards) described his irritation when another faculty member (I'll call him Professor Douglas) was listed as a fellow co-author on a student's paper. Professor Richards said he had "fed" the student "intellectually" and given the student financial support as well. The student had admitted to Richards that Douglas had had little input on the paper, but the student "wasn't in a position to assert." Richards's discomfort was mitigated, however, by the fact that Douglas had provided significant financial support early in the student's career, before Richards "took it over." Thus financial investment "counts" as a contribution.

A doctoral student put the issue rather more starkly. His advisor, he said, had given him little or no intellectual support. Why was the advisor listed as an author? "He is providing money for me so it's a little difficult to say, 'Hey, you're not getting on this paper' . . . He needs his name on papers to get more research grants coming in . . . Tenure is completely based on whether they're bringing in money. In order to bring in money you have to have a huge list of papers you've published." Several other students echoed these comments, though most felt that funding was not the only reason their advisors deserved co-author credit. "[Publications are] the real mechanisms for demonstrating to [sponsors] that you've spent their money and actually done something with it" said one doctoral student. "Everybody has a vested interest in it, it's just sort of part of the game, of the system, it's kind of the ring you have to jump through in addition to your oral exams." Some professors were equally candid. "I will not let a student put out a paper without my name on it . . . because I had to bring in the money for that student," said one. "And I think that's an unspoken rule of the culture."

The *Chicago Tribune* characterized the academic architecture of human relations as feudal: in exchange for minimal financial support, the "serfs" till the soil while the "lords" reap the profits. The comments of professors and students suggest that the academic process more closely parallels corporate authorship, whereby corporations claim copyright in works produced under their auspices. The presumption is that the work is produced under the direction of the corporate body, which is therefore the point of origination. Ill-paid students, as "employees," are permitted to claim authorial status, but must also be sure to acknowledge their professors as points of origination, providing their professors and the professors' sponsors with a profit.

Labor

If "investment" often determines "last place" in situations of structural hierarchy, first place appears to be determined by labor as much as by originality. As in copyright doctrine, a creative spark is crucial, but the more prevalent phrase is "doing the work" or putting the "hours" in. I asked several professors what counted as the kind of "work" that earned authorship credit. One professor's comments, echoed by others, precisely distinguished "the work" from "the idea": "In all areas there is schlep work . . . once you've had the major idea and you've set it down on paper exactly what you're doing, someone has to do it. And very often it's students. It is good, students have to learn how to do it. So that's the work, even though they may not have thought about [the problem] enough themselves."

On this account, *labor* is invested in carrying out the "major idea" and authorship credit is the fruit of that labor. This paradigm is further emphasized in discussions of expression. Students draft papers, often with editorial help from their advisors, but in technoscience "writing" is often the least valued aspect of "doing the work." It *is* taken seriously. Many scientists do not consider themselves to be good writers, and some view writing as "painful," so they respect those who are successful at it and see writing as a significant contribution to "the work." But writing is still a secondary process: one "writes up" the research, after the creative activity of formulating the problem and the lesser but crucial work of testing it. Thus expression is still a matter of labor, rather than, as copyright doctrine might have it, the essence of originality. And while first authorship is often tied to describing the work for the community, that expressive activity is not necessarily equivalent to being the primary creative force behind it.

The relationship of labor to first authorship is somewhat curious, for it would appear to contradict scientific priorities. "Work," as Weber said, "is no substitute for imaginative insight" (1919/1974, 59). If authorship credit is supposed to reward original scientific insight rather than technical work, why has a labor theory of authorial claims emerged in this arena? Better, what cultural work is it performing?

Copyright law indicates at least a partial answer. In this body of law, a labor theory of property is sometimes used to resolve political problems on moral terms. Labor, argued William Enfield in 1774, "gives a man a natural right of property in that which he produces: literary compositions are the effect of labor; authors have therefore a natural right of property in their works" (quoted in Rose, 1993, 85). This "natural rights" justification for IP has been overtly rejected in U.S. courts in favor of a utilitarian theory that portrays IP rights as an incentive for creators to make their work available to the public (Goldstein, 1992a). Yet labor justifications persistently reappear when the author-subject eludes easy definition, as in disputes over whether corporate persons can be authors and whether historical and scientific facts can be authored.[15] A labor theory of property focuses attention on moral precepts (the moral rights of creators to reap where they have sown) rather than political questions (such as whether a corporate person's investment of money is equivalent to a "natural" person's investment of labor).

The same principle may obtain here. In technoscience, decisionmaking about authorship is an uncomfortable and highly politicized process that potentially brings into relief the tensions *between* gift and market rhetorics of scholarship and *within* trust relationships. The language of labor bridges that dualism by introducing a seemingly neutral category— "the work"—which can be represented as quantifiable and which invokes the familiar moral power of natural rights discourse. The assignment of authorship can therefore be represented as a technical and/or moral problem rather than an economic and political decision.

In sum, it would seem that Judge Cardamone was right to refuse to treat academic authorship as "special," given the alliance of academic science's rhetorical strategies with those of copyright law. In this sense, perhaps, the *Tribune*'s hyperbolic celebration of the academy's entrance into "the modern" was right on target, to the extent that modernity can be taken to denote the ascendance of a rhetoric of creativity that assumes and affirms private property rights. The appellate court's opinion dislodged the "gift economy" model of academic scholarship in favor of a market-oriented model. In so doing, it replicated the academy's own production of scientific authors as individualized, legally if not structurally "equal," and morally autonomous property owners—a creation which exists simultaneously with the "gift model" of authorship. A more "modern" academy was thereby produced and normalized. Or was it?

THE SPECTER OF THE GIFT

In a final twist, the specter of the gift continued to haunt the case, providing the means for a partial reconciliation of gift and market models. Having resolved the question of ownership, the Second Circuit was faced with another question: Even if Weissmann could legitimately claim copyright in the work, did Freeman's use of it for educational purposes constitute a "fair use"? Judge Pollack had paid comparatively little attention to this issue in the first phase of the case, but Judge Cardamone took it seriously indeed.

Fair uses are those uses of a copyrighted expression which are treated as exceptional under the law and therefore noninfringing. The quotations in this book are fair uses; unauthorized reproductions of entire copyrighted films are not. Four factors determine fair use: (1) the purpose and character of the use, including whether it is of a commercial nature or is for nonprofit educational purposes; (2) the nature of the copyrighted work; (3) the portion used in relation to the copyrighted work as a whole; and (4) the effect of the use upon the potential market for or value of the copyrighted work.[16] Judge Pollack had argued that the syllabus was intended for nonprofit "educational use." Further, because the piece was "factual and scientific" the law was predisposed to facilitate its free dissemination over, for example, "works of fiction or fantasy." Because it was not in fact used in the class, moreover, that syllabus had "no market value"; thus its use could have no effect on any potential market for the work (1262). In short, Pollack concluded, Freeman's reproduction was fair use.

Again, the Second Circuit Court of Appeals came to a rather different conclusion, and the logic of that conclusion rested upon a conceptualization of the community of scholarship in both gift and market terms. "Monetary gain is not the sole criterion" of profit, Judge Cardamone argued: "Dr. Freeman stood to gain recognition among his peers in the profession and authorship credit . . . he did so without paying the usual price that accompanies scientific research and writing, that is, by the sweat of his brow. Particularly in an academic setting, profit is ill-measured in dollars. Instead what is valuable is recognition" (1324). Judge Cardamone's assertion that monetary gain was irrelevant to academic work was contradicted, somewhat, by his insistence a few sentences later on the importance of the economic incentives of copyright protection to scientific production. Truly curious reasoning, however, emerged in his assessment of the "market value" of the syllabus. "The particular market at issue here—namely, the world of scientific research and publication," he said, operated to encourage the circulation of scientific work through incentives of promotion and advancement. Recognition, in this formulation, was the "fruit of one's labor" (1326). The syllabus was a way of producing recognition for Weissmann, and therefore had a market value aside from any direct monetary remuneration.

This claim, when made in the context of a property rights dispute, represents a rather startling bit of boundary work. Looking to adjudicate academic authorship on the terrain of property, the Second Circuit located the "academic setting" outside of the money economy and simultaneously reconstructed that setting as a market. This marks a potentially significant shift in fair use reasoning. With some significant exceptions—such as large-scale photocopying of course materials—courts have often been predisposed to treat most educational reproduction as meeting, by definition, the minimal fair use requirement of noncommerciality.[17] Universities may increasingly "mean business," as the brochure of one prominent university declares, but the courts have usually preferred to imagine that universities "mean" something more akin to public service. Yet if economic rights inhere in reputation (as the court said they did) and pedagogy can be construed as a kind of marketing tool, then it follows that academic uses should not be presumptively treated as nonprofit, fair, uses. The Second Circuit tried to sidestep the implication of its argument by portraying the academic market as unique—profit motives might exist, the court suggested, but the desired payoff was a rise in status rather than in one's bank balance. In other words, the academic market was simultaneously an identifiable entity and a contradiction in terms.

It is telling that here, as elsewhere in copyright history, a labor theory of property was deployed to resolve and partially conceal the contradiction. As noted, rhetorics of ownership rooted in the investment of labor help recast political disputes in moralist terms by characterizing economic claims as natural rights rather than objects of contest. Ironically enough, however, the court's approach actually highlights the striking similarity between academic and other markets. The economic rights the court identified were not, of course, entirely new in the history of the professions (Larson, 1977). But the construction of scholarly "recognition," or reputation, as "the fruit of one's labor," and therefore a form of intellectual property, should have been startling. More directly, what should have been startling was the application of such reasoning to the professoriate, for this logic has been more often found in the rather different context of battles over the publicity rights of celebrities.

The right of publicity is the right of a person to control the commercial use of his or her identity. In the mid-twentieth century, courts began to reason that since celebrities invest time, labor, and money in the construction of their public selves, they have a moral right to reap "the fruits of their labor" by exclusively controlling the use of those public personas. Advertisers, for their part, have a moral obligation not to "reap where they have not sown" through unauthorized invocations of a celebrity image to promote a product (Nimmer, 1954). Once sharply limited, publicity rights have become "real" private property rights in the past several decades, "fully assignable and descendible, as well as potentially perpetual" (Gordon, 1993, 153n14). The scope of publicity rights has also been dramatically broadened. Publicity rights once were narrowly construed to cover only name, likeness, photograph, voice, and signature. Today, rights can be claimed in "evocations" of identity, including phrases and objects associated with a celebrity (such as a car), singing styles, and so on.[18]

As noted previously, the production of the author and work as tightly linked yet simultaneously autonomous was crucial to the commodification of information. Publicity rights take this operation a step further: "the work" is, literally, the objectification of the author's self, the "star persona." In essence, publicity rights inhere in elements of celebrity identity so distinctively personal that they can be propertized. In *Weissmann* it is the academic persona—professional identity—that is produced as property. Just as Johnny Carson and the heirs of Elvis Presley have a right to prevent the appropriation of personas to which they lay claim, so too did Heidi Weissmann have a right to reap the profit of her investment in her academic reputation. After all, as many scholars pointedly told me, a scholar's reputation is all she has. If defense of that reputation comes in the form of the kind of property right more commonly associated with Hollywood than with Harvard, so be it.[19]

But this defensive strategy comes at a cost, one that points to the broader implications of Judge Cardamone's opinion. The rhetorical force of publicity rights, like that of academic reputation, rests upon the "unquestionable truth" of individual labor. And the question is, or should be, What kinds of labor, performed by whom, are construed to be valuable, and for what purposes? Judicial opinions in publicity rights consistently treat fame as a product of individual achievement: celebrities "painstakingly build" their public personalities through years of effort, "assiduously cultivating" their reputations.[20] One court declared in 1970 that "a celebrity must be considered to have invested his years of practice and competition in a public personality."[21]

And yet it is not clear why, exactly, a celebrity—or an academic—*must* be considered to be the sole investor in her public persona. Fame is conferred by others: one does not become famous on one's own (Madow, 1993). Audiences, including scholarly audiences, make selections among alternate meanings, and their selections influence the reproduction of authorized identities. For example, fan clubs, fan magazines, and audience research techniques channel practices of reception into practices of production (Dyer, 1986). These practices are even more evident in the academy, where the value of the work (and therefore the value of the scholar's reputation) depends on reading practices (such as perceptions of order of authorship), experimental testing, and citation. Technicians, research assistants, and colleagues all help produce reputation, and especially the economic value thereof.

Judge Pollack's opinion, misguided as it may have been, sought to recognize at least some portion of this shared productive activity. Judge Cardamone's more faithful representation of IP law's basic assumptions did not. Instead, the opinion implicitly acknowledged that the discourse of individual creativity and labor upon which the propertization of the public persona is based resonates with both gift and market model of authorship. The gift model of authorship is concerned with locating individual responsibility and enhancing individual reputation, for how else can the gift return honor to the giver? Plagiarism is frightening, after all, because it disrupts the author-work connection that guarantees the truth of science as surely as it secures the author's—and the celebrity's—position at the center of a world of commodities (Rose, 1993). Thus a shared commitment to individuated creation facilitates the interweaving of market and gift rhetoric as much as does the language of investment. The relative ease of that operation suggests that a blurred line between professors and celebrities may not be exceptional but rather typical of the consequences of invoking property rights to define and defend academic authorship—an issue to which we will return in subsequent chapters.

RESCUE OPERATIONS

"In what ways and with what effects," asked Robert Young, "can the university, both inside and outside the market economy, useful and useless, function as a surplus that the economy cannot comprehend?" (1992, 121–122). My intention in this chapter has been to partially answer this query in order to reframe it. Young posed this question in the context of the "culture wars" of the late 1980s and early 1990s, and his central concern was the potential subordination of the liberal arts to the contradictory logic of free-market capitalism. I have been concerned with a related cultural struggle and the mobilization of shared assumptions—encapsulated in the boundary object "authorship"—to manage that struggle. The Weissmann case indicates a need to ask, In what ways and with what effects can the market economy comprehend the university precisely because of its uselessness? How are the organizing principles of market and gift economies of knowledge necessarily polarized and interwoven?

Set against the background of academic discourse, the concept of "authorship" appears to be embedded in competing visions of scholarly work and to be flexible enough to circulate between these notions and across legal and extra-legal contexts. But it would be a mistake to imagine that these competing visions are reconciled. Rather they maintain an uneasy coexistence. Heidi Weissmann's lawsuit threatened to disrupt this coexistence because its resolution seemed to demand the displacement of the gift in favor of the market. Faced with this visible transgression, the district court sought to reinscribe a gift model of scientific authorship. The appellate court recognized the impossibility of this strategy and repositioned Weissmann and Freeman as proper liberal subjects, equal and autonomous property owners. That repositioning, it is worth noting, helped Weissmann force Montefiore and Einstein to settle her sex-discrimination lawsuit for $900,000. But her violation of the "trust relations" of the gift economy was not forgotten: seven years after filing the suit, she was still unable to find professional work in academia or private practice (Spector, 1994).

Yet the Second Circuit, too, was finally unable to leave the gift behind, choosing instead to awkwardly knit the two models together. Indeed, the appellate court, in the space of a few sentences, constructed academic science and the market as both distinct and hopelessly intermingled. This final turn of the Weissmann case is symptomatic as well as productive of academic authorship's multivalence. Again and again, in policy statements, interviews, and legal disputes, gift and market models are treated as oppositional, mutually constitutive, and overlapping.

This confusion of meaning lends poignancy to the *Chicago Tribune's* search for signs of modernity in the academy, if we keep in mind Latour's observation that "the modern world has never happened" in the sense that its central tenets have never been fulfilled (1993, 39). By this he means that modernity is not built on dichotomies, such as that between gift and market. It is built, instead, on hybrids "made possible by absolute investment in dichotomies" (40). In other words, modernity is founded on boundary objects, rather than simply boundaries, for its social arrangements are stabilized by intermediating concepts.

To make all this activity work, however, these hybrids have to be concealed. One of the things that make authorship "work" as a boundary object between gift and market economies is the shared assumption that the two models do not share important assumptions. Heidi Weissmann's lawsuit challenged this assumption and thereby highlighted the productive tensions between gift and market economies and perhaps even the dangerous incursion of a "market mentality" into the public domain of the gift. If we read the case against the grain, however, we can discern another threat: that the hybridity of academic authorship might be exposed. It was this threat that produced a crisis of belief. Such crises occur, according to Elaine Scarry, when "the work of creation, which always has at its center the work of rescue, has broken down" (1988, 276). The academic author who is at once subject and object of creation was visibly overtaken by the "domain of the political" (Butler, 1991). The dichotomies that provided the academic author's conditions of possibility were thereby destabilized and the entity's rescue became an urgent task.

Heidi Weissmann's property claim, as an extraordinary instance of boundary crossing, demanded an equally extraordinary feat of reconstruction. The district court's argument was the first effort in this direction, but its importation of the gift model into a property context threatened the foundational opposition between gift and market. The Second Circuit's final argument was a more significant rescue operation, one that simultaneously recognized academic authors as private property owners and reconstructed the academic knowledge system as a gift economy. And this rescue was made possible by the final betrayal embedded in it: the very complex of shared assumptions that rescue attempted to conceal.

CHAPTER THREE

"University Lectures Are *Sui Generis*"

We have seen that hybrid concepts such as authorship can act as boundary objects, mediating but maintaining the opposition between legal paradigms designed to promote the circulation of commodities and academic paradigms designed to promote the exchange of gifts. Now I want to think more explicitly about how this boundary work has been performed over time and how that performance has shaped the definitions of the university, pedagogy, and the professoriate. To ground this discussion, I look closely at the legal linchpin of academic authorship—the "academic exception" to work-for-hire laws—and its application to ownership of teaching materials. At most U.S. universities, faculty members hold copyrights in the "traditional" creative works they produce. It is not clear, however, exactly why the faculty should be treated as knowledge owners rather than knowledge workers. As a general rule, copyright in works developed under the direction or with the resources of an employer—"works for hire"—rests with that employer. In the modern university, administrative staff typically fall under this rule and thus do not own most of the works they produce on the job. But faculty, students, and research associates whose work qualifies as "scholarly" are treated as exceptions, meaning they do own the literary works they produce, and this treatment has been left largely unquestioned by jurists and academicians alike.

Until recently, that is. Copyright ownership is fast becoming a major point of contention in universities across the United States. Consider, by way of example, the response of faculty, student, and librarian representatives to a draft report on copyright circulated at the University of the West in September 1998. In preparation for several months by a committee composed of senior faculty, librarians, and academic technology specialists, the report contained a set of fairly noncontroversial recommendations that had been carefully drafted to forestall any faculty objection. Or so the writers thought. Despite the committee's best efforts, many reviewers found the report very objectionable indeed. Although some readers applauded the report, their comments were muted by the extensive criticism from faculty associations, technology managers, and research administrators. Critics directly questioned the expertise, motivations, and especially the credibility of committee members, some going so far as to suggest that the committee was too responsive to the administration and insufficiently committed to scholarship, creativity, and academic freedom.

The draft report's treatment of ownership of the classroom was the primary locus of criticism. The draft report recommended that UW affirm faculty copyright ownership of "works of scholarship," but it also advised the university to "provide management services" that would "assist" faculty in exercising their copyrights and indicated that class materials and lectures might not always fall into the category of "works of scholarship."[1] Perhaps sensitized by a series of well-publicized controversies over ownership of distance-learning materials, UW faculty were quick to read these suggestions as an attempt by the university administration to frame faculty copyright in course materials as a privilege rather than a right. One widely circulated response also specifically rejected the report's suggestion that the administration and faculty might be partners in copyright "management," emphasizing that the interests of faculty and the administration were likely to conflict.

If UW faculty and administrators are squaring off in a battle for control of copyright, they are not alone. In the midst of significant shifts in the organization and possibly the object of higher education—a "second academic revolution"—faculty copyrights are being constructed as badges of autonomy, independence, and control. University administrators across the country, meanwhile, are observing the institutional investment and profit potential in Internet-based educational tools and software developed by faculty and students under university auspices, and are themselves moving to assert copyright ownership of some teaching materials.

Noting the depletion of library resources caused by skyrocketing subscription prices, administrators and librarians are also considering ways of "encouraging" faculty to retain copyright ownership of their publications rather than assigning full rights to the publishers. But many faculty are suspicious of administrative offers to assist faculty in "copyright management," reading these offers as threats to faculty property rights. According to education activists across the country, the faculty's suspicions are well founded. Pointing to agreements between major research universities and for-profit "learning corporations" to market teaching materials, activists warn faculty that they must carefully guard their copyrights if they wish to stave off the commodification of education and the proletarianization of the professoriate (Noble, 1998; Weiss, 1998).

Yet copyright law is a thin reed upon which to base this "counterrevolutionary" movement, for several reasons. The central problem is this: the position of faculty and the university itself as arbiters of true and valuable knowledge—the very position that, as we will see, justifies the academic exception—depends on the location of academia outside the realm of commodity production and circulation. Yet copyright law produces creative work(s) as commodities and academic creators as owners. Can faculty continue to position themselves as intellectual property owners while simultaneously retaining the "cognitive property" claims that accompany their "nonmarket" subject positions? Not to put too fine a point on it, can faculty use a body of law designed to promote the distribution of intellectual commodities to resist the commodification of intellectual work?

The short answer is yes, they can—indeed they *are*—but not easily and not without an enormous amount of cultural work that promises, in the long term, to redraw the very constitutive boundaries upon which the property claims of the professoriate rely. To see why, we need to locate professorial copyright within a legal history. Before we can do so, however, a more extended consideration of academic copyright battles and the "academic exception" is in order.

DIGITAL DIPLOMA MILLS OR DEMOCRATIZATION OF EDUCATION?

A 1995 monograph from the Society for University and College Planning offers the following "vignette" to illustrate its vision of a transformed higher education. A new student at a "distinguished liberal arts college" discovers that most of her professors have traded in textbooks for websites, from which students may download readings, notes, and other materials. Her writing and research are equally networked, incorporating CD-ROMs, videos, and simulations. At the end of her first year she collaborates with four other people to "develop" a multimedia research project that fulfills the requirements of three courses at once. She looks forward to demonstrating her "basic critical thinking skills" early, so that in her final year she can pursue a directed study under the joint direction of faculty "mentors" and her future employer. At no point in her years of "liberal" study can she expect to be "taught"—rather, she will enter a series of learning spaces in which critical thinking will be facilitated (Norris and Dolence, 1995, 16). And, the authors of this vignette suggest elsewhere, any fees she pays for this will be understood as "payment for exchange of intellectual property based on value added" (4). To what, precisely, the "value" is being added is unclear.

For some, such as the "technology strategist" Stephen Delong of the State University of New York at Albany, the "customized mentoring" model of learning is part of a much-needed democratization of education (Delong, 1997). Faculty authority will be challenged, he suggests, by students with easy access to multiple alternate sources of information. One of the most ancient privileges of the professor is the certification of knowledge and knowledge sources. Access to the World Wide Web allows a student who disagrees with a given lecturer's position on a topic to do her own research with relative ease, mobilizing statistics and opposing interpretations from "unauthorized" sources. Professors working with students who have access to massive electronic databases may look less like arbiters of knowledge—masters—in the classroom, and more like information "guides." Students, by extension, may look less like a receptive audience and more like active interpreters, new citizens in a more democratic republic of knowledge.

But many others—most visibly David F. Noble of York University—contend that the "democratization" of education looks very much like a process of commercialization. The commodification of instruction has begun, argues Noble in pieces widely circulated on the Web, and with it the Taylorization of scholarly work. As education becomes dominated by "digital diploma mills" that offer remote instruction from part-time professors using materials and lesson plans designed and owned by administrators, he warns: "The faculty have much more in common with the historic plight of other skilled workers than they care to acknowledge. Like these others, their activity is being restructured, via the technology, in order to reduce their autonomy, independence, and control over their work and to place workplace knowledge and control as much as possible into the hands of the administration" (1998). If what Noble says is true, the restructuring is not simply a matter of technological change; related challenges to the social mechanisms of academia, especially the traditions of tenure and shared governance, are being mounted all over the United States (Leatherman, 1998; Schmidt, 1998). Administrators are questioning the ability of consensus-oriented shared governance systems—which assign substantial control over curriculum, research, and faculty status to faculty boards or "senates"—to produce decisions in a fast-paced information economy, and they are looking to "streamline" governing authority by centralizing decisionmaking power. In addition, many universities are simply opting out of the shared governance tradition by hiring more part-time and full-time "nontenured" faculty—who are often not only poorly compensated but also excluded from academic senates. Taken together, these technological and organizational developments work to position faculty as employees in educational corporations rather than critical scholars pursuing a vocation.

Although my focus here is ownership of the classroom, these discussions overlap with an equally contentious issue: copyright transfer agreements between scholars and academic journals. Current practice requires that researchers sign contracts relinquishing all copyrights in a research article to the publisher of that article in advance of publication. Professors usually receive nothing in direct exchange except the status that comes from publication; in fact, researchers in some fields may even be asked to subsidize the publication by paying "per page" costs. As we saw in Chapter 2, researchers do gain credit and credibility that may be reinvested toward indirect benefits such as research funding. Publishers collect articles, coordinate peer reviews, and provide the means of production and distribution of the journal. Their profits are derived from paper and online journal subscriptions, database subscriptions, and fees for article reproductions in course readers and textbooks.

Until about twenty years ago this system worked reasonably well by most accounts (Okerson, 1996; Chodorow, 1997). Since 1970, however, the cost of scholarly journals in the United States and Western Europe has increased at a hyperinflationary rate (11 percent per year overall, 13.5 percent for scientific journals, as compared to an average inflation rate of 6.1 percent). Academic publishing has become an increasingly centralized, for-profit industry, and prices have risen accordingly. For example, a subscription to Reed Elsevier's leading publication, *Brain Research,* cost $15,000 per year in 1996. This journal is an extreme case, but in general journals produced by commercial rather than nonprofit entities are more expensive, according to the Association of Research Libraries, in part because their production costs are not subsidized by professional associations (Okerson, 1996).

Librarians say they cannot keep up with journal prices, at least not without dramatic budget increases. Forced to cut subscriptions or develop some creative strategies, they have enlisted the help of scholars in fields as disparate as chemistry, physics, and economics to find ways to maintain their journal collections. In 1998 an American Academy of Arts and Sciences working group used the pages of *Science* to call on federally funded authors to retain copyright in their works (Bachrach et al., 1998). Different visions for a new system are still under discussion, but the main idea is that publishers would receive a limited license to publish an article, rather than a full copyright in that and any subsequent reproductions of the article. Under this system, academic libraries could establish alternative access points for research (such as websites and electronic journals) that might allow universities and students to save money on teaching materials as well as subscription prices. Course readers, for example, would be less expensive because no fees would be paid to publishers for the reproduction of works composed at the professor's own university.

Publishers say they could not make reasonable profits under such a system. And many faculty members, eager to have their research published in prestigious journals, are reluctant to endanger a publication by insisting on copyright retention over a publisher's objections. A more effective tactic, therefore, might be for universities to enact policies *requiring* faculty to reserve copyright in their publications. If several "first-tier" schools did so, publishers would be forced to agree to the new terms or risk lowering the quality and value of their journals. The *New England Journal of Medicine* would be badly damaged if it could not publish research generated at Stanford, Harvard, and Yale. But such requirements would necessarily limit faculty autonomy. If the reactions to the draft report of the UW copyright committee are any indication, relatively few faculty members will be willing to consent to such limits.[2] The fundamental irony here, that many faculty insist on retaining copyright only to promptly assign those rights to a publisher, is not lost on librarians.

Parties involved in conversations about ownership of scholarly works are looking hard at the so-called academic exception to work-for-hire laws. The doctrine of work for hire establishes, in a nutshell, that copyrightable creative works produced by employees in the scope of their employment are the property of the employer. Commissioned works may also fall under this rule, depending on the nature of the work and the extent of direction and motivation supplied by the person commissioning the work. The legal question in both instances is who has the "right to control the manner and means by which the product is accomplished."[3] Control of production, in other words, secures right of distribution. Professors could be considered employees under work-for-hire doctrine because they are treated as employees for tax purposes, receive benefits, use materials and equipment provided by an employer, and cede substantial control in the hiring and remuneration of their assistants to their employer, the university (Kulkarni, 1995; Burk, 1997). Yet by policy and precedent "traditional scholarly works" made by "independent academic effort" are not considered works for hire, and the majority of professors own the knowledge they produce in the course of their employment as researchers and instructors.

The academic exception was developed prior to the 1976 Copyright Act's substantial revision of copyright statutes, however, and it is not clear whether the exception survived those modifications. Some judicial decisions in the past decade (two of which were written by former university professors) seem to support it, and the majority of scholars, not surprisingly, insist the exception should and will be preserved (Meyer, 1998; Reichman, 1989).[4] But a vigorous minority of commentators and some district courts disagree (Simon, 1982; Duboff, 1984).[5] What is clear is that without an explicit statutory foundation the exception can no longer simply be assumed. Further, interested parties looking to reinforce the claim quickly find that it is no longer even clear what sits inside the category of "traditional scholarly works," nor is it certain where "independent academic effort" ends and collaborative effort between a faculty member and an institution begins. Extensive university resources (staff, computers, software) may be needed to develop and use new media technologies for teaching. For example, university staff may be heavily involved in designing a website. Their involvement could provide a basis for a university to assert that it substantially controlled the production of the work, meaning the work in question would look more like a work for hire than an "independent" work of authorship. If so, a website developed for a class might be copyrighted by a university and sold to a distance-learning corporation, and the professor who taught the class could be forbidden to rework subsequent expressions of the material. This scenario is already being enacted or contemplated at several universities, including the University of Colorado and Princeton, and it rouses faculty associations to the clarion cry of academic freedom—even as, on the publishing front, individual faculty ownership of copyright in "traditional" works is starting to look like a hindrance to free academic inquiry (Schiller, 1999; Guernsey and Young, 1998). It is not surprising, therefore, that there is a perceived need to define and defend professorial copyright in the classroom.

Defense of the professorial copyright is defense of the profession itself. Professors, like other professionals, are always engaged in an effort to, as Magali Larson puts it, "constitute *and control* a market for their expertise" and thereby sustain a "monopoly of competence" (1977, xvi). This monopoly is maintained in and through the reproduction of experts themselves as knowledge owners whose skills are the result of years of training and effectively inalienable. As noted in Chapter 1, Larson refers to this monopoly of competence as "cognitive property" (CP), and she notes that this form of property, and the "autonomy and 'intelligence of the whole'" it represents, are "uncertain privileges" at best (244). Work-for-hire laws, if applied to academics, would threaten these privileges directly by threatening professional autonomy. The test of whether a work is a "work for hire" is based on principles of agency law, and it seeks to determine if the creator was an independent autonomous agent. The academic exception assumes and protects a special kind of agency for faculty and helps establish a legal foundation for the professoriate's monopoly of competence. The comments of the law professor Jerome H. Reichman are telling in this regard: "To equate a general duty to write with a duty to produce specific works for a university distorts the nature of academic employment and downgrades the professorial rank to that of an ordinary staff member" (1989, 674). Just so.

The application of work-for-hire reasoning to professors could very well provide the legal basis for the Taylorization of education by permitting cognitive property to be firmly detached from the professional, appropriated by an employer, and commodified. Once course materials are digitized and published in websites, Noble (1998) contends, the faculty knowledge and skill embodied in those materials are effectively "transferred to the machinery and placed in the hands of [the university] administration." That transfer signals a breach in the professorial knowledge monopoly. The professor retains the knowledge and training required to organize and transmit information, but loses much of her command of the uses to which that knowledge and training are put. Her profession, by extension, loses an important strategy of control over the market for its expertise.

The defense of the market for cognitive property (CP) by way of intellectual property (IP) law involves a seductively "natural" use of one monopoly to protect another. To the extent that IP discourse constructs professors as autonomous knowledge owners rather than subordinated knowledge workers, moreover, its use picks up on a long history of depicting professors as "appointees" rather than employees, who work for "administrators" rather than bosses, to create "works of scholarship" rather than work products (Metzger, 1987). Too, it reflects the conflation of freedom with property ownership that pervades U.S. political and legal discourse. This excerpt from the American Association of University Professors (AAUP) Statement on Copyright (1999) encapsulates the argument: "In the typical work-for-hire situation, the content and purpose of the employee-prepared works are under the control and direction of the employer; the employee is accountable to the employer for the content and design of the work. In the case of traditional academic works, however, the faculty member rather than the institution determines the subject matter, the intellectual approach and direction, and the conclusions. This is the very essence of academic freedom." In the name of freedom of inquiry, then, professors must be granted limited monopolies on knowledge. Following this logic, if the university's reason for being is free and rational inquiry, then full professorial copyright is the *sine qua non* of the research university itself.

The AAUP's statement goes on: "Were the institution to own the copyright in such works, under a work-made-for-hire theory, it would have the powers, for example, to decide where the work is to be published, to edit and otherwise revise it, to prepare derivative works based thereon (such as translations, abridgments, and literary, musical, or artistic variations), and indeed to censor and forbid dissemination of the work altogether. Such powers, so deeply inconsistent with fundamental principles of academic freedom, cannot rest with the institution." But if there is something offensive about an institution controlling the dissemination of a work (including, by implication, its commercialization), it is not clear that there is anything inherently less offensive about an individual professor being able to do so. As noted, professors are supposed to be producing gifts, not commodities, and scholarship is supposed to be "disinterested." The cognitive property of professors (as well as other professionals) depends, in part, on the location of its producers at the margins of the commercial sphere, in the "gift economy" described in Chapter 2. I will have more to say about this positioning in a moment, but for now we need only recall Judge Pollack's sense of unease and irritation at Heidi Weissmann's effort to claim copyright in her research, and his repeated challenges to her "credibility." Ascribing property rights in lectures inevitably "propertizes" academic work in general, helping to reposition scholarship and pedagogy at the center of a web of commercial relations—a market economy. Once lectures and other scholarly works are overtly identified by their creators as objects of private ownership, we are encouraged to stop worrying about the commodification of the professional knowledge and training of academics and focus instead on who will own that commodity. At that point, a great deal of cultural work must be performed before the academy can be reconstructed as a place where reputation matters more than economic power.

The use of IP to defend CP is not, therefore, a simple exercise. How, then, are these two rhetorics of property bridged? One clue may be found in the simple observation, made by two *Chronicle of Higher Education* reporters, that for academicians "the most important issue is not ownership but control" (Guernsey and Young, 1998, A23). The trope of control is an old one in copyright discourse, and, as we will see, it is infused with even older commitments to honor and reputation. Borrowing from Mark Rose (1993), I will call this infusion the discourse of propriety. "Propriety," like authorship, is a hybrid concept embodying both "property" and "right conduct," and this concept, Rose demonstrates, helped mediate competing ethics of authorship in the early years of modern copyright. In the following section I draw on Rose to briefly present a line of cases that established the intersection between propriety and intellectual property, and then I consider how "propriety" might ease the use of IP to defend the privileges of the professoriate.

MASTERING THE USE OF THE NAME

Propriety and Property

Scholars date the birth of modern copyright to the 1710 Statute of Anne in England, which granted to authors a copyright in their registered works for fourteen to twenty-eight years. The exact nature of literary property, however, took several decades to define, and that definition had more to do with the common law than the statute itself (Rose, 1993). Drawing on contradictory precedents, copyright advocates tried to argue that the short-term statutory right merely supplemented a preexisting, perpetual, common law right. The resulting debates over the nature, scope, and duration of the common law right provided the ground for a broader reformulation of the relationship between authorship and ownership.

That reformulation depended in large part on the invocation of a discourse of dignity, or propriety. Today we usually think of "propriety" as "right conduct," or appropriate social behavior and speech. In this sense, the term refers to a public self—the disciplining of one's persona to accord with custom, in order to protect the honor and reputation of oneself and (harking back to Roman law) one's family. In premodern Europe, however, the term also signified a private self, one's "true nature" or character, that which was "peculiar" to a self. Further, propriety was synonymous with property: as late as the eighteenth century one's real estate holdings might be called one's "propriety."

The premodern meanings may strike us as contradictory—one's propriety was at once an essential nature and a mask, or even, in the form of real estate, alienable private property. Yet in the medieval and even early modern periods, when property ownership was linked to familial status and conduct and the administration of property was coded as duty and privilege rather than individual natural right, no direct contradiction existed. Property, especially property in land, was tied to a role—that which was "proper" to a particular family—and a fixed place in a hierarchy. According to Carol Rose, one's propriety was a domain to be guarded for subsequent generations and thus property claims carried "the authority, but also the responsibility, of a trust to the larger community" (1994, 65).

In the seventeenth and eighteenth centuries, as "public" and "private" were reconstructed and property ownership was firmly tied to a private sphere of individuals, these meanings diverged sharply. The community of the self-possessed liberal subject is based on economic interest rather than honor or trust, and the property of that subject a matter of right and freedom rather than privilege and obligation. In this community "true nature" is a purely private matter, to be carefully isolated from any public persona. As this vision of subjectivity took hold, propriety came to embody and mediate a built-in tension between public and private rather than an identity-relation between conduct, duty, property, and particularity.

The illusion of consistency in legal reasoning is achieved through the grafting of new concepts onto old traditions (Kairys, 1982). The hybrid concept of propriety offered one such grafting tool to copyright law. Medieval precursors to copyright, Mark Rose observes, drew on the nonmarket values of honor and reputation to justify limited authorial control of publication (which implied a right to license publication for money, a form of property). The earliest form of copyright, a state privilege granted to the Stationer's Company (see Chapter 1), took up and reshaped this discourse, binding principles of honor, fidelity, and service to censorship. By granting copyrights to a few publishers and requiring that the authors of texts be specifically identified on the title page of a manuscript, the state could effectively censor heretical or seditious writings. In exchange, the Stationers were allowed to regulate the book trade. In this "regime of regulation," copyright was more closely linked to guild power, "right conduct," and integrity—propriety in the older sense— than to private property and individual right. Some individual printing privileges were granted, Rose notes, but they were understood as highly provisional "honors" rather than "rights."

In the seventeenth century, however, authors began to argue more vigorously that protection of individual integrity might depend on individual control of publication rights. This position was perhaps most famously encapsulated in John Milton's *Areopagitica* (1644), which protested the licensing system as, among other things, an assault on authorial honor. Rose points as well to *Eikonoklastes* (1649), in which Milton compares King Charles's use of a prayer written by Sir Philip Sidney, without acknowledgment, to the levying of a tax upon the author. Milton thus framed unauthorized reproductions as both assaults on an author's honor and a kind of "takings," appropriation of property.

Though Milton's notion of "takings" was a far cry from the vision of literary products as commodities that would soon emerge, the link he and other authors established between personal honor and alienable private property would persist as a source of persuasion and contradiction. Consider, for example, the 1741 case of *Pope v. Curll* (Rose, 1993).[6] The defendant in the case, Edmund Curll, had published a volume of letters written by the poet Alexander Pope without Pope's permission. Because they were not identified as "publications," letters did not clearly fall under the Statute of Anne's provisions, and booksellers took advantage of this fact to solicit the letters of prominent individuals from their correspondents. This practice, argued Pope, was an unconscionable invasion of privacy and a threat to an author's property and reputation. "Your Fame and your Property suffer alike; you are at once expos'd and plunder'd," he declared (quoted in Rose, 62). Curll, for his part, relied on the language of the gift to support his entrance into the market. Letters were a gift to the recipient, he insisted, and, as such, became the recipient's property.

Pope won, and his victory had two effects relevant to our concerns here. First, it actively constructed the author as a solitary creator rather than a participant in a social exchange, and reading as a "private act of consumption" (Rose, 1993, 66). In so doing, the case helped clear the way for a larger refiguration of cultural producer and audience as radically divided (Lury, 1993). Second, Pope's property right in the letters was treated as a way to protect his fame and his property at once: to prevent the "exposure" of his peculiar self and the "plunder" of his wealth. The decision thus confirmed the salience of "propriety," in all its senses, to the emergent regime of property.

A discourse of propriety was again dispositive almost thirty years later, in *Millar v. Taylor* (1769).[7] Seeking to determine whether a common law copyright survived publication, the Court of Chancery looked to *Pope v. Curll* and its progeny. If a copyright existed prior to publication, the court reasoned, its evisceration at publication signified the loss of both profit and dignity. Speaking for the majority, Lord Mansfield argued that if an author could not retain copyright in his work, "He is no more master of the use of his own name. He has no control over the correctness of his own work . . . Any one may print, pirate, and perpetuate the imperfections, to the disgrace and against the will of the author; may propagate sentiments under his name, which he disapproves, repents and is ashamed of" (quoted in Rose, 80). Rose describes Mansfield's argument as reaching "deep into history" to find a common law right of property rooted in honor rather than economic interest (81). Attached to a representation of self (the name), the right was also naturally perpetual—after all, who could put a limit on honor? The notion of perpetual copyright was later overturned in *Donaldson v. Becket* (1774), but the *Millar* reasoning would continue to be influential in common law copyright doctrine. It was also echoed by the Romantic movement, which invoked the public and private dimensions of propriety by turn to link authorship with nobility (in the spiritual as well as the aristocratic sense) and to characterize expression as "peculiar" to the self (Rose, 1993; Woodmansee, 1994b).

These invocations had consequences that would have surprised many early advocates of copyright. Despite the rather high-flown celebration of personal honor in the cases described here, copyright was originally intended to protect the profits of booksellers and printing guilds, not the interests of individual authors (Bettig, 1996). And in fact it did so, once publishers persuaded authors to assign their copyrights in literary works. Nevertheless, by facilitating the emergence of the individual author-subject and obscuring the contradictions between individual copyrights and traditional notions of books as objects of mixed rather than absolute property, the discourse of propriety helped promote the author-owner at the expense of other entities who also contributed to bookmaking—the printing guilds among them (Davis, 1983). Thus one of the fundamental assumptions of the regime of regulation under which these guilds operated—the linkage of the text to reputation, responsibility, and control—was deployed to clear the way for a regime of property based on individual right rather than guild privilege. By acting as midwife at the birth of the individual author-owner, the discourse of propriety assisted as well in the demise of communal claims to the book.

Cognitive Exclusiveness

The boundary work of the discourse of propriety did not end with copyright. Just as it mediated guild-based and individualist conceptions of authorship, "propriety" would also bridge guild-based and professionalizing rhetorics of labor, including new forms of academic labor. In the pre-industrial period the acknowledged professions (law, theology, and medicine) were distinguished from the craft guilds by university education. Industrialization, political revolution, and the rise of the middle class in the United States and in Europe undermined the traditional hierarchies and premises of both organizational forms. The guilds would never regain their socioeconomic power, but the professions would thrive and multiply. That growth would be assisted by the use of the discourse of propriety to define and defend a professional market for cognitive property.

The ascendance of the professions was based, in part, on strategic use of medieval and early modern ethics of propriety to link professional knowledge and the professional personality. Larson identifies three conceptual underpinnings for the cognitive exclusiveness upon which the market value of the professional depended, each of which was a kind of "residue" of a pre-industrial ideal. The notion of a "calling," or a vocation, was derived from a craft-based work ethic that constructed work as intrinsically valuable. An individual felt herself to have been chosen, to have an affinity for a particular kind of work. Certainly many nonprofessionals felt this way, and many professionals did not, but the point is that the rhetoric of professional identity told aspiring professionals they *should* have a sense of "calling." Further, professionalism was tied to a rhetoric of superiority built on a distinct aversion to commercial pursuits, and thus bespoke the feudal notion of *noblesse oblige*, itself partially rooted in even older notions of honor and family reputation. Finally, and particularly salient here, the ideal of universal service toward which professionals were trained to strive responded to values of community bonds and responsibility, while simultaneously joining those values to a model of gentlemanly disinterestedness. In a binary liberal frame, the obligation of universal service (disinterest) worked also to mark the space of non-obligation (self-interest).

The guild-based discourse of academic work was mobilized to reframe the academic profession with relative ease, and this mobilization was crucial to the rise of the professions in general. Having given up the trappings of commerce for "higher learning," professors had long been positioned as the true "experts," qualified to train others and evaluate the importance of developments within specialized monopolies of competence. As we saw in Chapter 1, by the end of the nineteenth century this role was not confined to the traditional professions of law, medicine, and theology but extended to the many forms of professionalizing labor.

Every profession necessarily claimed a distinctive set of skills and knowledge, and therefore needed arbiters of that set who were "called" to apply principles of reason to the development and dissemination of distinct competencies. Professors were particularly well suited to this role, for they were also publicly committed to ideals of "teaching, research, and service," as specifically opposed to commerce and self-interest. As research and scholarship themselves became more specialized, meanwhile, economic and social rewards became more tightly attached to individual names—persons who were responsible, by way of their individual skills, competence, and reputations, for producing and certifying results. Professors were evaluated by their fellow masters, and that process helped affirm the competence and legitimacy of their respective disciplines and the professoriate as a whole. In the case of professors, then, the link between personality and knowledge was crucial to multiple cognitive property claims.

Both cognitive and intellectual property claims, then, were strategically coded in terms of controlling the production of reputation and honor. The professional commodity, like the authorial copyright, depended on the deployment of a rhetoric of individual propriety (honor, vocation, reputation) to underwrite property (the intangible services that the professor could provide, the quality of which was underwritten by his personal history). And, as in the case of copyright, propriety intermediated traditional guild-based and professional representations of work.

It must not be supposed, however, that this bridging mechanism was, or is, stable. In fact, it has been continually remade to account for new paradoxes and the reappearance of old tensions. Further, these remakings have shaped representations of the university, the professoriate, and the "nature" of education. To show how, I turn now to two foundational cases for professorial copyright in the classroom to consider how the discourse of propriety was deployed to stitch the common sense back together. Each of these cases, as we will see, made and contained an argument about the nature of academic work at crucial moments in the history of the university and the professoriate.

PUBLIC AND PRIVATE AUTHORITIES

The time was the late nineteenth century and the place, the University of Glasgow. Once an acknowledged center of Enlightenment thought, the Scottish university had become less influential and by the 1880s was reforming itself along the lines of the German university ideal (Rothblatt, 1993; Wittrock, 1993; Phillipson, 1974). Notwithstanding its waning prestige, though, the Scottish university, as a public institution, was at the cutting edge of one trend in higher education: toward secularization and popularization. One indicator of the University of Glasgow's position with respect to the latter was its fees: seventeen pounds, as compared to Cambridge's two hundred pounds (Rudy, 1984).

The populist vision behind the fee policy was imperfectly aligned, however, with both the principles of autonomy that underlay the German model and the Scottish university's own aristocratic traditions. Shaped as it was by several competing visions of academia, the Scottish professoriate owed allegiance to the university, to the scholarly community, to students, and even to the general public. Within the web of these allegiances, the professor was alternately constructed as an autonomous reasoning individual, a public servant, a member of an ancient guild, and, possibly, an employee. But it was not yet obvious that the professor was an intellectual property owner.

Or at least it was not obvious to a bookseller in Glasgow named William S. Sime. Without permission, this bookseller used a student's notes to reproduce the lectures of a philosophy professor, Edward Caird. The "reproductions" were sold under the title "Aids to the Study of Moral Philosophy," with the student, William Finlay Brown, listed as the author. In his preface, Brown observed that the subject of moral philosophy "entails such an amount of reading that no student, if left to himself, can undertake it successfully."[8] The notes might help. Apparently preferring that his students struggle on unassisted, Professor Caird promptly sued for infringement of his common law copyright. The sheriff found in Caird's favor and seized all copies of the work. Bookseller Sime appealed to the Second Division of the Court of Session, which deemed the issue important enough to be considered by the whole court. In a close decision, Sime won on the theory that a professor in a public university was a public official, and his lectures were therefore public domain material. Outraged, Caird turned to the House of Lords and the Privy Council for relief.[9]

The case presented to the Peers raised two interwoven questions. First, did a professor in a public university own his lectures? And second, did delivery of the lecture constitute a "publication to the world," an act that would vacate any existing common law right in the lectures?

The bookseller's advocates, Lorimer and MacClymont, argued that the professor was "clothed with a public office" and was therefore obligated to deliver lectures to the students and members of the public as part of that office. "The university exists for national ends and the diffusion of knowledge, which knowledge is not to be confined to students" (333). Noting that students "attended the lectures in the exercise of a public right" and that the only bar to entry at the lecture was the payment of a fee, they contended that the lectures were themselves public documents and therefore available for appropriation (333). In other words, the professor was a public figure rather than a private individual, and his words were also "dedicated to the public," meaning that they were effectively allocated to the public domain the moment they were spoken to an audience.

This argument had been successful in the lower Court of Session: Lord-President Inglis, for example, had insisted that the universities were "national institutions . . . open to every member of the community" and their professors obligated to teach "not for [their] own benefit" but for "the benefit of . . . students and, through them, of the public" (34). Lord Young had added that it was "too clear to admit of dispute that the prelections of a public teacher in a public institution are publicly delivered" (62).

Among the Peers, however, only Lord Fitzgerald sided with Sime on this point. Indeed, he extended the argument considerably by insisting that the public had a right to hear, use, and judge public university lectures. "[The] universities of Scotland," he noted, "are all ancient public endowed corporations established by public authority" (352).[10] The obligation of the professor, he added, was to "teach the nation through its youth," and the citizens of that nation had a right to evaluate the training their children were receiving. It was therefore "essential to the public safety that university teaching should be exposed to comment, to searching criticism and the full blaze of public opinion" lest the nation be left in "Cimmerian darkness as to the teachings of its youth" (353, 355). The likelihood that those teachings might look rather different filtered through a student's notetaking hand did not apparently trouble the Peer.

The Solicitor-General for Scotland, James Bannerman Robertson, relied on another lecture-ownership case, *Abernethy v. Hutchinson*, to refute these high-minded democratic claims.[11] In that case, Lord Eldon looked to no less a luminary than Sir William Blackstone for guidance regarding the dissemination of lecture notes. Blackstone's *Commentaries on the Laws of England*, the principal foundational text of Anglo-American law, were based on his lectures. How, Lord Eldon asked, could Blackstone have retained copyright in his lectures for twenty years if no such professorial copyright existed? "We used to take notes at his lectures" the Peer said, "but it never was understood that those lectures could be published" (quoted in *Caird*, 330–331). The application of Eldon's analogy to *Caird* was no doubt effective: it must have seemed that denying Caird's property right would be tantamount to denying Blackstone's own authority.[12]

The Court of Session, too, had considered the relevance of *Abernethy* to Caird's claim, but had rejected the precedent on the theory that Caird, unlike the injured parties in *Abernethy*, was a public official. To refute that theory, Robertson argued on appeal that, once within the university walls, the student became a member of a specialized group, rather than simply a member of the undifferentiated general public. To cap the argument, he invoked the image of the gentleman scholar, emphasizing that a student's right to gain intellectually from his master should not be construed as a right to gain financially. The professor, in sum, was not a public figure speaking to a public body, but rather a private individual speaking to other private individuals (or apprentices) on the basis of an implicit contract.[13]

Labor and Dignity

Sime's activities offered a direct challenge to the professoriate's "monopoly of competence." Court of Session Justice Shand had put the point rather baldly, noting that a ruling for Sime would directly threaten the professor's livelihood: "He might find his usefulness restricted and his income impaired by competition in the delivery of his own lectures by some student who might, at reduced fees, and at an hour suitable to a great number, deliver his former professor's course of lectures, skilfully taken down verbatim in shorthand" (41). If, as Lord Fitzgerald suggested, the nation should be able to judge the worth of a professor's ideas and expression, and a common bookseller able to commodify them, how could the professoriate protect its market?

For Lord Fitzgerald, the professorial market was less important than the public interest. To show why Caird was obligated to serve that interest, Lord Fitzgerald called on one element of a then-emergent discourse of professionalism. The professional ideals of universal service and aversion to commercial pursuits, he suggested, did not jibe with the exclusivity and commerciality of intellectual property. A professor's lecture, delivered in a public university, he said, "may be likened to a gift from the university or the professor to the nation" (359). And there was something unseemly in asserting individual rights where national interests were at stake.

The Peer majority's response to this reasoning invoked a discourse of propriety to reframe property rights as mechanisms for the protection of professional honor. This tactic was already evident in the repeated references to the impropriety of a student's seeking financial gain (that gain, apparently, being payment for delivery of notes). These references were bolstered by the notion that a professor's copyright served most of all to secure his reputation. According to Lord Chancellor Halsbury, several members of the House were swayed by the poor quality of the reproduction of the professor's work and, by implication, the damage such a reproduction would do to Caird's reputation. Lord Watson, for his part, noted that if lectures were declared publications professors would be likely to withhold their most original thoughts from their classes until those ideas had "matured"—again, to protect risk to their reputations.

Crucial to the success of this reasoning was a continually shifting figure: the student notetaker who actually produced the notes. The Peers did not rule on the issue of whether the notes were "substantial reproductions" of the lectures such that they were effectively "copies" of the lectures. The issue had been hotly debated at the lower court level, however, with only a bare majority finding that the "Aids" were in fact reproductions. Brown insisted that he had merely relied on the notes in preparing the work, and that he had authored the work in dispute. Caird's own claims did not help his counterargument. The notes were so badly taken, Caird argued, that his reputation would be severely damaged by any association with them. Presumably, then, the language of the notes was easily distinguishable from that of the lectures. As Caird was unable to produce manuscripts of his own lectures, the testimony of former students was introduced to establish the language and substance of his delivery, and these witnesses conceded that there were several differences between the notes and the lectures as they remembered them. In short, Sime had a strong argument that the "Aids" were not reproductions of

Caird's lectures at all. But clear evidence that Sime had deliberately set out to reproduce the lectures, however short the final product may have fallen of the goal, persuaded the majority that the Aids should be treated as copies. The student-author was thus procedurally submerged that the professor-author might come into sharper relief—except when the jurists' concerns for Caird's reputation brought Brown back in as the vehicle of Caird's dishonor.

If students were not active participants in the reproduction of knowledge, neither could they be taken to constitute a public. "I do not think that students of moral philosophy in the University of Glasgow, or in any other Scotch university, either are or can with propriety be said to represent the general public . . . they must be members of the University" said Lord Watson, adding that those members should profit intellectually, not financially, from that membership. Indeed, following Lord Chancellor Halsbury's lead, Lord Watson noted that the "crib" provided by the bookseller would be likely to hamper the educational process by lessening the "intellectual effort" that students—except, presumably, Brown— expended in recording lectures.

But the students were at least members of the *universitas*, and thus a deserving audience for Caird's work. The general public, in contrast, was almost entirely dissociated from the products of the masters it supported. Answering the "public interest" argument, Lord Watson expressed doubt that most Scottish citizens were interested or equipped to evaluate university teaching. Dismissing Lord Fitzgerald's contention that a professor was obligated to make his views known to the nation, Lord Watson stated, "The capable critics are a small and by no means unanimous section of the community; and I doubt whether the governing body of the University or the professor would derive any assistance from their strictures; whilst experience has shewn that the public who are interested in it are not ignorant of the character of university teaching" (345). The public that counted, in other words, was not the "general public" that paid for the university but the "capable" educated few.

Lord Watson's comments applied traditional copyright assumptions to academic authorship, representing Caird as a solitary creator who needed no "assistance" from the "public," a self-authorizing *magister* rather than a *rhetor* whose argument might be responsive to and shaped by an audience (see Readings, 1996). This representation reflected the more widespread differentiation of audiences for creative works that occurred in the eighteenth century. Drawing on Walter Benjamin and Raymond Williams, Celia Lury (1993) has argued that the discursive production of the author as autonomous creator was related to the construction of an abstract audience dislocated from that creator. In premodern and early modern Europe, cultural reproduction depended on the co-presence of producer and audience. Mechanical reproductive technologies, however, helped foster a radical division between these entities. In the eighteenth century, as we have seen, this division was encoded into law through the construction of the author-work unit as the basis of property and the firm separation of that unit from the sphere of reception. Mechanisms of thrift were nevertheless present on the reception side, as elite publics formed to define standards of judgment and value. In the visual arts, for example, an "audience-as-public" (critics, dealers, patron organizations) claiming specialized knowledge worked as a moral and cultural gatekeeper for the abstract "audience-as-market," to which was relegated the simple act of consumption. In *Caird v. Sime,* Lord Watson treated the general public as the latter form of audience: passive consumers, whose task was to receive the products of the university—educated students—rather than evaluate and respond to an educational process. Caird's fellow masters, presumably, were the academic equivalent of Lury's "audience as public." Students occupied an in-between position, at once members of the university and consumers of the professional services and products of a solitary creator.

Corollary to the atomization of the professor-author was a contradictory representation of the institutional context for academic labor. On the one hand, Lords Watson and Halsbury invoked the traditional claims of the medieval master's guild to figure the public university itself as an autonomous institution, endowed by the public but not controlled by it. The *senatus academicus,* observed Lord Watson, had been authorized by the Scottish state for over a century to govern teaching and discipline at the University of Glasgow. Yet the image of the guild was ill-suited to the reality of the modern research university. By 1887 the university had long since ceased to be coextensive with a guild of teaching masters. In the medieval university the masters were the acknowledged center of the academy and the university corporation effectively a kind of housekeeping unit. In the emergent modern public university, the faculties were still responsible for teaching as well as research, but the institution as a whole was responsible for ensuring that state goals were accomplished. Meanwhile, as the historian Stanley Chodorow (1997) notes, the institution's functions were taking on greater weight and the masters becoming entrepreneurial employees within a larger corporate structure. The Lords' repeated references to the university-professor relationship as a "bargain" indicate that professors already looked more like employees than guild members. Equally prevalent references to an "implied contract" between professor and student (rather than between university and student), and Lord Halsbury's observation that the professor did not speak for the university but for himself, further emphasized the independence of the professor from his institutional home (337).

Monopolies of Competence

Considered against the background of the "first academic revolution," well under way by 1887, the invocation of the discourse of propriety to resolve this common law copyright case had three consequences. First, it constructed academic labor, in particular the act of teaching, as a private, producer-consumer relation, governed by implied contracts between student, professors, and administrators, and organized around "delivery" rather than participatory exchange. The view of the professor as a creative author, paired with the eradication of the hand of the student that made it possible to treat the "study aids" as copies of the original lectures, portrays lecturing as a highly autonomous, individual, one-way activity.

The importance of this portrayal comes into focus if we recall that specialization and professionalization were becoming the watchwords of scientific and even humanist work in universities in France, England, Denmark, the United States, and Scotland (Torstendahl, 1993). Although the process varied across disciplines, the professoriate as a whole was slowly taking on the dual role of teacher and researcher and reconstructing its monopoly of competence against the incursion of amateurs. Educational institutions were also rapidly replacing apprenticeship systems and thereby gaining new importance as guarantors of the cognitive property of new professions. Further, universities were being reconstructed as generators and arbiters of new knowledge. The treatment of lectures as private property offered a legal strategy for defense of multiple monopolies of competence, for it portrayed professors as sources and masters of knowledge, "principles of thrift," to use Foucault's phrase, in the proliferation of new meanings. But it also, and quite deliberately, constructed lectures as properties and commodities. Indeed, part of Caird's complaint was that he had hoped to publish his lectures and that Sime's edition would cut into his profit.

Second, the decision figured the public university as a fundamentally autonomous institution at a time when the nature of the university and its obligations to the nation were in flux. According to Björn Wittrock (1993), the rise of the modern research university was "coterminous with the formation of a modern nation-state," but that nationalist identity would exacerbate the paradox Kant outlined—the sense that only a fully autonomous, "useless" university could be useful to the state (321). Lord Fitzgerald's view of the university and its employees as obligated to the nation-state—a view shared by several members of the Court of Session—directly challenged that autonomy, and his words should have held special weight where, as in Glasgow, the university was sponsored by the taxpayers. Instead, the majority of the House of Lords rejected that obligation; further, Lord Watson's expression of that rejection emphasized the cognitive superiority (hence exclusiveness) of the capable few composing the university community over the less capable many composing the general public.

Finally, the opinion identified professors both as the essential authority of the university and as employees capable of bargaining with the university. Lord Chancellor Halsbury noted that he was "not aware" of any regulation or bargain between the university and its professors requiring professors to make their lectures public but that, where one existed, the university could sue a professor exercising his copyright for breach of contract (339). This comment figured the university and the professoriate as separate and potentially antagonistic entities, with potentially competing property claims. Lord Watson's opinion, in contrast, reunified the university and the professoriate by stressing faculty governance of teaching and discipline at the University of Glasgow. Taken together, these opinions demonstrate the incomplete reconciliation of the guild-based vision of the classical university with the specialized and professionalized modern research university. Both the medieval and the modern universities were organized around the assumption that masters were the primary authority of the university: only masters could judge masters and only reason could judge reason. *Caird* suggested that, in the modern university, authority was also vested in a space of non-reason, that is, the administration, which did not govern teaching but did govern the professoriate. The recognition of the increasing bureaucratization of the university corporation acknowledged as well that while the masters' guild remained the heart of the university, the guild was not its sole governor.

The reasoning advanced by the Peers can be read in two ways. They offer a form of provisional resolution, using the discourse of propriety to stitch together ancient and modern visions of the university into a cloak of autonomy. If they are read closely, however, a process of remaking can also be discerned. The professor is represented as a new kind of magister—an autonomous creator of alienable private property but also a member of a guild worried more about dignity than profit. The university is figured as a public (nonmarket) autonomous space but one which is necessarily exempt from public opinion. Finally the professoriate is portrayed as the heart of the university but not its brain. This process of remaking—and the contradictory images that accompany it—would surface once again some eighty years later, in response to another assault on the professorial monopoly of competence.

KNOWLEDGE WORKERS, KNOWLEDGE OWNERS

The paucity of cases on professorial ownership of lectures suggests that the *Caird v. Sime* outcome was left virtually unquestioned in British and American common law for several decades.[14] But in the late 1960s the issue reappeared some five thousand miles from Glasgow, in yet another moment of change, in yet another public university. While students in campuses across the United States were struggling for the right to speak, a professor at the University of California at Los Angeles (UCLA) was engaged in a quieter battle for the right not to speak, the significance of which is only now being understood.

The facts in the case were substantially similar to those of *Caird*. In 1962 Dr. J. Edwin Weisser, an enterprising optometrist and a UC Berkeley alumnus, started a lecture note–taking service ("Class Notes") at UCLA. With approval from the Dean of Students, Weisser hired students to audit over 150 courses between 1963 and 1965. These students submitted outlines of their notes to Weisser, who reproduced the outlines for sale. The courses included in the service were listed on the Class Notes office bulletin board, along with the names of instructors responsible for each course. Portions of the list were reproduced in advertisements for the service published in the student-run campus newspaper.

Dr. B. J. Williams joined the UCLA faculty in anthropology in 1965 and began teaching Introduction to Anthropology in the fall semester of that year. Several weeks into the semester he learned that Class Notes was publishing an outline of the course, including charts and diagrams he had drawn on the blackboard, based on notes taken by a student, Karen Allen. Through his attorney, Amil Roth, Williams demanded that Class Notes cease and desist. Weisser responded by offering to give Williams a share of the royalties. According to Weisser, Roth said his client might be interested. But a few weeks later, just as a formal offer landed on Roth's doorstep, the attorney was sitting in Weisser's office serving a temporary restraining order and complaint. Ultimately Williams sought a permanent injunction and compensation for general and punitive damages (273 Cal. App. 2d 726, 1969).

The case turned on three issues, each of which had also been raised in *Caird v. Sime*. First, did the professor own his lectures, or were they "works for hire"? Under the 1909 Copyright Act, an employer was considered the author of any work it had hired another to produce. Williams was an employee of the University of California, hired to teach anthropology; UC, therefore, was arguably the copyright owner of the course that resulted. A person hired by an advertising agency to "build" a radio show could not be said to own any part of the content of that show.[15] Why should a professor be treated any differently? Second, if Williams did own the lectures, had he released his expression into the public domain by presenting it to his students? Echoing Lord Fitzgerald's arguments in *Caird*, Weisser argued that the University of California was a public institution and the plaintiff was "a brilliant and highly trained educator, hired by the University to impart his knowledge and wisdom to any who might come to the University seeking such knowledge and wisdom" (Appellant's Opening Brief, 31). Having delivered this knowledge and wisdom, the plaintiff did not have a right to "take it back," to try to control its use. Third, was the professor a public or private figure? Williams argued that his reputation had been damaged by Weisser's use of his name to identify the set of notes taken from his lectures. Williams's delivery of the lectures was a matter of public record, Weisser countered. Professors, he added, especially those in a public university, were necessarily public figures who gave up the privacy rights afforded most citizens. "Even if plaintiff [Williams], like the exotic and secluded Queen of the Golden Era of Films, could be heard to plead that he only wanted to be left alone, anonymity is not his to have" (ibid., 34).

But apparently it was. In both trial and appellate courts, Williams won on all counts. On the first issue, ownership of the lectures, the California Court of Appeals gave little credence to the defendant's arguments. Partly on the basis of an amicus curiae brief filed by the University of California, the court concluded that "University lectures are *sui generis,*" meaning they were not like other works for hire. Judge Kaus's decision observed that, "[they] should not be blindly thrown into the same legal hopper with valve designs . . . motion picture background music . . . [and] high school murals" (735). As for the argument that lectures delivered in a public institution entered the public domain, Judge Kaus noted that *Caird* had established that oral delivery constituted a limited publication, to a limited class of "public" rather than the "general public." Because no tangible copies were distributed to the students, moreover, no true "publication" had occurred. Finally, the judge held that Williams's right of privacy had been violated. Against his will, his work had been commercially distributed and his name associated with that distribution, thereby potentially undermining his "professional standing." Looking to a 1955 case in which another professional—an attorney—had successfully sued a photocopier company for listing him as a "satisfied customer" in an advertisement (on the ground that the ad had damaged his professional reputation), Kaus suggested that plaintiff's personality, too, had been appropriated to Weisser's financial benefit.[16]

Williams v. Weisser in Context

To understand the implications of the decision, a few words about its historical context are in order, particularly with regard to the shifting relations between professor, student, university, and society. While the *Williams v. Weisser* trial was under way, the University of California was engaged in a bitter dispute with the state government over funding, itself colored by complaints about the "politicization" of the university. Demands for more active supervision of the university by the Regents and the state legislature pointed to conflicts between the "autonomy" of the Regents from the state government and the "autonomy" of the campuses themselves from the Regents (O'Neil, 1974). These struggles, moreover, were being replicated throughout the United States. As the chancellor of the State University of New York, Samuel B. Gould, declared before the New York Joint Legislative Committee on Higher Education in 1968, "Society, quite wisely, has granted the university freedom of internal governance, knowing the university is a social institution whose unique spirit must be preserved." One year earlier the president of Cornell, James A. Perkins (1967), had spoken against legal interference in university decisionmaking as threatening "fundamental damage" to the university. Meanwhile, this freedom of internal governance was being used to license the dismissal of professors on overtly political grounds.[17]

At stake in these battles was the definition of a public university. Who owned a public university, and what were the limits of that owner's "use and enjoyment"? What did "service to the state" mean when, as the political theorists Sheldon Wolin and John Schaar put it, the "dynamic" of the state administration depended "almost entirely upon its ability to sustain public anger against education" (1970, 147)? And what, finally, did academic freedom mean? Speaking to the student body of Kansas State University, Governor of California Ronald Reagan (1967) noted that that academic freedom, for the taxpayers, meant the "freedom to have some say in what they get for their money." It is hard to miss the echoes of Lord Fitzgerald's declaration that the general public, not only the "capable few," had a right to criticize and evaluate the teachings imparted to the nation's youth by a publicly endowed corporation.

Taxpayers and politicians weren't the only ones seeking a greater say in how the university was run. In fact, taxpayers' concerns about the university were, in large part, a response to the efforts of students to change what was perceived as an impersonal, bureaucratic, and corrupt system of education. While Karen Allen was busily taking notes on Williams's lectures, the University of California's Berkeley campus was the scene of a "middle-class crisis . . . spiritual and psychic rather than material" (Wolin and Schaar, 1970, 15–16). The year before, the Free Speech Movement had halted university activity in protests against restrictions of political speech on campus and, more broadly, the impersonality and conservatism of undergraduate education. In 1965 the university as a whole was ostensibly engaged in a process of self-assessment and limited instructional experimentation, even as political protests—this time directed at segregation and the escalation of the Vietnam war—continued.

Finally, and perhaps most important for our concerns here, the professoriate was engaged in an internal struggle over the nature of academic labor. Between 1960 and 1970, as the historian Walter Metzger notes, as many new academic posts were created as had existed since the founding of Harvard College. At the same time, large universities were growing into highly bureaucratized industrial corporations. As universities became physically dispersed, spurred by massive growth and a need "to teach and to hold a student torrent," administrative authority was seen as increasingly centralized in executive boards and/or statehouses (1987, 174). Enmeshed in massive systems, academics found it difficult to remember that they might be members of any "community of scholarship" outside their own specialized fields. In short, the university was becoming "too Westinghouse in look not to be treated as Westinghouse in fact" (174).

It was not surprising, in this context, that by 1969, 59 percent of new faculty agreed that collective bargaining had a place in the university (Ladd and Lipset, 1973, cited in Metzger, 1987). But for traditional faculty societies, especially the AAUP, unionization remained a profound threat to the professional status of academic workers. Union arguments for compensation based on seniority rather than "individual merit" challenged both the peer review system and the basic precepts that only faculty should determine the quality of professional work and that such determinations resisted standardization. More generally, the whole notion of legally binding collective bargaining implied that professors and administrators were not "partners" in a system of shared authority, but rather antagonists. In other words, it implied that professors were employees and workers, rather than highly autonomous professionals. The problem, for the AAUP, was that many of its members found that "adhering to old professional verities was rather like guarding an empty shrine" (Metzger, 1987, 175).

Nested Autonomies

Placed in context, the *Williams* decision, and especially the articulation of professorial work as private property, takes on particular resonance. *Williams v. Weisser* constructed the university and its inhabitants in terms of a nested set of autonomies. At the most abstract level, the decision set the limits of "the public university" in the name of evicting "the private," firmly positioning the university beyond the commercial sector with disdainful references to Weisser as an "outsider" and a businessman.

Perhaps more important in light of concurrent arguments about university and professorial power, the legal force of the university's memos and policies was also secured. The ownership of the lectures was officially governed by two documents cited in the opinion: The University's Copyright Policy (which referred specifically to writings), and a memo circulated by UCLA Vice Chancellor Charles E. Young that stated: "The common law copyright in a lecture is the property of the lecturer rather than of the University, and therefore any legal actions for the infringement of such right must be brought in the name of the aggrieved faculty member" (731). Weisser argued that the University of California, as a state university, was not permitted to allow its employees to "claim the absolute and exclusive right to preclude members of the public from free access to the product of his services for the University." Such a policy, he added, would be detrimental to the university itself as a public institution (Appellant's Opening Brief, 28). The university responded in its *amicus* brief that it knew very well what was and was not detrimental to its mission, and pointed to the broad discretion granted to it by the California Constitution, particularly with regard to employment.[18] In this area, the university asserted, referring to a 1940 case, *Wall v. Board of Regents*, "the conclusions reached by the Regents are final."[19] In making this assertion, the university failed to mention that the limits of its discretion were (and are still) undetermined. According to a 1952 decision in a loyalty oath dispute, the Regents' discretion applied only to "exclusively University affairs."[20] As numerous subsequent lawsuits involving academic tenure, collective bargaining rights, and freedom of speech would demonstrate, the affairs of an entity employing over 75,000 people in multiple cities can easily be imagined to be matters of statewide concern (Scully, 1987). But for the *Williams* court, at least, control of the circulation of a professor's speech certainly fell under the definition of a "University affair." Thus the treatment of lectures as *sui generis* implied and reproduced the autonomy of the university corporation.

Equally important, if less obvious, was the recapitulation of *Caird's* construction of teaching as a producer-consumer relationship. As some professors were busily evoking "ancestral memories of the ideal of a community of scholars bound together in the spirit of friendly persuasion" in the pages of the *New York Review of Books*, a member of a real academic community, with its support, was characterizing the student body as a consuming audience (Wolin and Schaar, 1965, 356). It is worth noting that four days after the *Williams* decision was handed down the Supreme Court affirmed the priority of audience interests with respect to broadcasting and in the process figured that audience as an active rights-holding public.[21] *Williams* by contrast imported copyright law's radical distinction between speaker and audience into the academic context and thereby constructed the student audience as passive consumers. Indeed, because both parties conceded there was a substantial similarity between the notes and Williams's lectures, the student who took the notes virtually disappeared in arguments about the case. As in *Caird*, the hand of the copyist was obscured, allowing the "delivery" of a lecture to be represented as a solitary act and activities of reception to be marginalized. In short, the classroom was treated as the exclusive domain and creation of the lecturer.

In assigning this domain to the lecturer, Judge Kaus was making a broader argument about academic work than any of the Peers had been prepared to mount in 1887. Government employees were not, as a rule, permitted to claim copyright for work carried out in the course of their employment, on the supposition that they were doing the public's business and were therefore obligated to make their products freely available to the public. The University of California, as a "fourth branch" of state government, might also have been required to make all of the work created under its auspices available to the public. Edwin Weisser demanded that it do so, and while it was certainly disingenuous on his part in light of his simultaneous suggestion that the university should assign that copyright in lectures to himself, the theory is not unreasonable. The obvious counterargument, that professors *do* make their work available to the public by publishing and lecturing, does little to explain why they should *own* that work and thereby retain the option of keeping it to themselves.

To reject Weisser's argument, the Court of Appeals had to construct Williams both as a consummate professional pursuing his vocation and as a rights-holding owner. The court proclaimed the matter a simple issue of weighing "undesirable consequences." "Professors are a peripatetic lot," Judge Kaus argued, "moving from campus to campus" (734). If universities could be said to own rights in lectures produced under their auspices, he suggested, a professor would be less able to change campuses and "take" his knowledge with him.[22] The primary distinguishing characteristic of professors, on this account, was their status as itinerant knowledge workers, a status that underwrote, in turn, their legal position as knowledge owners.

Beneath this utilitarian reasoning, however, lay the same assumptions about the nature of knowledge work and the "specialness" of these particular itinerant workers that informed the *Caird* decision. Williams's expression had to be his own solitary creation—and therefore his property—because, according to the vision of academic life offered by the court, it could not be anything else. Following Lord Watson's recognition of the power of the *senatus academicus,* and anticipating the AAUP's reasoning some thirty years later, Judge Kaus said that "neither the record in this case nor any custom known to us suggests" that universities could prescribe how their professors expressed the ideas they were hired to teach (734).[23] Again, in the modern research university the ancient guild-right of the masters to certify themselves (that is, grant titles) was transmuted into the foundation of reason: only reason may critique reason, only professors may judge other professors. Williams had mastered the unique skills and knowledge necessary to "profess," and nonexperts (university administrators as well as ambitious optometrists) were not qualified to dictate the terms of that communication. Thus that which tied the university most closely to the public domain—its claim to generate truth derived from and certified by the disinterested exercise of reason—was used to frame the products of that exercise as private property.

It would be singularly difficult, Judge Kaus went on to observe, to separate the knowledge a professor "brought" to a given job from knowledge gained in the course of his employment. To determine what a professor had learned and produced under its auspices, a university would have to delineate both the exact copyrightable property a professor owned when her employment commenced (to determine what was subsequently produced) and the exact hours of the day that would count as working hours.[24] The assertion of university copyright would require, in other words, that the university discipline its professors as it did its other employees. With ill-concealed irritation, Judge Kaus noted that "No one but the defendant, an outsider as far as the relationship between the plaintiff and UCLA are concerned, suggests that such a state of the law is desirable" (735).

But these statements, again, begged the question. Other employers presumed their new recruits brought some knowledge with them, and nevertheless managed to claim rights in work developed on their premises, and there was no reason that process should be any more or less difficult for a professor than for an industrial engineer. Referring to a line of cases in which other employees were found to be subject to work-for-hire provisions, Weisser pushed the point in an unsuccessful appeal to the California Supreme Court: "Surely the members of all of the professions, arts, and crafts . . . are as anxious to seek greener vocational pastures as the Court of Appeal seems to consider respondent's peers; and who would deny that all of them would find their careers greatly enhanced if they were but allowed to take with them the exclusive rights and title to the products of their former employment?" (Appellant's Petition for Hearing, 6). The Supreme Court chose not to hear Weisser's appeal, but the parameters of "work for hire" did come under review in many courts in the late 1960s, and, as Weisser's appeal suggests, the bulk of the judicial decisions favored expanding employer ownership.[25] The 1909 Copyright Act had failed to define "employer": filling that gap, the courts included entities that had motivated and/or supervised the work, or at whose expense the work had been created. Under these definitions, it would appear that one federal judge's 1987 observation that, in theory at least, every scholarly work could be a work for hire (for purposes of the 1976 Copyright Act) was equally true in 1967.[26] Given that academic workers were themselves finding reason to identify with other "bureaucratized white-collar cadres" outside of academe, why should they have been treated as "exceptional" with regard to copyright?

THE PROFESSOR AS CELEBRITY

A partial answer can be found in the disposition of the final issue in the case: the alleged violation of Williams's right of privacy. Though less obviously than in *Caird v. Sime,* here as well a discourse of propriety was deployed to clinch the decision. Williams argued that Weisser had violated his privacy in two ways. First, Williams's thoughts on the history of his discipline were disseminated more widely than he had intended. Some lecturers see the classroom as a testing ground for new ideas that may not yet be ready for peer review. Williams was one of those people, and the circulation of his ideas in print form, he argued, might undermine his reputation, particularly since the notes contained errors and omissions. Second, because his name was attached to this commercial product, implying his support of it, his personality had been appropriated for commercial gain. Again, his concern was that such an association might jeopardize his "professional standing" (741).

Williams thus anticipated the reasoning of the *Weissmann* case discussed in Chapter 2 by treating an academic's reputation like a celebrity's persona—as an object of appropriation. Indeed, *Williams* has been cited repeatedly in disputes over publicity rights in the star persona.[27] This development is not as surprising as it may initially seem, for publicity rights and the academic exception share more than just a technical connection. Publicity rights recognize a celebrity's right to control the use of her personality—her reputation—and the academic exception to work-for-hire doctrine does the same for the professoriate. Moreover, both publicity rights and the academic exception assume and reinforce the idea that some aspects of the persona are so particular (proper) to an individual that they may be commodified.

Publicity rights and the academic exception also share historical roots in common law copyright. Publicity rights derive from the right of privacy "discovered" in the United States with the publication of Samuel D. Warren and Louis Brandeis's article "The Right to Privacy" (1890).[28] Supposedly appalled by the willingness of the press to print embarrassing facts, Warren and Brandeis argued that human dignity depended upon protection from public intrusions as from physical assault (McCarthy, 1987). Pointing specifically to common law protection of an author's unpublished writings as precedent, Warren and Brandeis argued that just as an author had a right to keep his writings out of the public eye, so, too, did most persons have a right to keep facts about themselves private: "The intense intellectual and emotional life . . . which came with the advance of civilization, made it clear to men that only a part of the pain, pleasure, and profit of life lay in physical things. Thoughts, emotions, and sensations demanded legal recognition, and the beautiful capacity for growth which characterizes the common law enabled judges to afford the requisite protection" (Warren and Brandeis, 1890, 195). Common law intellectual property rights, they reasoned, should be understood as an instance of the right to be left alone. "The principle which protects personal writings and all other personal productions . . . against publication in any form . . . is in reality not the principle of private property, but that of an inviolate personality" (205). In their view, authors were protected before publication because no person should have his sentiments exposed to the public against his wishes. Property, in this context, was a matter of individual control—of one's labor but especially of one's reputation and dignity.

Early twentieth-century courts found that the right to privacy included a right not to have one's name or face used for commercial purposes. Beginning in the early 1950s, however, courts began to reframe this right of privacy to include a more proactive right to choose the commercial purposes to which one's public persona would be put, and thereby reap "the fruits of [one's] labor": a right of publicity.[29] Melville Nimmer (1954) summarized the argument like this:

> [It is] unquestionably true that in most instances a person achieves publicity values of a pecuniary worth only after he has expended considerable time, effort, skill, and even money. It would seem to be a first principle of Anglo American jurisprudence, an axiom of the most fundamental nature, that every person is entitled to the fruit of his labors unless there are important countervailing public policy considerations. Yet, because of the inadequacies of traditional legal theories . . . persons who have long and laboriously nurtured the fruit of publicity values may be deprived of them, unless judicial recognition is given to . . . the right of publicity. (216)

Note that Nimmer, like Judge Kaus, assumed that a property right was the only appropriate "desert" for individuals who had invested in their public selves. And in fact, as we have seen, the idea that reputation could be protected by a private property right dates to copyright's inception. But it was not until the 1970s that reputation, or the public persona, became the subject of a fully alienable private property right. The reasoning in *Williams* was instrumental in this transformation—the property claims of teachers, in other words, helped lay the foundation of new forms of property right for celebrities.

In *Williams v. Weisser,* then, the discourse of propriety comes full circle. In Roman law the person, or persona, referred to any entity with legal rights and duties. According to Marcel Mauss (1985), the Roman persona signified a role rather than an identity. Persons were the public representatives of families and organizing principles for honors, duties, and obligations—the subjects of propriety. *Williams* helped clear the way for honor, reputation, and privacy to be treated as property themselves rather than simply foundations for property claims. As a result, Jane Gaines comments, "privacy's personal monopoly becomes productive property" (1991, 203).[30]

Yet even as he affirmed "privacy's personal monopoly," shoring up in turn the professoriate's monopoly on competence, Judge Kaus set limits on that exclusive possession. Contrary to Vice Chancellor Young's assertion, case law did not necessarily establish that lectures were the property of the lecturer, only that if no other policy existed professorial ownership would be so assumed. Read against the grain, Judge Kaus's opinion concedes as much. Undermining his own statement that a university, by custom, could not prescribe means of expression and thereby claim ownership, Judge Kaus added, "no reason has been suggested why a university would want to retain ownership in a professor's expression. Such retention would be useless, except possibly for making a little profit" (734). In other words, the university did not want to own the expression. The implication was that if the institution did so desire, a different conclusion might be in order. Kaus noted that no "evidence one way or the other" had been presented regarding UCLA's ownership (733). The door was left open, therefore, for a university to establish policies and practices that might establish its claim to lectures. If evidence had been presented that the university had actively directed the preparation of the expression in question by providing syllabi and detailed outlines of material to be communicated, the case might have gone rather differently.

In sum, the *Williams v. Weisser* opinion called on individual honor, reputation, and, in a peculiarly American twist, privacy, to protect the cognitive and intellectual property of the professoriate. The invocation of Williams's right of privacy, in particular, allowed the case to be treated as a matter of personal injury rather than economic interest. One result was that wider controversies about the nature of academic labor could be ignored. Against a massive bureaucratization of the research university and a rising sense that professors might not be any more "special" than other knowledge workers, the sense that was fueling a unionization movement, stood Dr. B. J. Williams, an autonomous author-owner defending his individual honor. His defense offered an alternative story and strategy, in which academics were still exceptional professionals possessed of a monopoly of competence that could be protected by property rights rather than collective action.

However, the case also exposed the cultural work necessary to tell this story and make it persuasive. As Weisser rightly argued in his final appeal, the court's reasoning that university lectures were *sui generis* was flawed. The court warned of the "undesirable consequences" of Weisser's approach, but those consequences had not been deemed undesirable with regard to a host of other information workers (such as artists, musicians, and writers working in the private sector). Judge Kaus's acceptance of the "privacy" argument points to what is at stake in this treatment of lectures as *sui generis:* the sense that professors are uniquely situated in a separate sphere of honor and that their claim to their work is rooted as much in propriety as property. This sphere of honor included the university itself, which was characterized as a nonmarket institution with no reason to seek ownership in a professor's expression and no right to prescribe that expression.

The problem is, the court used this reasoning to construct the professor as an autonomous author-owner rather than a member of a gift community, delivering goods rather than fostering critical thinking. One could argue that production was itself an "undesirable consequence," given a historical backdrop of intense student criticism of the university teaching as impersonal and universities in general as "knowledge factories." Further, the resolution of the case not only followed *Caird v. Sime* in offering a vision of teaching modeled on commodity exchange, it broke new ground by carrying the *Caird* reasoning to its logical conclusion. It constructed the academic personality as an object of property, capable of "appropriation" by a commercial entity and therefore in need of protection. In so doing, it anticipated the reasoning we have already seen in the context of the *Weissmann* case; in *Williams* as in *Weissmann,* the protection of the academic personality was linked as closely to publicity as to privacy. Publicity rights permit the commodification of the star persona. Will the academic persona be far behind?

Today there is reason to think it will not, and to see why it is useful to briefly examine a recent controversy at UCLA. The central issues of *Williams* were raised again some thirty years later, when a deal between the junk bond king and convicted felon Michael Milken and UCLA went sour. Milken had paid the UCLA Anderson School of Management

$40,000 to allow him to lecture for one academic quarter and videotape the proceedings.[31] The university and Milken worked out a joint copyright agreement for the videotapes, set for broadcast on Milken's fledgling Education Entertainment Network (Mecoy, 1994; Harmon, 1993). Sharply rebuked by legislators, the UC Board of Regents, and the press (including the cartoonist Garry Trudeau, who lampooned the university in several *Doonesbury* strips), UCLA eventually got out of the deal. But the scandal called attention to contradictions and evasions in university policy regarding course materials. If a teacher owned the written lecture, who owned recordings of the performance of that lecture? The rationale for university ownership of recordings was not well developed, but a committee report responding to the Milken debacle suggested that ownership claims derived from the use of university property, such as buildings, staff, equipment, and the university name (Work Group on Commercialization of Lecture Materials, 1995). Did the same principle hold for performances by visual artists on the faculty? What about artists using university equipment? Faced with a proliferation of "recorded" forms and possibilities of commercialization, the committee was reduced to "reaffirming" an inferred policy granting copyright ownership of all recordings to the UC Regents, and calling for further guidance.

Faculty associations across the United States are now indirectly answering this call by turning to the language of contract. One comment on the UW copyright committee's 1998 draft report is a case in point. The letter notes that the copyright committee report implied that the university might have rights in lecture materials. Referring only briefly to a "tradition" to the contrary, the letter turns to the language of contract. Under the 1976 Copyright Act, copyright cannot be transferred involuntarily but must rather be deliberately assigned, in writing. New faculty employment contracts, the argument ran, would have to be written before the university could claim copyrights in works of scholarship, including lecture materials. The commentator's argument, which is echoed by the AAUP Statement on Copyright, is based on the belief that the academic exception will continue to be upheld by law. If faculty are indeed the legal authors of teaching materials, then it is true that their copyrights cannot be transferred involuntarily. Yet it is also true that tradition and a few legal decisions are less reliable than statutory law, especially when, as now, the professoriate's own activities are calling "tradition" into question. Without statutory protection, the "academic exception" rests on a shaky foundation.

Leaving that problem aside for the moment, a contract-based argument should be reassuring only to those who imagine new employment contracts would not be written, or that contracts are not available to multiple interpretations. Consider, for example, the shifting status of software. Until very recently, software was governed by the UW copyright policy, which permits faculty to claim rights in "scholarly or aesthetic works." In the course of my research, this policy was unofficially changed on one campus. A new technology transfer office director began informing faculty that software, or at least those aspects of it which are considered patentable, would be treated as works of technical utility rather than aesthetic works. Thus redefined, software may now be subject to the same university ownership claims as other patentable university research.

In other words, copyright ownership of lecture materials remains an open question. Against this backdrop, academics have strong incentives to turn to publicity rights, rather than copyright, to protect their cognitive property. Publicity rights deploy the moral force of "privacy" in the service of property. Unlike copyright, they are not subject to the vagaries of work-for-hire provisions—while the rights may be licensed to an employer or anyone else, no one has yet argued that an employer has a publicity right in an employee's public persona.

But publicity rights carry their own risks and losses. As noted in Chapter 2, they obscure the contribution of multiple sources to the production of knowledge. Further, their use may contribute to the very "propertization" of academic work that the professoriate may want to resist. In a digitized era, the celebrity persona works as a principle of unity across multiple media. For example, the face of Elvis Presley, displayed on lunch boxes and Web pages, reproduced in film clips, games, and paintings, ties these commodities by a common cultural thread that, not coincidentally, pulls in licensing fees for Factors, Inc., the company that owns the Presley persona (Gaines, 1993). Perhaps the academic persona, too, may begin to work as a principle of unity as classrooms become increasingly variegated. The sociologist James L. Wood worries that faculty who teach introductory courses will be displaced by "star professors" teaching courses online from distant campuses (Weiss, 1998).[32] How ironic that, if so, that operation could be substantially legitimated by and organized around the very discourse of propriety to which the professoriate has traditionally looked for protection from the market. Eighteenth-century publishers pushed for authorial copyright and used it to maintain their own control over the market in the face of a massive proliferation of texts. Twentieth-century media corporations have used the celebrity persona to protect their economic interests in the face of a proliferation of images. It is not hard to imagine that twenty-first-century educational corporations will look to the individual academic persona to provide an organizing principle across a proliferation of "learning environments" and happily use that persona to protect their economic interests.

RIGHTS, LOSSES, AND PROPERTY STORIES

As we have seen, the invocation of copyright to defend academic labor is not new, nor is it irreconcilable with the "nonmarket ethic of authorship" that, according to the UW copyright committee, defines academic creative work. In fact, the use of IP rights to defend the autonomy of the higher learning in America from the conduct of businessmen (including university administrators) dates at least to the making of the modern university.

We are now in a position to better evaluate the stakes of current property stories. It appears that, rather than traversing "knowledge frontiers," we are retelling old stories about the nature of academic work and the academy itself. Indeed, the demand for these tales seems to be increasing. Beginning in 1999, universities around the United States were confronted with a new practice: posting student-taken lecture notes online. Several companies were offering to pay students up to $400 per semester for class notes, much to the consternation of universities and professors alike (Kaplan, 1999). Some professors argued that publication of student notes would chill classroom speech and that it is an invasion of privacy (Schevitz, 1999). "There's nothing much more personal than your lecture material," one faculty member told the *Chronicle of Higher Education* (Blumenstyk, 1999). Others stressed that publication of student notes infringes on the professorial copyright. Summing up the views of many, one law professor stated: "[It] is outrageous morally and infringement legally" (ibid.). The companies publishing the notes counterargued that lectures are not personal at all, but rather summaries of facts or ideas and thus public domain material.

This debate covers increasingly familiar territory. It is crucial to notice, however, that this time university attorneys are leading the charge. In 1965 the University of California insisted that it was up to B. J. Williams to defend his copyright; in 1999 and 2000 it seemed the UC and other universities were prepared to declare their own interest in the material. Yale University threatened legal action against one company, and that company quickly removed all notes from Yale classes. Along with Harvard University, Yale also informed its students that selling notes violated university rules. Other universities promptly revised their regulations to forbid or at least monitor sales of notes (Sanders, 2000; LoLordo, 2000). In California, the state legislature passed a bill prohibiting the unauthorized recording or publication of lectures delivered by any professor in the state's public university system (Patel, 2000).[33]

These developments add dramatic tension to other new, or at least newly prominent, themes, for the "academic exception" is now being invoked by professors as a defense against employers as well as outside parties. Recall, for example, that the UW faculty, echoing concerns of activists such as David Noble, were worried that their university would ally with commercial entities against them. The faculty-university tension poses a concrete problem for faculty looking to claim property rights in expression, given the uncertain legal ground upon which those rights rest. To begin with, it is very possible that, absent a contract to the contrary, universities could claim copyright in most academic works, on the theory that those works fall within a professor's scope of employment. The policy of most universities, which is part of every professor's contract, gives copyright to professors—for now. But the AAUP's intense interest in copyright, not to mention the irate responses at UW to the mere suggestion that faculty might not own copyright in all of "their" work, indicates a growing suspicion that the academic exception is in need of a vigorous defense.

Curiously enough, given the uniqueness of the academic exception, that defense may put the professoriate at the cutting edge of an accelerating economic trend. Manuel Castells has argued persuasively that the capacities, working conditions, interests, and projects of workers are becoming increasingly individuated. The work process is organized through global networks of salaried employees, contractors, and subcontractors, whose sole point of contact, if any, will be a common product. As production grows ever more globally dispersed and relations of production ever more contingent and temporary, Castells observes, "labor loses its collective identity" (1996, 475). Labor is nevertheless as highly stratified as ever, divided between generic, replaceable operators who, for example, put microchips together (the knowledge workers) and highly individualized informational producers, who design the microchips (the knowledge owners).

Professors can hardly be blamed for choosing to align themselves with the latter category. Indeed, that choice is emerging as a basic survival strategy, as universities begin to question or even abandon shared-governance principles, recruit temporary lecturers to fill positions once held by tenured professors, and demonstrate a renewed interest in the creation and ownership of "scholarly works." Yet an embrace of knowledge ownership signals as well a pervasive rejection of a collective professional identity that the professoriate has often taken to be its hallmark—an identity upon which those very ownership claims are founded. The anthropologist Sally Engle Merry (1990) offers a useful analogy. She observes that when working-class people turn to the law to resolve problems, they often lose control of the process. Their experiences are reframed to fit legal categories and their lives are shaped by new forms of discipline (counseling, home visits by social service workers, or lectures on values, hygiene, relationships). Professors, too, risk losing control when they turn to the law. The ground of the claim to cognitive exclusiveness—the concepts of committed service to society, and aversion to commercial pursuits, what the historian Lawrence Veysey calls the "gentlemanly ideal" of scholarship—is necessarily loosened when the claimants are positioned as autonomous and litigious owners of alienable private property.

Thus far the contradictions of the academic exception to work-for-hire reasoning have been successfully mediated by a boundary object—the hybrid concept of propriety. This boundary object has allowed the property discourses of law and the academy to continue to appeal to each other for legitimation. It has also helped undermine the conceptual underpinnings of that appeal. The legal history of faculty ownership of lectures indicates that property rights are a treacherous foundation, at best, for political strategies that seek to defend the academy against "commercialization." In fact, the academic exception, whether an explicit matter of contract or ratified and concealed by the hybrid concept of propriety, may actually reinforce a vision of academic freedom organized around market principles and, by extension, the very commodification of learning that the professoriate may want to challenge.

CHAPTER FOUR

Metes and Bounds

The mathematician and prolific inventor Norbert Wiener wrote that the "real scientist of the first rank is by the nature of his own activity too busy to care much either for money or the ordinary signs of prosperity" (1993, 148). The real scientist was therefore not only the most productive source of profitable inventions but also "a core of possible defiance" to capital (35). "The man who is to be governed by a desperate curiosity about nature" and thus capable of discovering its rules, Wiener insisted, must be insulated from "better-paying worldly values" (36). Looking skeptically at the great industrial laboratories, he stated one of the foundational premises of industrial and information economies: capital needs scientific creativity, but scientific creativity requires seclusion from the needs of capital.

Thus the apparent contradiction of that constellation of activities known as technology transfer and the patent system upon which it partly depends. In return for publishing the details of an invention, patent law authorizes inventors to prevent others from making, using, selling, or offering to sell that invention for twenty years. This protection is supposed to encourage the dissemination of knowledge and promote progress in science and the useful arts. But because patents impose a model of ownership rather than stewardship on the circulation of ideas, Wiener argued, they actually "render sterile the soil of human intellect" (151). On this logic it is urgent to defend the one institution that, at least for Wiener, exists to maintain the fertility of that soil—namely, the academy.

Yet this institution is rapidly abandoning the position of "steward" for that of "owner." The end of the Cold War and the erosion of national culturalism have undermined the research university's traditional sources of funds and legitimacy. "Technology transfer," or the patenting and licensing of useful academic research to the private sector, seems to offer a persuasive set of alternative justificatory rhetorics. Throughout the United States, university administrators are looking to technology transfer offices for new sources of revenue and, more important, new ways to demonstrate university contributions to economic growth. Will the political and economic benefits of this repositioning come at the cost of depleting the soil of human intellect, what IP law calls the public domain?

Academics and industrialists alike fear the answer is yes, and their anxieties tend to focus on the erasure of boundaries between the academy and the market. Economics and sociology professor Martin Kenney, among others, contends that when universities and private companies work together, "the entire society is endangered . . . [for] industry will then discover that by being congenitally unable to control itself and having no restraints placed on it by the public sector, it has polluted its own reservoir" (quoted in Matkin, 1990, 4). Industry is also interested in boundary maintenance, for curiosity-driven academic science is seen as a source of economic value. As an executive of a major oil company told a senior Collingwood researcher: "You're worth a lot more to us working in the university coming up with good ideas than . . . on our research staff being forced to work on projects that have already been decided by management."

Yet the disappearance of boundaries is less striking than the almost desperate attempts by all parties concerned to affirm and stabilize difference in the face of transgression—to make sure, in other words, that technology transfer can continue to be represented *as transgression.* Rather than simply showing how the discourses of ownership and stewardship intermingle (which, as we shall see, they do), I investigate the processes in and through which the products of academic research as gifts and as private property are distinguished in spite of that intermingling. The "work" of patenting for technology transfer is two-fold. First, multiple actors and worldviews are enlisted in the stabilization, atomization, and propertization of knowledge—difference is mediated. Second, fundamental and mutually constitutive oppositions between some of these actors and worldviews are continually reestablished—difference is maintained.

My analysis of these processes extends paradigms developed to study the social construction of authorship to examine another governing system for the ordering, appropriation, and exclusion of knowledge: the realm of invention and inventorship. The task is made easier by a body of sociocultural studies of academic science produced by ethnographers, sociologists, and rhetoricians. Drawing on these divergent literatures and on in-depth, open-ended interviews with persons involved in various aspects of technology transfer, I pose a series of questions.[1] What is an invention? What is an inventor? As we will see, inventions and inventors are authorized through the cooperation of multiple social worlds—what meanings do those authorizations engage and foreclose? Finally, how do these multiple authorizations enroll social actors in the representation of technology transfer as necessary transgression?

To answer these questions, we need a better sense of their historical context. I begin, therefore, with an account of the changes in federal and university policy and law that laid the groundwork for the contemporary surge in technology transfer activities.

A PREHISTORY OF TECHNOLOGY TRANSFER

Public Patents

Some technology transfer advocates like to argue that universities have been involved in technology transfer, in the broadest sense of simply disseminating knowledge, since the Middle Ages. But I will take my cue from most of the technology transfer managers with whom I spoke, and define technology transfer as the patenting and licensing of inventions arising from university research. While these practices are much less ancient, their pedigree in the United States is almost as old as that of, say, academic freedom. As early as 1921 the chemist William J. Hale wrote in *Chemical and Metallurgical Engineering:* "There is nothing dishonorable in a university scientist seeking a patent. On the contrary, he gains enormously thereby in international prestige. Of course, he usually is condemned at home by the university drones unable to comprehend the value of ideas other than their own; but such childish criticisms are negligible. No true scientist doubts for a moment the right of a man to patent his own inventions" (quoted in Palmer, 1947, 681). Several U.S. universities, including UW, had limited programs and foundations dedicated to the administration of patents based on university research in place in the 1920s.[2] Most of these programs were small, reflecting profound institutional ambivalence about the patenting of inventions.[3] One famous exception is worth noting: the Wisconsin Alumni Research Foundation (WARF). WARF was founded in 1925 to administer patents resulting from University of Wisconsin Professor Harry Steenbock's research on vitamin D. Intended to provide a kind of buffer organization that could siphon profits to the university but prevent any taint of commerciality from attaching to the institution, WARF was nevertheless sharply criticized for bringing the university too close to industry (Matkin, 1990).[4]

As federal support of research mounted and the number of patentable inventions increased, however, administrative attitudes began to change. By 1944 the federal government was financing three-fourths of all research in the United States—and universities were taking in their share. Under the auspices of Vannevar Bush's (1945) vision of an "endless frontier" of knowledge, discussed in Chapter 1, that financing increased steadily and sometimes dramatically in the 1950s and 1960s (Lowen, 1996). With one end of the scale awash in money, the balance between teaching and research shifted in favor of the latter, and professional advancement began to depend on research and publication. Meanwhile, universities saw a slight but visible increase in academic patents. The increase in research funding does not necessarily explain the increased interest in patenting—researchers might just as easily have continued to ignore the patentability of their work—but it may suggest that more potential inventions were available to be identified as such. In 1943 UW, like several other U.S. universities, formed a patent board to administer faculty inventions and began to actively lobby for rights in government-sponsored inventions.

Ownership of federally sponsored research nevertheless remained an open question. In 1945 the Senate Committee on Military Affairs held a series of hearings on assigning patent rights in federally sponsored scientific research to contractors of all shapes and sizes (Eisenberg, 1996). Participants and commentators fell into two camps. Advocates of a "license policy" argued that the federal government should assign title in inventions arising from sponsored research to the organization performing the research and retain a right to a royalty-free license. Assignment of title permitted inventor-contractors to apply for a patent and prevent nongovernmental entities from making, using, or selling the invention. "Title policy" advocates, in contrast, proposed that the government retain full title in sponsored inventions and license them to several competing contractors at once.

There were few if any proposals to leave government-sponsored inventions unpatented altogether, and this absence points to one of the basic problems of modern conceptualizations of the public domain. Because the commons is understood as a kind of space of free appropriation, it is difficult to ensure that an idea, left "unprotected," will not be appropriated by a private entity as its own. Even published ideas can simply be reworked by new "inventors," and a patent on that "new" idea can be used to limit commercial and even noncommercial use of the original. "Title" or "public patent" advocates saw government ownership of patents as the only way to preserve the public's claim to the inventions for which it had paid (Eisenberg, 1996).

Appearing before the committee or commenting on its proceedings, professors from several major universities, as well as government officials (including President Harry Truman) and private-sector engineers argued against the "license" strategy. Articulating the basic argument against these patents still repeated today, Dr. Horace Gray, of the University of Illinois, contended that to "turn the results of [publicly funded] research over to some private corporation on an exclusive, monopoly basis . . . [amounted] to public taxation for private privilege" (quoted in Kreeger, 1947, 727). That argument was perhaps especially persuasive after it became known that several major defense contractors had licensed military technologies to Germany just prior to World War II (Kevles, 1977/1996). In 1947 the U.S. attorney general recommended that the federal government reserve all rights to inventions produced by employees and contractors under its auspices.

The title advocates had prevailed. In the end, though, the attorney general's recommendation was only partially adopted. In effect, what emerged in that decade was a kind of double system under which some federally sponsored inventions were effectively assigned to the public domain while others were handled by federal "license agencies." These license agencies permitted universities to assert patent rights in an invention, subject to the granting of a royalty-free license for government use of the invention (Matkin, 1990). In order to claim such rights, universities had to demonstrate an organizational capacity to license and market inventions, and many were increasingly inclined to do so.

Still, patents remained a fairly marginal pursuit with few substantial payoffs through the 1960s, and a nearly universal refusal to defend university patent rights against infringement indicates that patenting of university-based research was still construed as inappropriate. The work may have seemed more trouble than it was worth: in a 1951 letter to the head of a committee assigned to review UW patent policy, the president of UW observed that patent "problems [were] constantly arising to plague both the President and the Regents." And when UW began to require faculty to disclose and assign to the university inventions arising from their research, it was feared that a faculty rebellion to "rival the Oath incident" would occur (Letter from UW Vice President to UW President, January 1952). The faculty did not rebel, perhaps because the policy was not actively enforced. Few inventions were "disclosed," still fewer pursued.

Delivering Genius to the Market

In the 1970s the major forces pushing technology transfer began to coalesce. First, the growth of new technology-based businesses around the University of California at Berkeley, Stanford University, and the Massachusetts Institute of Technology highlighted the potential contribution of university research to economic growth—and astute National Science Foundation (NSF) officials looking to protect their funding started gathering the numbers to prove it (Matkin, 1990; Atkinson, 1996a). Second, private companies looking to be part of that economic growth by developing inventions arising from federally sponsored research found their efforts frustrated by complex and sometimes arbitrary licensing rules. Meanwhile, industrial investment in university research increased, and private companies began to push harder for intellectual property rights in the research they themselves sponsored. Finally, the economic growth of Japan and Germany, coupled with high inflation and recession in the United States, sparked a national (and nationalist) discussion of the sources of U.S. economic growth or lack thereof—including one of the accepted pillars of American ingenuity, the patent system.

Against this background, a dispute between Department of Health, Education, and Welfare (HEW) patent counsel Norman Latker and his superiors became a major public controversy. With the support of Republican-appointed administrators, Latker had developed a streamlined approach to licensing HEW-owned inventions. New officers appointed by Democratic President Jimmy Carter were suspicious of this strategy and began to review all of Latker's decisions, thereby delaying transfer of the technology.[5] Lobbied by Latker and research contractors who had assignment decisions pending, in 1978 Senators Birch Bayh (D-Indiana) and Robert Dole (R-Kansas) attacked HEW for undermining important biomedical research. The officials released some of the pending assignments, but they also fired Latker.

Bayh and Dole introduced the University and Small Business Patent Procedures Act to bring all government agencies under one policy. In 1979 hearings on the bill, witnesses stressed that the existing regime was destroying America's inventive spirit. Bayh's opening statement expressed his deep concern that the United States was losing ground in technological development. More and more foreigners were being granted patents (35 percent of the total U.S. patents in 1973), investment in research was stagnating, and the number of U.S. patents was declining. For the United States to compete, Bayh argued, the U.S. government had to do its part "to insure that the fruits of American inventive genius are delivered to the marketplace" (Hearings, 3). More specifically, the federal government had to facilitate the commodification of the research it paid for by allowing universities and the private sector to easily patent and license inventions arising from federally sponsored science. "Unless universities and small businesses receive the right to retain the patent in these inventions," Bayh declared, "valuable discoveries wind up wasting away on the funding agency's shelves, benefiting no one" (Hearings, 2).

Witnesses took up the refrain. "Rules and regulations . . . which cause doubt about the ownership and disposition of the fruits of the brain, the intellectual property of creative people," said the pediatrics professor Leland C. Clark Jr., "have a repressive and chilling effect on the inventor" (71). Prompted by Dole, Clark also noted that foreign industrial scientists were free to use U.S. research to develop new products, which were then sold back to U.S. consumers. Looking to the Bible for support, General Motors Vice-President for Environmental Activities Betsey Ancker Johnson likened the patent system to Samson's hair: the system was the key to America's strength, and its importance would not be felt until it was lost. Passage of the bill, she contended, would demonstrate "our firm determination to remain first in a peaceful but brutally competitive world" (149).

Underneath this nationalist rhetoric, the argument for private patents was simple: no firm would be willing to invest the resources needed to bring an invention to market (to fund, for example, the clinical trials necessary for Food and Drug Administration approval of a new drug) without some protection from competition.[6] Admiral Hyman Rickover (head of the navy's nuclear propulsion laboratory and the sole opposing witness) attempted to remind Congress that the taxpayers had already provided substantial incentives for innovation. Inventions resulting from government-sponsored research were paid for by public citizens, he argued, and should therefore be available for use by those citizens as they saw fit. Moreover, he suggested, the bill embodied an important contradiction: "In private industry, the company that pays for the work generally gets the patent rights. Similarly, companies generally claim title to the inventions of their employees on the basis that the company generally pays their wages. In doing business with the Government, however, these same companies reverse the standard, contending that the patent rights should belong to the one who comes up with the idea, not the one who foots the bill" (158). This contention conflated the university and small business owner with the inventive employee, but the point was well taken. It reflected, moreover, the sentiments of such diverse critics as the consumer advocate Ralph Nader, the Justice Department's antitrust division, and Senator Gaylord Nelson, chair of the Senate Subcommittee on Monopoly and Anticompetitive Activities (Roark, 1979).

The bill's proponents answered Rickover's invocation of the taxpaying citizen with an equally powerful American symbol: the pioneering individual inventor. The testimony of a General Motors executive notwithstanding, the Bayh-Dole Act was touted as a tool for the promotion of small business interests (think Ben Franklin and Eli Whitney). The emphasis on granting rights to such virtuous figures as small business and universities, Rebecca Eisenberg (1996) argues, effectively defused the still powerful public aversion to granting monopoly rights to large government contractors. Protests, like that of Senator Russell B. Long against what he termed a "radical and far-reaching giveaway" of tax dollars, were less forceful when the "giveaway" was ostensibly directed toward worthy individual entrepreneurs and university corporations (*Chronicle of Higher Education*, 1980).

The bill was passed in 1980, and thus was born what Dole characterized as a new "true and genuine partnership, a partnership in which the Government can act as impresario in bringing industry and universities together with new fields of knowledge" (Hearings, 29). The implementation of the bill's provisions took a few years to work out, but for universities the process now usually works like this: the research institution has first claim to patent rights in inventions that emerge from research financed by the federal government. If the institution chooses not to pursue a patent, ownership reverts to the funding agency, which may assign it back to the inventor.

Several other developments in the 1980s laid the final groundwork for a surge in technology transfer. First, the Supreme Court declared in *Diamond v. Chakrabarty* (1980) and *Diamond v. Diehr* (1981) that living organisms and software, respectively, could be patented.[7] These decisions substantially expanded the subject matter available to university technology transfer offices. Second, the Cold War ended, and universities scrambling to respond to an anticipated dramatic decrease in federal funding for research became more interested in patenting and licensing as a way to generate revenue, demonstrate the continuing usefulness of the university to the nation, and develop relationships with potential industrial "partners." Major federal funding agencies stepped up efforts to protect their budgets from the congressional chopping block by pointing to commercial success stories arising from publicly financed research. Third, the Tax Reform Act, passed in 1986, required public universities to retain title to any inventions created using public resources or risk losing their nonprofit tax status. Public universities were also forbidden to assign monetary value to any invention in advance of its creation and, therefore, to grant a "license" to any products of research as part of a research agreement.

Finally, many of the large industrial laboratories involved in basic as well as commercially driven research began to shut down. IBM and AT&T, to take two prominent examples, began to pull out of basic research in the late 1980s. Some of their scientists took positions in research universities but maintained relationships with their old colleagues. These relationships, the private sector's continuing need for basic research, and the development of several highly profitable commodities based on academic research in bio- and information technologies, encouraged private industry to remember the value of the university to economic development.

By 1996 industry support for university research had reached $2.5 billion per year and, in line with the nationalist rhetorics that shaped the Bayh-Dole Act, technology transfer had been recoded as a kind of national service (Navarro, 1996). The success of that representation, however, required an often unacknowledged but profound redefinition of "service." Under the German model of the research university, "useful" meant "in service to the national culture." The American version incorporated economic and political as well as cultural benefit, but these divergent missions were still framed as a continuing struggle rather than a fait accompli, particularly during the Cold War. By the early 1990s the struggle was largely over and the university legitimated its activities primarily in terms of economic rather than cultural growth.

Thus the uselessness of the university made it useful again—so long as mechanisms were in place to ensure that what UW's patent policy called the "fortuitous by-products" of that useless work were made available for commercialization. Nevertheless, to the extent that it positions the university as beholden to the concerns of businessmen, technology transfer still represents a powerful threat to both the epistemic regime that the modern research university helped found and the economic and political interests that benefit from that regime. Significant boundary work has to be done, therefore, to refigure the "useful uselessness" paradox and thereby maintain the value of the university and its technologies.

UW was deeply involved in the changes described here, and in the last two decades it has come to take technology transfer, and particularly the patenting of research, very seriously indeed. Its current president has actively promoted university-industry partnerships for decades, and it is likely that he was chosen as president in part because of his perceived ability to lead the university into the "second academic revolution" that technology transfer both heralds and promotes. Managing patent activities is a complex business, requiring the enlistment of several divergent and sometimes antagonistic social worlds, all of which are interested in simultaneously crossing and maintaining the conceptual boundaries of the university. Technology transfer requires, therefore, the production of boundary objects. Let us turn now to the specifics of this production.

INVENTION IS A SOCIAL ACT

Overview of Technology Transfer

At UW, the process of technology transfer begins with a disclosure, filled out by the inventor(s) and submitted to a technology transfer associate.[8] This form describes ("discloses") the invention, and its completion marks the first step in the translation of research into a patent. In truth, the faculty member does not have to disclose the invention at all. There are no "patent police" and it is likely that the technology transfer office will never know if she chooses not to disclose. Thus the submission of the forms signals a kind of enlistment in the process as well. Further, because the researcher is asked to identify inventors and potential licensees in addition to describing the invention, the disclosure form begins to create a map of the invention and its cultural landscape.

Disclosure in hand, the TTA will determine who has a legitimate claim to the invention, and it is here that the boundary work of technology transfer begins. Was the research funded by the federal or state government, or a commercial entity, or some combination thereof? Did its development require university resources? Was a researcher from another university involved? Were materials from a for-profit or nonprofit entity used in the research and, if so, was an agreement regarding rights in inventions arising from use of the materials signed by all parties? These questions reflect the numerous contributory sources that might stake property claims and the genuine difficulty of setting the borders of the university. As a general policy, the university claims all rights in any invention developed using its resources—but this policy is sometimes more of a starting point for negotiation than a firm rule. Under some circumstances, for example, an industrial group might contract for a specific piece of research and obtain rights in any invention arising therefrom. Faculty are encouraged to take on research contracts and otherwise consult with private and public entities as a form of public service, but they are not usually permitted to release rights in inventions that might arise from the consultation.

Funding is not the only source of property claims. Several companies that provide materials for research have tried to "reach through" and claim rights in inventions arising from research in which the materials were used. The semiconductor industry is particularly notorious for attempting to "reach through" and claim rights in both technology arising from research it funds and technologies in other laboratories peripherally related to the funded research. These "peripheral" researchers may have worked out their own research agreements, and then, noted one senior TTA, "we have sold the same horse to two different funding entities." The DuPont corporation is equally notorious. It sought to force all universities using its Crelox technology in research to sign a license assigning to DuPont rights in inventions developed using the technology, and it forbade researchers to provide the materials to any university that had refused to sign the agreement (Commission on Life Sciences, 1999). Many universities agreed to sign, but the National Institutes of Health, Harvard, and the University of California refused—much to the consternation of their research scientists. Researchers, especially those in strong competition with other scientists, see administrative refusal to permit "reach-through" clauses in research contracts as an unnecessary impediment to their work. Grant officers and research boards, however, must weigh pressures from faculty against complex political, legal, and contractual obligations that enforce what is assumed—the fundamentally noncommercial nature of university research. Faced with formidable opposition, DuPont eventually backed off.

The problem, though, remains—rights in many inventions must be negotiated with several parties: providers of research tools, private and public research sponsors, and university administrators. To forestall conflicting claims, scholars are asked to compartmentalize their knowledge by keeping track of the uses of their professional knowledge and skills, not to mention university equipment. For example, they are asked to consult only in areas divorced from their primary research projects, and to spend no more than one day per week on "outside professional activities." The problems of this arrangement are obvious. Why would a company want faculty expertise on topics outside that professor's research interests?

Contract and grant offices, conflict-of-interest (COI) committees, and TTAs share the uncomfortable task of policing this compartmentalization. The most serious problem, at least for TTAs, is that faculty may report an invention to the technology transfer office (TTO) but insist that it was created as part of their outside professional activities. Or they may never report the invention at all. One TTA found out from a magazine article about a patent that had been issued to a university researcher and licensed to a private entity. Confronted, the professor insisted the work had arisen from a consulting arrangement. The work was clearly related to his primary research area, however, and it was likely that he had used university resources in some aspect of its development. The TTA cried foul: "We just simply said we're not going to let the company steal this from the university. You're going to have to license it and if you want to fight over it, we'll fight. And if you don't want to fight, we'll license it to you, we won't charge a lot, we'll get some reasonable return and you'll have your technology. So it's a win-win situation. If you want to argue, then we're going to have an argument. And small companies don't like that. We don't like it either . . . [but] there are people going through the back door with their technology." As it happened, the professor was also a co-founder of the company claiming the technology.

In cases like this, COI committees may also get involved by monitoring consulting arrangements between the researcher and the company. But as this example also indicates, COI committees cannot fully monitor the flow of knowledge between faculty and private entities. It does not help that even sympathetic faculty members see COI efforts to do so as a nuisance at best and a threat to their autonomy at worst. One senior researcher explained: "You have to sign a form that says, basically, [you] haven't spent more than X hours, X days doing consulting. I think I find that somewhat offensive . . . I guess it's a legitimate question but [we're] in an environment where you're not used to being questioned or having to answer." University COI policy implicitly reinforces this view by insisting that a faculty member's own ethics are the first line of defense against conflicts of interest—affirming the university as a space of honor, even as its bureaucrats busily work to police the intersecting sphere of contract.[9]

Having determined university ownership claims, the TTA will assess potential industry interest and the likelihood of writing a defensible patent. She may be assisted in this endeavor by the inventor, who may already have a potential licensee in mind.[10] If she decides to proceed with a patent application, the associate will (1) get in touch with possible licensees to determine "marketability" and (2) send the disclosure and supporting documents to outside counsel for patent prosecution—the composition, filing, and revision of patent applications. The attorney will then investigate the patent and scientific literature ("prior art") to determine the "newness" of the invention. The attorney may draw on the knowledge of the inventor herself at this point because she is likely to know the field well. Based on the supporting materials and conversations with the inventor, the attorney will draft an application for the patent that describes the invention. The inventor will be asked to review it and suggest any needed changes. After a few iterations, the application is sent to the patent examiner for review. Once the application is filed, the inventor can publish and/or speak publicly about the work without fear of losing patent rights.[11]

Patents are rarely granted on the first try. Often the examiner will return the application to the attorney and suggest that the invention has been anticipated by prior work in the field. The attorney will revise it accordingly and send it back for another review. And so on. The entire process can take as long as a decade, though the average is between one and three years.[12]

Meanwhile, the TTA has (very often) negotiated a license with a private company to "bring the invention to market." Such negotiations often begin before an application has been filed, because the university prefers to have licensees pay the filing fees and legal costs of patent prosecution. Depending on the technology, bringing the invention to market can mean further testing and experimentation, clinical trials, market research, and so on. The TTA is supposed to monitor these activities and ensure that the company is diligently developing the invention. If all goes well, the patent is issued, the invention becomes a profitable commercial product, and the licensee starts paying royalties, to be divided (after remaining patenting and licensing expenses are deducted) between UW (50 percent), the inventor's campus (15 percent), and the inventors themselves (35 percent).

The Social Worlds of Invention

As this sketch of the process indicates, intellectual property formation for technology transfer requires the cooperation of at least three social worlds: academic research, technology transfer, and law. Although these worlds overlap, I want to conceptually separate them for descrip-

tive purposes before discussing their interaction. First, a caveat. In my research I did not seek to develop detailed accounts of the commitments,
histories, and vocabularies of each of these worlds. Instead, I constructed
a panel of knowledgeable informants with experience in various aspects
of technology transfer, and focused the interviews on the identification
of inventions and their translation into patents. This involved a necessary sacrifice—I might have confined my interviews to lawyers, for example, and learned a great deal about how they understand patenting or,
as some researchers have done, focused on the views of scientists (Packer
and Webster, 1996; Webster and Packer, 1997). I chose instead to develop a cross-sectional sample, and through it sought to understand how
interested groups cooperate.

The world of academic research discussed here includes several disciplines: electrical engineering, neuroscience, biological science, earth science, and oceanography. In addition to researchers, students, and technicians, this social world is occupied by diverse administrative bodies:
contract and grant officers, conflict-of-interest committees, support staff,
technology policy committees, and department administrators. These individuals, overall, construct themselves and the university as invested in
long-term, "curiosity-driven" investigations, as specifically distinct from
short-term commercial research. Even investigators who frequently consult with private industry and/or use private funds to help support their
projects said they prefer government funding because they see it as more
supportive of long-term study. Yet while most of the people with whom I
spoke share a commitment to the university's traditional mission of basic, disinterested research, teaching, and service—indeed, researchers,
students and staff alike referred often to that mission to explain why
they chose not to work in the private sector—they disagree sharply on
how that mission is to be accomplished. For example, researchers suggest that the university's IP and COI policies interfere with the progress
of science and, not coincidentally, faculty autonomy.[13] Research administrators, for their part, portray faculty as either cavalier or deliberately
mercenary in their willingness to "give away" new inventions in exchange for research funding and consulting fees and/or to use university
facilities for commercial purposes.

A second social world, that of the technology transfer office, handles
the patenting and licensing of inventions that are not "given away."
Technology transfer is coordinated by two entities: a parent organization

that oversees technology transfer throughout the university, and campus offices with varying degrees of autonomy from the parent organization. At both levels, TTOs are populated by managers, support staff, and senior and junior technology transfer associates who specialize in engineering, life, or chemical sciences. Some TTAs have advanced degrees in science; most also have law degrees. The system-wide TTO works closely with research administrators on policy issues as well as troubleshooting. The research administrators and TTAs are slightly more estranged at the local Collingwood office, and this estrangement may be related to the latter's pro-business orientation. The TTAs and the director pride themselves on their knowledge of "how business works" and refer to licensees as well as inventors as "customers." The system-wide TTO takes a more antagonistic attitude toward business, treating good licensee relations as a priority but one tempered by a perception that industrial representatives may try to take advantage of the university and undervalue its technologies. TTAs in both offices feel overburdened. They may be responsible for as many as two hundred inventions at once, and while only a fraction of those inventions may need active attention at any one time, just maintaining good relations with the "primary resource"—the faculty—can be very time-consuming.

Like research administrators, TTAs have a kind of love-hate relationship with faculty. On the one hand, technology transfer at UW is imbued with a rhetoric of service to faculty and a commitment to working out deals that make faculty members happy. While many TTAs emphasize their good relations with "their" inventors, they also portray faculty as arrogant, individualistic, sometimes mercenary, and often naive. TTAs referred often to the need to work with faculty "ego" and the importance of not taking faculty complaints "personally." Faculty have higher status in the university and can use that status to pressure TTAs, especially those at the local level. For example, some TTAs reported that faculty had pushed them to "give away" inventions, meaning license them on very good terms, to companies that were providing research support. Faculty can also simply refuse to disclose inventions.

Faculty, for their part, give equally mixed views of TTAs. Faculty members complained of mismanagement of inventions, assignments to untrustworthy licensees, interference in research support, and overly conservative decisionmaking regarding the marketability of inventions. One prominent faculty member, for example, felt his invention had been licensed to a company that lacked the expertise and interest necessary to develop it. Unless and until the terms of the licensing agreement were violated, however, he could do little but complain.[14] Another researcher described long delays in the patentability evaluation of two closely related inventions due to repeated miscommunications between TTAs at the system-wide office. TTAs have no way to prevent the main source of contention, however—namely, their responsibility, underscored by financial need, to find and license *profitable* inventions. As one senior researcher put it, "Really good ideas they don't want to patent until a company is banging on the door saying we want to spend a million dollars on this."[15] TTAs do prefer to file patents when they can persuade a licensee to pay the filing costs and attorney's fees, which can easily run to $20,000 or more, especially when foreign as well as U.S. rights are sought. Technology transfer is supposed to pay for itself and generate revenue for the faculty, the campuses, and the university. In practice, the system-wide TTO's own documents referred to revenue generation (albeit with tongue in cheek) as a "pyramid of disappointment": of 400 reported inventions, 100 applications are filed and 50 inventions licensed. Of these, only 16 will produce significant income, but one will pull in more than $1 million (undated memo, UW TTO to UW president). It is no surprise, then, that TTAs look for the "big hit."

TTA relations with faculty are partially mediated by the activities of a third social world, the lawyers. The job of in-house counsel is to protect the university, by which is meant the university as a whole rather than the interests of specific faculty. This task has grown more difficult in recent years, according to one experienced in-house counsel, as the university has come to be viewed by potential plaintiffs as just one more deep-pocketed corporation. UW's relatively new willingness to sue for patent infringement (to "defend the patent") has also complicated their jobs. These attorneys also work with the second group, outside counsel, on patent interferences (which arise when one patent application "interferes" with another, or claims the same invention) and patent infringement litigation. But outside counsel are more often engaged in the more mundane activity of patent prosecution.

Patent prosecution is a specialized legal skill, and to be licensed in it one must be educated in science as well as law and also pass an exam given by the Patent and Trademark Office. Many of the outside counsel with whom I spoke held advanced degrees in science, often Ph.D.'s, and chose patent law after becoming dissatisfied with academic or industrial research. Patent law practice allows them to stay engaged with new scientific developments but offers greater security and control over their professional lives than does scientific work. Working with university researchers is rewarding in this regard, and they also gain some satisfaction from "getting research to the public." But the researchers are not the clients—the university is. Explaining this is part of the educational work they must do with faculty inventors, in addition to the main task of defining the invention and translating it from "science" to "patent law."

All of these social worlds must collaborate in some fashion for a technology to be successfully transferred.[16] Attorneys need faculty help to write and prosecute an effective patent application. TTAs often need faculty investment of time and social capital to get a piece of research licensed; faculty willingness to suggest potential licensees and/or to advise a licensee during product development helps "get the deal done." Faculty inventors interested in developing or maintaining relationships with private companies may need the TTAs to make sure that a licensing negotiation does not alienate their industrial "partners." And faculty who license the technology themselves may need help from attorneys to make the patenting process as fast and inexpensive as possible.

A Contact Zone

Technology transfer is often characterized in ecological or biological terms. Speaking at a 1997 UW conference on the matter, a dean of engineering described university-industry relationships as "a new ecosystem." The term "triple helix," coined to describe the university-government-industry knowledge complex, deliberately evokes the generative force of the "double helix" of DNA (Etzkowitz and Leydesdorff, 1997). The prevailing metaphor for the subject matter of technology transfer among attorneys, technology transfer associates (TTAs), and inventors is that of the infant. As the president of the American Patent Law Association declared to the House of Representatives in 1979, "An invention . . . requires a lot of loving care and attention to raise it to the point where it can be self-sufficient and productive" (quoted in Eisenberg, 1996, 1697n146). TTAs, too, embrace biological metaphors, characterizing related inventions as "families" of "parents" and "children" and promising "cradle to grave" management of those inventions.

A less naturalizing image of the interaction between these social worlds is Mary Louise Pratt's (1992) concept of a "contact zone," developed in her discussion of the discourses of colonization. Pratt uses the term to characterize "the spatial and temporal co-presence of subjects previously separated by geographic and historical disjunctures whose trajectories now intersect." Her intent, like my own, is to "foreground the interactive, improvisational dimensions" of contact zones, emphasizing "how subjects are constituted in and by their relations to each other" (7). I do not imagine the technology transfer process to be one of colonization—differences in historical, political, and racial dynamics preclude any easy analogy. Recalling the binary opposition (outlined in Chapter 1) between private and public domains of knowledge, and the role of IP law and the university, respectively, in policing those domains, I do want to suggest that researchers, attorneys, and TTAs negotiate a set of "interlocking understandings and practices" in and through which the law of patents and the law of nature (as discerned by academic science) are (re)constituted (Pratt, 1992, 7). And the crux of this operation is the continual representation of this mutually constitutive relationship as transgressive.

CONSTRUCTING PATENTABLE SUBJECT MATTER

As Stanley Fish (1991) observes, law is often represented as a matter of ordering a problem according to established procedures such that its solution becomes evident. Persons attached to this representation can be irritated to find that, once applied to local and specific disputes, legal forms are inevitably "infected by interpretation" (162). Patent law illustrates this point, despite its practical reputation—indeed it is a paradigm case. Patent statutes lay out a simple set of criteria for patentable subject matter: a patent must be a human creation, and it must be novel, useful, and nonobvious.[17] If a given process, machine, article of manufacture, composition of matter, or any new or useful improvement thereof, fits those criteria, a property right should be granted.[18] The problem is, standards of human creativity, novelty, utility, and nonobviousness are always contextual, determined by the "state of the art" and a set of prior assumptions about the relationship between facts and artifacts, nature and culture. A "natural" operation of a human gene, for example, can only be patented if that operation can be used to accomplish a task useful to humans, such as the identification of a disease. The same operation, in other words, can be constructed as an observation (a fact) or an application (an artifact).

This determined indeterminacy frustrates lawyers, who want to establish a clear and defensible claim to an idea. Yet it is also precisely what makes the technology transfer possible, for it allows legal concepts to work as boundary objects. In the abstract, property criteria are crucial to the collaboration of TTAs, researchers, and attorneys in the production of "patentable subject matter" as a boundary object. Because these criteria embody basic scientific as well as legal norms, they help mediate difference. When these criteria are rendered concrete in the actual patent application, however, members of distinct social worlds discover they do not share important definitional assumptions. Thus these same criteria also permit the discourses of science and intellectual property law to be reconstructed as distinct, even oppositional—allowing difference to be maintained.

Patentable Subject Matter

Facts and Artifacts Before an academic invention can be propertized, it must first be represented as patentable subject matter. First, the idea must be conceived and made by a human. Indeed, one of the remarkable features of patent rights is that, unlike copyrights and trademarks, they cannot be granted to a corporate person. UW cannot patent anything in its own name—it can only require that its human employees assign their patent rights to the university as a condition of employment.

The idea that "people conceive, not companies" reflects the historical context of the emergence of modern patent law, and bespeaks as well one of the shared premises of patent law and modern science.[19] The legitimacy of modern science substantially relies on its claim to facts—nature's creations. Patent law, as we saw in Chapter 1, confines property claims to the opposite realm of artifacts—human creations. With patent rights limited to identifiable human creations, patent proponents could point to a vast public domain of "nature" as partial proof of the narrowness of the monopoly. Thus legal and scientific discourses worked together to locate humanity "outside" nature, in the realm of culture, legitimating, in turn, property claims in identifiably cultural products. As a contemporary text puts it, an invention must be "non-natural," "for a product of human effort is by definition something other than a product of nature" (Miller and Davis, 2000, 30).

This boundary is, of course, highly unstable, for inventions have a way of escaping their categorizations. A piece of research is categorized as a "product of nature" until a human "utility" for it is identified, at which point it becomes a potentially patentable invention. But the line between nature and utility can be exceedingly fine, as the following example, given by a biologist with decades of patenting experience, attests:

> We found . . . a new gene that was activated when cells attached to [the protein] as opposed to another [protein] . . . It turned out that this gene fits on a chromosome . . . which is very frequently amplified in cancer . . . I predicted that this gene would have a role in cancer progressions. So the technology transfer person started working on this. [But then we did] other experiments and [found] that the activity of this gene product was actually the opposite, it would actually promote differentiation of the cell . . . So then I told [the technology transfer person] you have to forget about this for now. But we have a story, and we may have a scientific story but we don't have a patent story.

As the research progressed, in other words, it shifted in and out of a "patent position," coded first as a discovery (the "scientific story"), then a potential property (a patent story), and finally, when the expected human benefit could not be proven, as a mere discovery once again.[20] But it remained poised to turn back into property—an artifact rather than a fact—if a new "utility" could be found.[21] This account suggests that the differentiation of the invention from "nature" is an intricate and gradual process of classification organized around the mutually constitutive opposition of academic science and intellectual property, one with powerful corollary effects. By defining the subject matter of intellectual property stories in terms of practical benefit to society, the law helps configure the stories of academic science as, in contrast, "impractical" narratives of objective exploration—curiosity-driven discovery rather than market-driven creativity. Yet this researcher's experience demonstrates that good patent and scientific stories both depend quite directly on human interventions, for even the return of this invention to nature (and therefore to the public domain) depended on human effort and creativity. In other words, the more thoroughly a scientist catalogues, collects, and maps nature, the better able she will be to determine where it ends and where culture (and private property) begins.

Novelty, Nonobviousness, Utility   Scientific and legal discourses also share an investment in novelty, nonobviousness, and utility. Scientific fame usually goes to the first person to solve a problem—to advance knowledge. Patents are also supposed to foster progress, and any inventor will have to prove that her idea is a new contribution to the human fund of knowledge. Thus while the idea may be a small thing scientifically, a patent will at least certify it as *novel*. For this reason, patenting is read by researchers as a validation of creativity, a sign that one can "come up with an original idea," as one researcher put it. And come up with it *first:* only the person who can prove she thought of it first can patent an invention.

This shared interest in novelty helps enlist the researcher in technology transfer. For example, TTAs and attorneys frequently rely on the researcher herself to distinguish the invention from previous work in the same area, or "prior art." Determining novelty is a way of drawing a line in time, locating the invention in a particular community's tradition. "I think I put a lot of faith in the inventor," said one patent attorney. "But these are people who are working in this area, doing nothing but research in this area, so they know what's going on a lot better than I do." As this example suggests, the involvement of the scientist in representing the research as "novel" also produces the inventor as expert. The researcher's position signifies an ability to define the "field of the invention" (in patent parlance) and mastery of the "contents" of that field.

Indeed, this mastery of the field can be deployed in the service of a broader monopoly than would be available to a commercial researcher. Patent examiners often challenge a patent claim by suggesting either that it is not supported or that it has been anticipated by prior literature. University researchers are well equipped to refute such claims. Whereas a commercial company is likely to have focused on and tested only a few specific applications, a scientist may have data available to demonstrate applicability in a number of areas. Perhaps more important, a scientist may also be linked to a certifying community of scholarship. One experienced attorney gave the following example: "At one point, an examiner asked about a particular article from [Professor X] and [my academic client] said, 'Oh I know her, what do you want to know?' [The examiner said] 'Well, what about this and this and this?' [The client answered]

'Oh, I think I know, but I'll just call her up and ask her and have her call you.' The examiner was sort of in shock . . . In commercial research . . . most people may know people from other companies but they don't communicate." In other words, the gift community can be mobilized to help define novelty and, by extension, to help create private property.

For both academic science and law, however, novelty is not enough: the idea must be nonobvious or, as an engineer might say, nontrivial. This is a trickier legal test when university inventors are involved because it invites the question, "obvious to whom?" The legal answer is, persons of "ordinary skill in the art"—meaning that if such a person would view the invention as a trivial adaptation of an existing technology, the invention is considered obvious. Professors are persons of extraordinary skill almost by definition, and they tend to work with other persons of extraordinary skill. Should their insights be compared to those of their peers or to those of the less skilled? One senior researcher expressed some discomfort about the defensibility of his patent because, to him, the invention was an obvious answer to a new problem posed to him by an industrial colleague:

> We started to talk about what we wanted to do and [environmental factors] and I realized that the traditional equipment wasn't going to work, we'd have to do something else. And I thought of something you could do. It wasn't rocket science, as they say. Once you'd decided that you wanted to do this particular thing, and recognized the limitations of the equipment, it wasn't very difficult to say what to try . . . except the key point here is I'd had access to [certain technology] . . . The way I understand it, if something's obvious, you can't patent it. But I think that to me it was clear what to try, but that's because of my position as an expert in the field with access to this fairly esoteric stuff.

This researcher was uneasy about the legitimacy of his patent, but found reassurance in the very representation of the academic scientist as "extraordinary" that produced the dilemma in the first place. The invention was obvious to *him*, but only because of his distinctive access to and mastery of "esoteric stuff." Attorneys emphasize this point as well. As one patent attorney put it: "A lot of very superior scientists, things come so easy to them . . . that they don't think of them as innovations. [They'll say] 'Of course, this is just a logical offshoot of the last project I did.' And you say, 'No, no, you took this thing to a higher plane.'" The operating assumption is that academic scientists are, by definition, "expert in the field," indeed help define the field, and thus while their ideas might be obvious to other "experts," they would not occur to a person of "ordinary skill." Thus a potential conflict can become, instead, a basis for reconciliation.

But as we have seen, the law requires something more from inventors: a demonstration of utility. The invention must "do" something—it must accomplish a useful task.[22] Utility should be another point of contradiction between academic and IP discourses, insofar as basic research is supposed to ignore commercial utility. An emphasis on the "accidental" nature of academic invention, however, effectively ameliorates this problem. So long as an invention is a "fortuitous by-product" of curiosity-driven research, its "usefulness" can be viewed as evidence of service to society. Indeed, several of the scientists with whom I spoke characterized patenting as proof of "impact." Pointing to the tenure and promotion process, one researcher noted: "It's a lot more important than a lot of activities that [Collingwood] documents [in promotion applications] . . . and it's the one that has in many cases the greatest effect on society, on the community . . . I'm very proud of my patents, some of them brought $5 million to the company that was to sell them. I didn't get any of it, but OK, that's a validation that somebody at some point in time thought they could be useful." Much of the work academic scientists do may have important long-term effects in medicine, computing, and so on. But there are few substitutes for the more immediate pleasure that developing a useful product brings. "It's a thrill," said one senior researcher, "if you can do something people recognize the value of." Not surprisingly, this is particularly true for engineers, for whom utility as such is not a sin (though direct *commercial* utility is still discouraged as an explicit research goal). But inventors in biology, neuroscience, and geology also emphasized their pleasure at inventing something tangibly "useful" to their peers or to the general public.

The fourth, extralegal criterion for patentable subject matter is marketability or, as one TTA put it, "Who wants it"? A market for the invention must exist; the invention must respond to and is therefore limited by the needs of the private sector. Some Collingwood scientists take an entrepreneurial approach by arranging to license the invention to a company they themselves form, or by discussing it with industrial contacts and using it to cement relationships which may result in research funding as well as licensing royalties. TTAs are grateful for the help. As one senior TTA said: "Particularly in life sciences, the scientific contacts are the most important factor in determining whether a case gets licensed or not . . . I remember a woman [whose former student] went to work at this company. It's as simple as that, there's that connection . . . The student is probably at this point simply a bench scientist, but the high-level executives know that there is a fit in their company for this product and someone there who can work on it."

For other scientists, however, the need to respond to "the market" is a source of enormous irritation, and conflicts between this criterion and the other three underscore the source of the others' efficacy. Novelty, nonobviousness, and even utility align, in principle, with scientific norms of inspiration and creativity, but commerciality may not. Researchers argued that these standards were detrimental to UW's image. One said, "You can't look to them to find ownership and creativity, to get the [university] stamp on a development." As recently as 1986 UW's stated policy was to pursue patents on the basis of technical merit rather than simply commercial viability. The apparent abandonment of that policy may frustrate scientists' efforts to patent, but it also helps draw a line between scientific and intellectual property stories.

In sum, the legal concepts of novelty, nonobviousness, and utility make up a set of "interlocking understandings and practices" between scientific, legal, and technology transfer social worlds that allow those worlds to work together to construct a representation of a "by-product" of research as patentable subject matter (Pratt, 1992). But a great deal more work must be done before the research is fully "propertized." Once an invention has been constructed as patentable subject matter, it must be transformed into an autonomous object. This process turns on the definition of its "metes and bounds" in an application for a patent, and it requires the participation of attorneys, researchers, and, to a lesser extent, TTAs. In the following section, we will see that as the invention is finally specified in a patent application, the principles that in their general sense enlisted the various social worlds in collective work are rendered concrete. A successful patent application accomplishes three tasks: it transforms the research into private property, it reaffirms the autonomy of the social worlds that collaborate in its propertization, and, most important, it reestablishes clear distinctions and oppositions between the academic science and intellectual property.

The Problem of Language

At first glance, patent law is a rather dry and imposing body of literature. Whereas copyright law is full of sexy battles over music and art and legal opinions that are almost equally artful, patent cases tend to hinge on technical differences between mechanical widgets, chemical compositions, gene sequences, and so on. They tell stories only a scientist or a lawyer could love. Yet closer examination of this technical literature reveals deep-seated anxieties about language that would intrigue the most technophobic cultural theorist. Patent claims and lawsuits almost always involve struggles for meaning, for patents are themselves inventions in the rhetorical sense of topics for further discussion. Judges embroiled in such discussions describe themselves as wading in the "deep and murky waters" of interpretation and openly concede their inability to provide stable definitions for even such basic concepts as "invention."[23]

It is not hard to see why. Patent applications are always arguments, bound by a set of contested rhetorical rules. The application is organized around descriptions and claims that "put the public on notice" of the "metes and bounds of the exclusive right" (O'Shaughnessy, 1996, 47). The object is to gain legal possession of an invention by asserting its mental possession.

Title 35 § 112 sets the requirements for "claiming" the invention. Applications consist of three parts: an abstract (which summarizes the invention), a specification (which describes the invention in such a way as to enable its replication by a person of ordinary skill in the art and outlines the best method of practicing the invention), and a set of claims (which describe the crucial elements of the invention). Inventions must be "definitely" described: the nature of the invention must be clear and clearly limited so that inventors cannot use one vague patent to claim a broad range of peripherally related inventions. Claims usually consist of a preamble or broad classification, a transitional phrase, and a body that lists the elements of the invention and how they interact.[24] If the argument is successful, those claims define the "metes and bounds" of the property right.

In this effort to establish the "bounds" of knowledge, patents reinstantiate the basic dichotomy we have already seen in copyright, between idea and expression. Descriptions and claims attempt to "embody" the idea ("fix it in a tangible means of expression" in copyright terms)—and thereby give it a kind of materiality. This "fixing" can involve the use of charts, graphs, diagrams, and photographs, but mostly it depends on the written description. As in copyright law, the goal is to contain meaning and to stabilize a reciprocal relationship between creator and work. But copyright grants ownership only in the expression. Because patent rights, in contrast, apply to the thing described, the relation between idea and expression must also be stabilized.

Case law and commentary emphasize that the idea is always put at risk by the inherent disconnect between idea and expression. As one claim-drafting handbook puts it: "The only known (or at least acceptable) way so far to particularly point out and distinctly claim an invention . . . is by means of an English sentence. This is unfortunate, because many of the problems in claims drafting stem from problems in the meaning of words" (Landis, 1970, 5). Patent lawyers and judges are perennially frustrated by the basic "problem" that written words, like all representational forms, are often multivalent. A word, wrote one judge in 1918, "is the skin of living thought and may vary greatly in color and content according to the circumstances and the time in which it is used."[25] No matter how carefully a given idea is specified, as it must be for a property right in the idea to be created, alternate interpretations of that specification are usually available. For example, Alexander Graham Bell's patent on the telephone claimed a machine for "transmitting vocal or other sounds telegraphically, as herein described, by causing electrical undulations, similar in form to the vibrations of the air accompanying the said vocal or other sounds." Bell's patent referred to an electromagnetic apparatus, but the U.S. Supreme Court interpreted the patent to cover a variable-resistance machine for causing "electrical undulations" as well.[26] This kind of broad interpretation may appeal to existing patent holders, but it terrifies patent prosecutors and litigators by rendering patent law more unpredictable.

Despite a great deal of judicial hand-wringing about plain and clear meanings, however, patent law's answer to the flexibility of language is to make it more flexible still via the doctrine of equivalents. This doctrine states, in essence, that devices that perform an equivalent function to one described in an issued patent, in an equivalent manner, infringe the issued patent. This doctrine allows ambiguity to become a valuable tool for broadening property claims rather than a liability.

The ambiguity of language is also counterbalanced, in principle, by the specificity of the audience. Interpretation of the meaning of patent language in any legal dispute rests with the judge rather than with scientific experts or juries. It is a "matter of law" rather than fact. And therein lies the rub, for researchers at least. Science is supposed to concern matters of fact, and scientific persuasion depends on a claim to truth rooted in scientific method. Thus the researchers with whom I spoke, too, found language to be a problem. But they represented the problem as a disconnect between legal structures and reality. One senior researcher put it this way: "There's a whole body of law that's associated with patents that has nothing to with technology and has to do with how you call things . . . What constitutes a claim, and prior art, and what a means is, and what means plus function is. So [attorneys] write [the patent application] in this very cryptic, bizarre fashion . . . I always found it hard to kind of wade through the verbiage to get at [whether] they really represented what I [did] properly."

Attorneys, meanwhile, insisted that their goal was to make the language as simple as possible. As one patent attorney said:

> I think part of the problem is inventors look at patent attorneys as knowing everything, knowing all these legal words, and they aren't legal words necessarily, they are words that are meant to explain it to somebody who is in that particular field of technology. And we're not experts in that technology, so the question is, am I accurate in describing this as a square when you would describe it as a semicube or something? A lot of [application drafting] is trying to put in terms that are as broad as possible so they will not be, down the line, restricted to a specific meaning.

At stake in this exchange is more than the usual professional identity construction inherent in any use of jargon. Read in the context of a contact zone organized around transgression, the indeterminacy of language may allow researchers to affirm the truth-status of the "scientific story" by constructing the "patent story" as effectively "false."

Attorneys and scientists often compared the classic forms these scientific and patent stories take: the journal article and the patent application, respectively. Though they emphasized the differences between these forms, to which I will turn in a moment, it is worth noting that many commonalities exist. Both forms of expression take some portion of the research activity deemed to advance existing knowledge, describe that portion such that it can be replicated, and rely in that description on tables and figures that condense the orchestrated movement of multiple "objective" instruments (Gross, 1996). Both expressions should demonstrate newness, interest, and value to scientific progress. Both are finally authorized by multiple sources: researchers, attorneys, and patent examiners shape the final issued patent, just as researchers, peer reviewers, editors, typesetters, and editorial assistants shape a scientific publication. Further, both forms are primarily written in an object-centered style that mutes human action and works, as the rhetorician Alan Gross puts it, "to create a world of quantified, causally arranged physical objects" (1996, 79). Indeed, an attorney will read a draft version of a research article to get an initial sense of what the invention might be, and, often after some discussion with the researcher, will use the manuscript to draft the application.

Despite these shared rhetorical conventions, the rearticulation of a manuscript in a patent application involves a series of interventions that install sharp boundaries between science and intellectual property. Most obviously, patent applications finally and overtly construct a human subject as a creator. Scientists are supposed to be creative, but ultimately their task is to analyze facts, not construct artifacts, and their products are ostensibly authorized by nature and reason. Patent claims are authorized, in the first instance, by their creators, and that authority is inscribed in the claims. Though patents are written almost entirely in an impersonal, formulaic voice ("it will be evident that . . ."; "it is an object of the present invention to . . ."), rather suddenly, just at the end, a first and true inventor may step in. It is not a requirement, but many patent applications begin the final section (listing the actual components of the invention) with the single declaration "I claim," reminding the reader that only a human subject can create and define patentable subject matter. Appropriately, it is here that the "metes and bounds" of the invention are set—only a human can measure the human hand.

When a researcher gives a draft article to an attorney, she considers it a specific and truthful description of the invention. But the attorney's goal is to make the broadest claims possible: the broader the claims of the issued patent, the more property the client owns. She will therefore use the description given to her by the researcher as a kind of baseline rather than a summary. A senior TTA told me: "Manuscripts and scientific publications are very conservative, they won't speculate. They'll say 'we have observed that if you add compound A you get effect Y.' Well the patent application is going to say, 'You can add compounds A, B, C, D, E, and F and get effects X, Y, and Z.' You broaden it out." If, for example, a device is supposed to be made of steel—might it be made of some other material? Could the drug in question be used to treat X as well as Y? This process can involve the attorney in shaping the research itself. One attorney noted that she tried to "look a little bit beyond exactly what they thought . . . Sometimes I send the scientists back in the lab and say, 'You found this in colon cancer, did you look in other tissues?' So I will very often try and help them pinpoint both the science and the invention."

For the attorney, the object is not to lie but rather to include *all* possible truths. For the researcher, the process may seem either invasive or so much sophistry, and in any case an affront to some traditional academic principles. Performance of necessary tests, when undertaken at the encouragement of a patent attorney and directed toward establishing ownership of more aspects of an invention, looks more like the activity of a industrial researcher than a curiosity-driven academic. But if the invention has not been tested for the treatment of X, the researcher does not know, with scientific certainty, if it works or not. To claim otherwise in a public document seems to threaten her scientific integrity. One researcher described the process as follows: "There's a lot of back and forth until you come up with something you really believe. We would end up having a lot of conference calls to really go through this and get it so we felt comfortable with what they had written . . . These lawyers put in things like, 'This is a possible cure for cancer,' which is OK if they say possible, but they can't claim that we'd done it . . . So we've always been very careful that they don't put anything in that isn't true." By the time a patent is issued, many of the broader claims may be tested and verified. But applications are written in the present tense—the inventor is asking the law to recognize her possession of an existing invention, not a projected one—and this rhetorical strategy helps produce these broad claims as fundamentally dishonest. As one researcher described it, "Basically, it's a different way of communicating. You don't mean what you are saying."

The researchers' discomfort may be exacerbated in the case of "technique" claims, which, as the legal theorist John R. Thomas notes, track behaviors rather than objects as such. A technique claim applies to a method or process: a "series of steps that act to manipulate the physical subject matter" (1998, 220). Technique claims seem to demand, therefore, that a researcher implicitly pretend to have engaged in specific behaviors, in person or by proxy, and this demand directly challenges the fundamental principles of scientific method. A scientific manuscript describes what a researcher *did* and emphasizes both accomplishment and method. A patent application describes what a researcher "possesses" and takes full advantage of the conceptual difficulty of "possessing" ideas. If one can *imagine* related applications of an idea and/or related behaviors, apparently, one "possesses" those applications and behaviors.[27]

The assertion of novelty and nonobviousness, relatively easy in the abstract, is also more troubling in practice. A successful patent application, unlike a successful scientific article, must radically decontextualize the research.[28] A TTA put the issue in this way:

> Once you've established that this is not obvious to one of ordinary skill . . . you don't need to gild the lily by laying out all the additional knowledge and understanding . . . [Attorneys] prefer that you make every invention by accident . . . What the patent attorney's trying to do is establish that there's no mechanism, [that] you couldn't have foreseen this. Which is the exact opposite of the faculty inventor who's trying to establish that their understanding of the mechanism and predictability led to this discovery . . . That scares patent attorneys to death. People could say "Wait a minute, you mean anybody could have formed this hypothesis based on what Professor Joe Schmoe said in this paper and that all you did was test [that idea]?"

Dissociated from prior literatures, the invention and by implication the inventor are dissociated as well from both the community of science and the process of creation. The same professor who felt his invention was nonobvious to a person of ordinary skill also noted that he was not sure his scholarly community—persons of extraordinary skill—would agree. He feared they would not, and would therefore view his patent claim as offensive, an exclusive ownership claim on communal knowledge. At issue was not only the propertization of an idea, therefore, but also the limits of a community's knowledge.[29] The researcher's discomfort at the prospect that other similarly situated persons might hear of his claim betrays an abiding awareness of the contextuality of "obviousness," a contextuality which is crucial to scientific discourse. A scientific publication insists on a degree of modesty in its claims (even if that modesty is feigned), diligent acknowledgement of previous work, and some circumspection as to future research directions. Gross points, for example, to

Watson and Crick's characterization of the structure of deoxyribonucleic acid as "of considerable biological interest" (1996, 62). Gross reads this as irony, but it only works as irony in the context of a prevailing rhetorical mode. One senior scientist characterized that mode as a combination of training, humility, and political acumen: "We're trained [not to] speak up, we don't make claims. So when we publish papers, we sort of hide, basically, inventions, and we're really humble about things and we make sure to give credit to our peers. For one thing they are going to review the paper." A patent application asks for the opposite: immodesty, virtual rejection of previous work, and the characterization of future research as already accomplished.[30]

Finally, while both patent applications and scientific articles are supposed to "enable" replication, researchers see the description of the invention, or "the preferred embodiment," presented in a patent application as a rather emaciated figure. Said one junior researcher: "With a patent you try to be broad and shallow, I guess, [while] with a technical paper you try to be narrow and deep." A senior researcher drew a firm line between the informational needs of scientists and those of patent examiners:

> The material involved is not even necessarily scientific. The person evaluating it is not my peer, and basically doesn't have the same qualifications as the peer review system has. [The patent is] not designed to disseminate scientific knowledge so that other people can repeat experiments and repeat ideas . . . What it's trying to do is protect the ideas at the same time as not giving away trade secrets. [If] I want somebody to be able to repeat my work, I'll give them information such as, "We've tried this material and it doesn't work" . . . In a paper you might include [that information because] until some other lab has been able to do the same experiment, it's not considered to be real.

Thus, despite the stated object of patent law—to reveal best practices to the public—scientists believe patents obscure and/or ignore method and are therefore illegitimate vehicles for scientific knowledge. The patent application can never make a claim to truth because, no matter how carefully evaluated by a patent examiner, it cannot be verified. Part of the invention, intentionally or not, will remain "secret."

This definition of secrecy depends on the management of competing representations of "the public." One of the most widely held objections to patenting research is that it "privatizes the public domain." Yet, from an attorney's perspective, the "public domain" actually constituted by scientific communication is very small indeed. Scientific stories are very often told in peer-reviewed journals to specific communities that are defined and affirmed by the circulation of the story. The value of that publication is based in part on providing a detailed description of the research that enables its reproduction. If one accomplishes these tasks, one has made the story "public" according to the norms of science and thereby promoted scientific progress.

Patents are supposed to accomplish the same goal but, in theory at least, target a much broader audience. Patents ostensibly encourage inventors to reveal their work to the public, and a patent application is supposed to include a specific description that will enable (or "teach") a person skilled in the art (nominally a peer) to reproduce the invention. The object is to promote technoscientific and commercial progress. And, according to attorneys and TTAs, the audience for patented research is a more "public" body than the community of scholarship. An attorney put it this way:

> People can say, "Well, it will come out anyway because even if the professor does not patent something, he'll write it up in an academic journal." But who reads those? . . . How many people outside a very small group of people who are focused on one subject even know it's there? . . . In order to get this thing out into the public, you have to have a vehicle for . . . bringing it into some sort of prominent communication so that it doesn't get buried in some journal that's on the back shelf of the science and engineering library that will be read by three grad students . . . It doesn't do anybody any good if it doesn't get out and get known and get used.

As this comment suggests, scientific and legal discourses construct very different versions of "the public." In academic science, "the public" is often coextensive with "the scientific community," a relatively small group of persons who share the level of expertise necessary to certify a researcher's gift and "use" it. For the more entrepreneurial researchers, attorneys, and TTAs interviewed, however, "the public" also included consumers, interested industrial researchers, and venture capitalists prepared to commercialize the research. One attorney noted that she wrote for the "average guy, not for your intellectual peers," and added: "You really have to move from that academic publication to doing what the patent laws require you to do: What is it, how do I make it, how do I use it? . . . And you're not thinking of your fellow scientists, you simply have to write a document that will take what you are able to do and put it within reach of the average person." Thus the multivalence of "public" allows all three of these social worlds to be certain that they are helping ideas "get out and get known and get used."

Once submitted, the application is reviewed by a patent examiner, who may either allow or reject the claim. The application is usually rejected initially, on the basis of the examiner's own search of prior art. (In fact, immediate acceptance of an application is taken as a sign that the claims have been cast too narrowly.) The examiner will issue an "office action" explaining why the application was rejected, and the attorney will rewrite it on the basis of this response. The attorney may enlist the inventor's help at this point to clarify prior art and the invention's relation to that art, and the application may be modified and resubmitted. This process is repeated (with some minor variations, as when new data call for a substantially reformulated application) until the patent is issued or issuance seems hopeless.

In sum, the patent application is itself a boundary object, a densely coded but finally ambiguous text with multiple audiences; it is, above all, an argument. Figured as such, it facilitates the production and circulation of an invention while simultaneously helping secure the autonomy and heterogeneity of the social worlds participating in that circulation. Scientists are learning to identify research agendas that will generate technology transfer, but the value of that technology and the research agenda as a whole still depends on those scientists' continuing autonomy from the market. The movement and value of those ideas beyond the ivory tower in the form of bounded and stable private property thus requires a simultaneous investment in cooperation and diversity. The invocation of shared values and premises accomplishes the first task, while the construction of scientific and legal discourses as mutually exclusive in their content, audience, and purpose accomplishes the latter. Because it allows scientific discourse to be constructed as true in contrast to the ambiguity of legal discourse, then, the "problem" of language is also a solution.

The movement of the invention across this contact zone, however, is secured by another boundary mechanism: the inventor, the individual whose voice authorizes the single "I claim." In the following section I examine this elusive voice and the discursive formations within which inventorship, like authorship, can operate as a hybrid concept. That operation, we will discover, relies on the concomitant reversal of the assumptions mobilized elsewhere in the patent process, for disputes about inventorship produce law, rather than science, as the arbiter of fact.

CONCEIVING INVENTORSHIP

Thus far we have focused on the construction of "invention as thing," that is, the production of a patented idea and the development of boundary objects that mediate and distinguish social worlds. I want to turn now to the construction of "invention as process" and the development of a final boundary object: inventorship. Attorneys and TTAs say two things about inventorship with respect to academic researchers. First, they characterize inventorship as a matter of education—once the *legal* criteria are explained, identification of the "true" inventors is relatively easy. Yet they also say that inventorship is a regular subject of dispute. At a 1999 meeting of the Association of University Technology Managers (AUTM), for example, the management of inventorship issues was a recurrent theme, with an attorney on one panel observing that inventorship disputes are becoming a growth industry for patent lawyers. Inventorship is so contentious, in fact, that TTAs interested in maintaining good relations with faculty prefer that outside legal counsel determine "true inventorship." The UW disclosure form advises the researcher that "actual inventorship will be determined as *a matter of law* by a patent attorney" (my italics) and emphasizes that "the rules for inclusion are not the same as a scientific publication."

These rules must be enforced because U.S. patent law takes inventorship very seriously. Unlike copyright law, which allows more than one individual to own a song if those individuals can prove they produced it independently, patent law only permits the "original and first" inventor(s) to claim property rights.[31] Applications must be filed in the name(s) of the inventor(s), who take an oath affirming that they indeed fit the statutory description. If the inventorship is incorrect, the patent can be invalidated.[32]

The act of conception is the key factor in the construction of "true inventorship." Following Karen LeFevre (1987), I find that Hannah Arendt's (1958) definition of "action" illuminates the legal understanding of this factor and its relationship to "the inventive faculty." Arendt observes that an action contains two parts: "the beginning made by a single person, and the achievement in which many may join by 'bearing' and 'finishing' the enterprise, by seeing it through" (189). Under patent law, inventive action is similarly bifurcated, into "conception" and "reduction to practice." Both must be accomplished for an individual to claim inventorship: patents reward "the doer not the dreamer" (Tresansky, 1974, 557). But while one may claim inventorship without having actually participated in the "reduction to practice" (for example by asking another to build and test a prototype), one must have participated in conception to be certified as an inventor, for "invention is the work of the brain, not the hands."[33] Thus LeFevre's observation that "invention is a social act" has relatively little place in patent discourse. The law prefers the beginner of the action over the many who may assist in "seeing it through."

Under U.S. doctrine, first articulated in 1897 and affirmed in 1986, conception is the "formation in the mind of a definite and permanent idea" in sufficient detail that a person with ordinary skill in the art could reduce that idea to practice.[34] It is concluded when the "work of the inventor ceases and the work of the mechanic begins."[35] This identification of conception as the heart of invention links the discourse of inventorship, like that of authorship, to the idealized individual originary genius.[36] Even Norbert Wiener, who conceded that the significant ideas emerge from interaction and ferment, was deeply committed to the notion that "new ideas are conceived in the intellects of individual scientists." "It is easy to stand the egg of Columbus on one end," Wiener added, "after Columbus has shown the proper way to do it. This takes one brain, not a thousand cramped half-brains" (1993, 96). Invention, then, is the province of heroic individuals who are able to observe the works of nature and man and recombine those works to nonobvious, novel, and useful effect.

This heroic activity is surprisingly difficult to track. Ideally, conception, like reduction to practice, can be verified by its material traces, such as an entry in a laboratory notebook. In practice, though, objective evidence of conception is often scanty, particularly in an academic context where patentable inventions are carefully described in employee agreements as merely "fortuitous by-products" of the real work. Consider the following story of invention told by a senior researcher:

Always, when you invent something, it does 90 percent of what you want and then it exposes the next thing you want . . . [With this invention] the thinking was mostly solo on my part. And it happened over the months before the [research] trip . . . I told the guys if we could transmit this funny transmission, I could try processing it to see if it improved things at all, and the electrical engineer said, "Gee, if I re-solder this here and here and here, I can trick what we've got into doing that." . . . In the end of the work part of the [trip], when we [had] a little breathing time, we shifted things around to try oddball ideas. And this [was] about the third or fourth oddball idea I tried. And it worked, boy did it work, and we knew it worked right then. There was a big crowd gathered around and it was one of these classic moments of "Come here Watson, I've got it!"

A lawyer presented with this story would have to ask several questions to determine who really conceived the invention. Previous inventions led to this one—did conception begin with those earlier inventions? The legal answer is no, because identification of a need does not signify "completion" of an idea. The researcher is not certain the concept will work until it is tested—it is one of several "oddball" ideas—and he is not required to know it will work for the conception to be "complete." But it can only count as a complete "definite and permanent idea" if he could have explained it in detail to persons of ordinary skill in his field. If the details of the invention were not spelled out in the scientist's mind, several individuals might have participated in conceiving the invention, beginning with the electrical engineer who figured out how to re-solder existing equipment. Legally, inventorship will also depend on what exactly is claimed, which means that if changes in the equipment are part of the invention, the engineer is more likely to be considered an inventor. Yet the researcher was certain that the "thinking" was "mostly solo" and that he was the inventor.

Recognizing the messiness of conception, Collingwood's technology transfer office attempted to enlist the tools of scientific production in the service of technology transfer by encouraging scientists to "keep good research notebooks," meaning legally useful research notebooks. Ideally, notebook entries become the first traces of the inventor-invention relationship that will help secure its mobilization across centers of calculation (Latour 1987). The Collingwood TTO provided the faculty with a detailed description of what should be included in such a notebook and emphasized the notebook's value for both "peer review and patenting activities." The advice included such suggestions as having a witness sign and date all entries (preferably "someone who is not connected to your invention or project but has the ability to understand your entries") and using "definite terms" such as "prove, demonstrate, shown" rather than ambivalent terms like "suggest." But many scientists do not keep clear and legally acceptable notebooks, and many have their laboratory assistants keep them. In the latter case, a good record of the reduction to practice may exist, but probably not one of conception.

Inventorship and Authorship

Problems of academic inventorship are often coded as a disconnect between inventorship and authorship. According to attorneys and TTAs, academics tend to equate inventorship with authorship and name too many inventors when they turn in their disclosure forms despite the form's explicit warning not to "list any inventor gratuitously." Attorneys view a long inventor list as a sure sign that "ego" and "politics" have been allowed into what should be "a matter of law" and not a matter of status or reputation.

For attorneys and TTAs, inventorship is a "fact-driven legal decision." Curiously, just as scientists view legal conclusions regarding invention as effectively "false," so too do attorneys view many scientific conclusions regarding inventorship as false, in the sense of manufactured, subjective, and political. The attorneys' invocations of legal expertise would be more reassuring if the waters of patent law weren't, as judicial opinions and law reviews agree, so very "deep and often murky."[37] For example, a claim of joint inventorship only obtains, in theory, "where the same single, unitary idea of means is the product of two or more minds, working *pari passu*, and in communication with each other" (Fasse, 1992, 159). It is hard to imagine such an ideal situation, and attorneys may instead parse out aspects of the invention according to the specialized knowledge each might require. More often, however, attorneys and TTAs must rely on the stories they are told by the self-named inventors to determine who contributed to conception.

This dependence means that, in practice, inventorship is often very much a matter of status and reputation, for the most effective bridging mechanism between inventorship and authorship is the academy's own enactment of the discourse of originary genius. In theory, because anyone can and must be listed as an inventor if she has contributed an "inventive concept," patent law could provide an even more effective equalizing mechanism than does copyright. For example, a TTA learned of an invention a professor had taken "out the back door" when a graduate student who believed she was a co-inventor called him. A private company, the student said, was filing a patent application on research done by an academic group of which she had been a member. The TTA called the professor, who denied everything and said the student was "crazy." The recipient company, having apparently investigated the inventorship itself, subsequently contacted the graduate student to ask for assignment of her co-inventorship rights. Told of the contact, the TTA investigated further and found that the work should have been assigned to the university. The company was then forced to negotiate to license the technology from the university, and the graduate student received some inventorship credit.

But this was an exceptional case. The graduate student had left the academy to work in the private sector, and her career was not beholden to the goodwill of her former professor. More often, inventorship, like authorship, is closely allied to academic hierarchy. Because the inventive act is parsed into two components—conception and reduction to practice—and only the former marks one as an originator, the legal discourse of invention maps easily onto the relatively common sense that students and technicians follow the direction of a principal investigator. A laboratory technician, for example, was characterized by one attorney as "kind of like a mechanic, somebody who has a special skill that enables the reduction to practice but they're not doing anything new, they're just using their own special skills." Another attorney told me this story:

> This is a situation where you had two scientists [talking] over a beer in a bar . . . about [treating] an infectious disease. And they came up mutually with the idea, apparently, of using a piece of DNA . . . [Later, one scientist suggested using X as a control.] So they used it . . . When they unblinded the experiments it turned out it was the *control* that worked and not the other one. That was what we were filing [a patent application] on. So who was the inventor and when was the point of conception? The answer is I haven't the faintest idea. You can make the argument that it [was] the technician that unblinded the results [who] first made the connection.

You know you really, just gutwise, don't want that technician to be an inventor, you just don't . . . even though she may have been the first who did or did not put it together, there's certainly nothing of what you would consider an inventive concept in that.

This attorney conceded she didn't have "the faintest idea" who the inventor was in this situation, but in fact she did have a good idea who was *not* an inventor. Her gut told her the technician must be eliminated; technicians are not, by definition, theorists—they do not make a beginning but rather invest labor in bearing out the project.

As we saw in Chapter 2, in situations of unequal status, researchers also want to distinguish between originality and labor. The researchers to whom I spoke were virtually unanimous in their belief that they alone had been the originators of the ideas, partly by virtue of their structural position. One senior researcher had this to say:

> I think there's rarely more than one inventor. I mean, if you wake up and you have an idea, that's the invention. And then there's all this work around it of course . . . [The postdoctoral researchers] contributed to the work, but they didn't do any really innovative work [such as] contributing new concepts, coming up with something that, in my lab, I haven't thought about. It doesn't happen . . . It's not that they aren't innovative people. I think the reason it doesn't happen very often is they don't have time to think as much, they have a lot of manual labor to do.

This reasoning helps explain a 1982 case heard by the Court of Customs and Patent Appeals (CCPA), *In re Katz*.[38] David Harvey Katz, a Harvard Medical School professor, had filed a patent application on a therapeutic immunosuppressive agent and a method of preparing it. He claimed he was the sole inventor but listed as prior art an article co-authored with two of his graduate students. The patent examiner rejected the application, arguing that either the students should be listed as co-inventors or they should file affidavits disclaiming the invention. Katz refused to do either, or even provide evidence of his sole inventorship. In essence, he insisted the Patent Board take his word that the "inventive" aspects of the work described in the publication had been conceived by him. The CCPA agreed to do so, stating that the examiner should have accepted Katz's declaration that the other two inventors were working under his supervision rather than engaging in "speculation" (456). It is hard to imagine that the CCPA would have made the same decision had a graduate student refused to list two professors as co-inventors. Like the district court in *Weissmann v. Freeman,* the CCPA thereby assumed and affirmed academic hierarchy. Dissenting from the opinion, Judge Miller observed that the majority's acceptance of the word of a decidedly interested "inventive entity" (Katz) about the potential existence of another "inventive entity" (the students) indicated that coauthorship was no longer reasonably indicative of coinventorship.

The alignment of conception with hierarchy is highlighted as well by the comments of one researcher who admitted acknowledging another's inventive contribution primarily because the other was the principal investigator of the laboratory in which she worked:

Researcher: The idea was mine, he never heard of [the process], but he allowed me to do it in his lab. I mean, I would never dream of publishing without his name on it, that's the way it is . . . And I know they say it's the conceptualization and everything, but on the other hand you could say that my boss, we talk all the time about the science, and we always knew we had to come up with a better way of [doing this] so we would always think about well, what could we do. So I had a prime mind when I heard this talk [that sparked the conception of the invention] . . . [Often] somebody comes up with a bright idea but there's a lot of interaction going on . . . The lawyers always ask me, "Are you certain that they [individuals listed on a publication from the same research] had nothing to do with the conceptualization of this work," and I say, quite honestly, "Yes, they did some technical things, but they didn't have anything to do with the conceptualization."

CM: But it would make sense in your mind to think of [him] as being part of the conceptualization?

Researcher: Yes, because we talk about our work together all the time so he's put ideas into my mind, I can put ideas in his mind.

CM: Would he list you? Say the positions were reversed?

Researcher: Probably not . . . It's different if you're the head of a department, if you really think you came up with the idea. He might.

This researcher's response was typical in that she moved very quickly from emphasizing the difficulty of delineating the inventor ("there's a lot of interaction") to asserting her ability to know who was *not* an inventor. Further, though inventorship was clearly a strategic matter for her, she was willing to do the cultural work necessary to bridge "law" and "politics," to identify the potential creative contribution of her superior. But she was less willing to do this work for people she regarded as doing only "technical things." A technician who had been listed as a co-author on the published work, but not as a co-inventor, was described by the same researcher as specifically noncreative: "It's always a relationship of, I write up the experiments and she does them, and occasionally she might say, do you think we should try such and such. Very rarely. She's just very happy to carry out the experiment."

"Stratification by status," Max Weber notes, "goes hand in hand with a monopolization of ideal and material goods or opportunities" (1946/ 1966, 25). A corollary is also true: the negotiation of knowledge monopolies is the negotiation of status. So perhaps it should not be surprising that the stories TTAs and attorneys tell about problems of inventorship are very often disputes about hierarchy. A particularly contentious example, described at a 1999 AUTM workshop on faculty relations, involved a graduate student's claim of sole inventorship of an invention arising from his thesis work. His advisor insisted on being named a joint inventor, over the vigorous protests of the student, who felt he had received very little guidance from the advisor.[39] In another controversy among several researchers from two different universities, a powerful professor effectively eliminated an adjunct professor as a named inventor, in the absence of strong documentation either way, and pushed to make sure his own name was listed "first" on the patent. Under patent law all inventors are equal, and under university policy all receive the same percentage of the royalties unless they themselves arrange otherwise. Nevertheless, the professor tried to treat "first inventorship" like "first authorship," as a matter of honor. According to the TTA who told me the story, the dispute "was about status." And so on. No wonder these disputes are characterized by non-academics as "political" battles over "ego" and can be so frustrating that, as the title of the AUTM workshop put it, "team building with faculty" is rather like "herding cats."

Matters of Law

Inventorship disputes might be read as assertions of autonomy and control in the face of legal and administrative efforts to "manage" researchers' intellectual property. In the context of a deliberate effort to objectify, stabilize, and thereby transfer knowledge outside the contact zone, researchers attempt to retain "possession" of it by linking it to their personas. Tracing a similar operation in a French computing research culture, the anthropologist Georgina Born argues that it instantiates a gift-oriented, "'purely ethical and social' realm" that resists the "profane drive to objectify and commodify" scientific work (1996, 112). Where the agreed end point is a commodity, however, this is a form of resistance that does little to challenge the premises of intellectual property law and explicitly rejects LeFevre's idea that "invention is a social act." Invention may be social, but inventorship is not: researchers are perfectly capable of compartmentalizing ideas and relationships to determine for themselves what counts as conception and who counts as inventive. They may disagree in their determinations, and their decisions may not be legally correct, but even their disagreements help construct an individualized inventor-subject as the source, rather than the vehicle, of knowledge.

Yet these disputes also disrupt the foundations of that construction. When academics position themselves as intellectual property owners, their necessary role in policing and defining the public domain—and, by extension, the raw material of invention—is undermined. The university betrays its own anxiety about this role in its efforts to characterize patenting as a kind of community activity. UW publications devoted to technology transfer try to promote a sense of community investment in inventions, noting that the university provides the conditions of possibility for the invention by "bringing together multiple disciplines" and that royalties from inventions benefit the university as a whole as well as named inventors. These efforts to shore up the university's traditional alignment with a vibrant knowledge commons, necessary for the continued legitimation of both itself and IP law, are nevertheless abraded when the university's own faculty insist on treating knowledge as private and individuated. At the same time, the frequent alignment of conception with hierarchy threatens the egalitarian discourse of inventorship that permeates U.S. patent law. Despite claims of scientists and attorneys to the contrary, the inventive entity is not discovered but rather determined in and through social relationships.

The figure of the inventor is rescued, at least temporarily, by the simultaneous construction of scientific decisionmaking on inventorship as a "matter of ego," and legal decisionmaking on the same subject as a "matter of law." Not coincidentally, in this regard the law *is* treated as objective, or at least rigorous. As one attorney put it, "It's very difficult, and it's really not a matter of mental state . . . It's supposed to be an objective standard of the idea in the mind of the inventors in such full and complete form that it can be reduced to practice without undue experimentation. So that really comes down to a *factual* thing, of what is the invention and then when were they in on it" (my italics). TTAs characterize the legal standard as "strict," rather than "gratuitous," "political," or even fair. A senior TTA said: "It's a tough sell, but most of the time we can convince people that the law is an ass . . . and they understand that, and fairness, and [that] who did the work really doesn't count." What does count is paperwork—research notebooks, disclosure forms, answers to questionnaires, memoranda, and so on. And while scientists may not always like the answers the law gives on inventorship, it is removed from their province. Thus, just as researchers view law as irrational with respect to the invention itself, thereby affirming the rationality of science, attorneys treat science as irrational with respect to inventorship, thereby affirming the rationality of law. As long as legal determinations of inventorship are treated as "factual" and objective, the discourse of originary genius that provided the underpinnings of that investigation can also be treated as objectively "true." At the same time, because the law has already been constructed as false in scientific terms, researchers can strategically characterize legal determinations as unfair but ultimately irrelevant to what really matters in the academic hierarchy—authorship. Academic science, in turn, can be reconstructed as a separate realm. As one senior researcher who had been involved in litigation observed, "I have to worry about my papers. That's more important in my career than having patents."

Ironically, even the limited objectivity of law is undermined by the insistent sociality of the patent process. Despite all the effort that goes into establishing a first and true inventor early in the process, inventorship is not certain until the patent issues. It is often asserted in law and cultural studies that audiences also "author" the text by participating in the construction of its meaning. The same principle holds for inventions—indeed, this is the final sense in which patent applications work as boundary objects. As a set of claims is redefined in response to challenges from the Patent and Trademark Office (the actual audience for the application, if not the issued patent), the inventorship may change as well.

For example, if the changes made by the electrical engineer who re-soldered ship equipment to allow the oceanographer's idea to be tested were included in the claims, he or she might "count" as an inventor. If those changes were later considered unpatentable, and those specific claims disallowed, that electrical engineer could be removed as an inventor. As the argument changes, therefore, so does the author, and the contingency of both is revealed.

Firmly tied to "conception" rather than "reduction to practice," inventorship can work as a boundary object. Strategically linked to the academy's own individualist rhetorics of creativity, academic hierarchy, and a rationalist representation of law, this production allows inventorship to be managed and continually reproduced as "true." It also assists a larger effort to partially reconcile the domains of academic technoscience and intellectual property law while simultaneously reconstructing the heterogeneity of those domains. Legal and scientific truth-claims are affirmed, as is their opposition. Thus the construction of the inventor who can authorize the single "I claim" in a patent application alternately assumes, defends, and undermines the rationality and integrity of academic science, law, and even technology transfer. It assumes, defends, and undermines as well the discourse of originary genius that finally authorizes this entire complex of activities, precisely where the intense collaborations involved in technology transfer might cause that discourse to be challenged.

The construction of invention and inventorship such that these categories can be mobilized in support of the propertization of academic research and that propertization simultaneously figured as transgressive requires extraordinary cultural work. As we have seen, a set of legal, economic, and cultural shifts have helped create a kind of contact zone between several social worlds on the "new frontier of technology transfer," each of which is invested in the notion that their very contact is inherently subversive but socially necessary (Erickson and Baldwin, 1988). In this contact zone, as in the spaces of co-presence Mary Louise Pratt explored, subjects and objects are constituted in and through social relations. The character of those relations suggests that the "new frontier of technology transfer" will be navigated with a set of very old maps.

These old maps allow us to ignore dangerous and interesting terrain, at least until someone falls into a stream that was not on the original survey. Contrary to the assumptions of legal, scientific, and technology transfer discourses, all of which tend to construct patenting as a matter of careful "identification," inventions and inventors are not discovered—they are negotiated and produced. We have seen, for example, that a piece of research may be coded as scientific story or a patent story. According to the former tale, the research is a fact about nature, the discovery of which is made possible by and is at least partially responsive to multiple sources and relations. In the second tale, the research is an atomized and decontextualized artifact, conceived by an individual.

To keep these stories intact, technology transfer associates, patent attorneys, and researchers themselves must actively police the boundaries between science and law, public and private, and academy and industry. Ironically, the tools of that police work are found in the very categories and assumptions that, by facilitating collaboration between social worlds, call attention to the permeability of those borders. The boundary work I have been describing brings into sharp relief, indeed depends on, the kinds of inconsistencies that legal and technoscientific discourses dislike. Patentable subject matter, the patent application, inventorship—all are exposed as leaky and highly contingent productions, at once boundary markers and unstable channels.

CHAPTER FIVE

Telling Tales Out of School

The "discoverer" of a scientific fact as to the nature of the physical world, an historical fact, a contemporary news event, or any other "fact" may not claim to be the "author" of that fact. If anyone may claim authorship of facts, it must be the Supreme Author of us all. The discoverer merely finds and records.
—*Melville Nimmer, 1977*

What, in short, is the strange unit designated by the term, work? . . . If we wish to publish the complete works of Nietzsche, for example, where do we draw the line? . . . What if, in a notebook filled with aphorisms, we find a reference, a reminder of an appointment, an address, or a laundry bill, should this be included in his works? Why not?
—*Michel Foucault, 1977*

So far I have mapped a few of the battle lines of the "second academic revolution" and indicated some of what is—and what is not—revolutionary about it. We have seen how IP law makes trouble for the academy, how the academy makes trouble for IP law, and how the production of academic intellectual property builds, maintains, and partially subverts a series of common boundaries. Now let us turn to what is emerging as the most dramatic and troubling border skirmish for both academia and the law: the propertization of scientific data.

FACTS AND ARTIFACTS

To think about the contours and effects of treating data as property and the boundary work upon which that process relies, let us return to the story with which we began: the case of the purloined protein. As the reader may recall, this case involved the alleged misappropriation of a set of procedures for crystallizing a protein, polymerase ß. Huguette Pelletier, a postdoctoral researcher, claimed that her research on pol ß was her trade secret, and that it was "stolen" from her laboratory by a former colleague, Michele McTigue, and given to Agouron Pharmaceuticals. Agouron allegedly used that research to publish a paper describing the crystal structure of pol ß before Pelletier could publish her own work. That publication, Pelletier argued, deprived her of the "credit" she needed to launch her postgraduate career. The stated aim of Pelletier's lawsuit was to protect her investment in her reputation.

In the end, the suit itself may have done greater damage to that reputation than the alleged misappropriation. Since filing the suit, Pelletier has been accused of seducing her mentor, hysteria, paranoia, juvenile behavior, irrational hostility toward her fellow students, and general sour grapes. The tenor of these accusations is not entirely surprising: in taking this issue to the law for resolution, Pelletier was definitely telling tales out of school.

Pelletier presented her lawsuit as, among other things, a defense of academic freedom, by which was meant the freedom to pursue knowledge and receive credit for that pursuit without interference from commercial interests. At the very least, the case was an effort to defend a gift economy of academic science by punishing individuals who had broken some of the rules of exchange. Yet Pelletier's lawsuit redrew the borders of that economy once again, for its success rested on her ability to construct scientific data as private property and stabilize her relationship to that property. She had to demonstrate that the data were trade secrets, that they were *her* trade secrets, and that the theft of those secrets had caused her economic harm. And to do that she had to step right in the middle of the legal quagmire of data ownership.

The Problem of Data

Data, especially scientific data, are classic public domain material, largely because they are legally treated as synonymous with "facts."

Both patent and copyright law base property claims on the demonstration of some modicum of human originality. Facts, in contrast, are assumed to originate elsewhere, usually in nature or a Supreme Being. Thus authors may copyright their expression of historical fact but not the fact itself, nor theories about facts, nor the research that yields those facts (Litman, 1990). Inventors may patent a particular application of scientific information—a human invention—but not the information itself, which is nature's invention.

The location of facts in the public domain is a powerful legitimating mechanism. From a utilitarian perspective, putting facts in the commons provides authors and inventors with the raw material for new works and justifies the temporary propertization of those works. Following Jessica Litman's reasoning discussed in Chapter 1, consigning facts to the public domain also allows judges, lawyers, and authors to maintain the legal fiction of "originality." Authorial expression draws on the author's experiences—things she has read, seen, and heard, her memories thereof—and that expression is extraordinarily difficult to parse into borrowed and "truly original" elements. A public domain allows authors and jurists to "avoid the harsh light of a genuine search for provenance" or originality (Litman, 1990, 1012). Litman focuses on copyright, but a similar dynamic is evident in patent law. Although a genuine search for provenance is undertaken by attorneys and patent examiners, the legal distinction between unpatentable facts about nature and patentable applications of those facts allows inventors to claim that they are only propertizing their own creations.

Treating research findings as factual and therefore public information supports the basic "useful uselessness" paradox upon which the modern university relies by affirming the public service component of academic research and the academy's devotion to progress rather than profit. In a comment that is especially telling in light of *Weissmann, Weisser,* and, as we shall see, *Pelletier,* Robert Merton insists that the ethos of academic science, in particular, rests on the assignment of scientific findings to a community rather than to individuals. Stating the norm, if not necessarily the reality, Merton observes that "recognition and esteem" are the sole property rights of a scientist in her discoveries and that these "property rights" are fundamentally incompatible with the private property rights granted in artifacts by IP law (1942/1973, 273). The location of research findings on the public side of the distinction between private artifacts and public facts helps reproduce the image of academic science as a matter of disinterested pursuit and discovery rather than interested manufacture—as a usefully useless activity (see Biagioli, 1998). Thus the production of data as factual and their concomitant assignment to the commons supports the conceptual underpinnings of both IP law and academia.

New technologies promise an enrichment of that portion of the commons which data represent. The development of new database systems and an Internet infrastructure that can facilitate widespread access to those systems has created extraordinary opportunities for information exchange within and across academic communities. For example, neurobiologists and laypersons interested in olfactory research can log on to the Yale University Medical School's SenseLab databases and use those databases to peruse the latest published sequences, models, and other research. Scientists are also experimenting with placing preliminary data online to garner early comments and suggestions regarding potential pitfalls and research directions (Wilson, 1998). It remains to be seen whether those forums will take on the "time-stamping" function of conference papers and publications, but in the meantime Internet bulletin boards do offer a way of increasing open communication.

At the same time, data are being relocated from the commons to the public/private border. Database publishers are pushing legislation granting property rights in collections of facts. Several database "protection" bills have been introduced in Congress, and it is very likely that some form of database legislation will be enacted within the next few years. Outside Washington, D.C., publishers, universities, and other research institutions are using legal and electronic means to assert and police their ownership of data.

Indeed, as the physical boundaries of the university seem to dissolve, access to data serves as the new boundary mechanism. Credentialed scholars—community members—have access to certified resources from which the uncredentialed are excluded. At UW, for example, contracts with electronic publishers spurred proposals for elaborate password systems that would ensure that the terms of those contracts, in particular rules limiting access to library databases to students, faculty, and staff, were met. Librarians also quizzed walk-in users of some electronic databases to certify that they were faculty, staff, or students of the university. In this regard, the UW technology management office's use (on its website) of the word "citizen" to describe its constituency is telling. When I asked the director of the office to explain the term, he said it meant someone who "is a member of our community who can, to use an old phrase from a British passport, roam without let or hindrance in the university's domain."[1] In a very real sense, then, university citizenship signifies access to information commodities as much as participation in a system of gift exchange.

The relocation of data to the private domain depends on the ability of multiple entities to tell meaningful and persuasive property stories about data. Like other property stories, these tales speak to, construct, and defend particular communities, protagonists, and points of exclusion. Because the narratives are also arguments, their success depends on the teller's ability to convince relevant audiences that no important discontinuities exist between old and new academic property/propriety claims. That kind of persuasion demands skillful boundary work, and specifically the production of scientific data as a common object—at once fact and artifact, gift and private property—through which multiple discursive fields may continue to appeal to one another for authority.

Secrets and Lies

Such was Huguette Pelletier's task, and its accomplishment depended on the formation of a link between scientific data and trade secrets—though before Pelletier was done she would touch on copyright, patent, and publicity law as well. As noted, data are usually located in the public domain, but there are some exceptions. If a person, corporate or otherwise, has information that is useful to that person's business (such as a recipe) and can keep it secret, that information becomes a form of intellectual property known as a trade secret. To qualify as a trade secret in most states (trade secrets are primarily governed by state law), the information must be treated as confidential, meaning its "owner" must use reasonable means to prevent its disclosure, and the information must gain present or potential independent economic value from being withheld.[2] Some case law also suggests that the secret should be at least minimally "novel." If these standards are met, others are still free to discover the secret on their own, through independent research or reverse engineering, but they may not use "improper means" such as espionage.

Scientists and legal scholars have long viewed trade secrecy as the most fundamental barrier between academic and industrial science, for secrecy violates the basic scientific norm of openness.[3] Academic scientists condemn, for example, the private sector's refusal to share data on the genetic blueprint of *Staphylococcus aureus* (the most common source of life-threatening bacterial infections in hospitals) despite the appearance of a new strain that resists all known antibiotics. To an academic, this refusal is fundamentally immoral; for the companies involved, it is simply an effort to protect an investment (Cimons and Jacobs, 1999).

However, the academy's increasing dependence on private industry as a source of both funding and research materials is eroding that moral high ground. The physicist Irving Lerch of the American Association for the Advancement of Science recently complained that the "commercialization of science has led to a new regimen of secrecy . . . of an entirely new scope and scale" (quoted in Hotz, 1999). Across the United States, universities, scientists, and private corporations are negotiating research contracts that include modified and unmodified secrecy clauses. As a result, researchers have been prevented by their own institutions from publishing their findings, even where those findings might save lives. Others have violated their contracts and lost faculty positions in consequence.[4]

Pelletier v. Agouron marked a new turning, an effort by a scientist to use trade secret law against a private company. The misappropriation of scientific data can be prosecuted under various fraud statutes, or punished through withdrawal of funding and fines (Burk, 1995; Frammolino, 1994, Hilts, 1993a; Gladwell, 1991). It can also be punished with the informal but still potent weapons of rumor and gossip. Comments regarding a scientist's lack of integrity, circulated through a given research community, can irreparably damage that scholar's reputation, rendering her accumulated academic capital worthless. Those means would not repair the damage done to Pelletier. Existing statutes governing scientific fraud tend to be directed toward the presentation of faulty data to justify federal or state research funding, and therefore only marginally applicable to the misconduct of a private company (Burk, 1995). As a commercial enterprise, Agouron Pharmaceuticals was also relatively immune to informal community policing mechanisms, even if Pelletier had had the necessary clout within her discipline to take advantage of those mechanisms.[5] Without a major publication under her belt, Pelletier was simply a vulnerable and mostly unknown postdoctoral researcher, with little academic credit to invest in her own defense.

Trade secret law seemed to offer another weapon. To fit her experience into trade secret law's categories, however, Pelletier had to create and manage a boundary object to translate across the now familiar borders of public/private, gift/market, and especially fact/artifact, while keeping those borders intact. That process of translation would rely as well on the management of a series of contradictory images of academic science: as a cutthroat struggle between individual entrepreneurs; as a free and open space of creative exchange; and as a closed community of communities ruled by a complicated mixture of trust, authority, and autonomy. The boundary object Pelletier found to accomplish all of these tasks was a representation of scientific data as private property.

In the following pages I examine this complex bounding operation and its impact on contests for the meaning of academic freedom. At a minimum, Pelletier's production of data as a boundary object exposed and contained the instability of scientific data. It also reconfigured a wider set of narratives about the nature of academia, and academic freedom, in "revolutionary" times.

AUTHORIZED AND UNAUTHORIZED ACTIVITIES

It seems appropriate to begin this property story with the few data points on which everyone involved in *Pelletier* agreed.[6] In 1988 the University of California, San Diego, biochemistry professor Joseph Kraut and Dr. Samuel Wilson of the University of Texas at Galveston agreed to collaborate on solving the crystal structure of polymerase ß, or pol ß. Wilson had previously directed research isolating the gene that expresses pol ß and defining its role in the repair of DNA. A crystallographic study would produce a kind of three-dimensional snapshot of the protein which could be used to determine both the properties of the protein and how it interacted with other molecules—information that would be useful, in turn, for drug design and other medical applications.

Kraut asked Michele McTigue, a second-year doctoral student in his lab, to take on the pol ß project as an addition to her thesis work. Assisted by Dr. Janet Grimsley, a technician who had been specially trained by the Wilson lab to purify pol ß, McTigue obtained a few crystals of the protein. But her progress was slow, and in 1990 Kraut and Wilson learned that a Japanese research group was also working on pol ß. Anxious to speed things up, Kraut asked a fourth-year doctoral candidate, Huguette Pelletier, and a new student, Michael Sawaya, to get involved in the research.

Hostility between Pelletier and McTigue had once led the former to refuse to work on the pol ß project. This time, Pelletier, McTigue, and Sawaya negotiated an oral agreement to divide the research. McTigue continued to work on the areas on which she had already begun, but was more focused on finishing her dissertation. In 1992 she graduated and began a postdoctoral fellowship at The Scripps Research Institute (TSRI) in La Jolla, California.

During her tenure at TSRI, McTigue continued to visit the Kraut lab. She wrote an article describing her initial research on pol ß and presented the research at two crystallography conferences. The research paper was reviewed by Pelletier, who found it contained "fabrications" as well as results actually discovered by Pelletier. An independent arbitrator assigned by UCSD approved the submission, but Kraut refused to be a co-author, and the article was ultimately withdrawn. McTigue also showed some of the data produced in the Kraut lab to David Matthews, an Agouron Pharmaceuticals researcher who had also been trained by Kraut. In 1995 McTigue went to work for Agouron.

Meanwhile, Pelletier and Sawaya began work on their portion—which for Sawaya would comprise his dissertation research—and made rapid progress. In 1992 Pelletier received her Ph.D. and Kraut asked her to stay in the lab to work on the pol ß project. She agreed, expecting to use the research to launch her postgraduate academic career. A year later Kraut learned that Agouron Pharmaceuticals was also working on pol ß and had been doing so since 1991; McTigue's husband, Jay Davies (also Kraut's former graduate student), was part of the effort. The company hoped the research would lead to a commercially lucrative delivery mechanism for anti-cancer drugs.

McTigue had never mentioned this competitive effort to Kraut. On the basis of subsequent conversations and correspondence between Kraut and Agouron, McTigue's failure to mention the competing project, and other circumstantial evidence, Kraut and Pelletier became convinced that McTigue had given Pelletier's research results to Agouron. Kraut and Pelletier filed complaints in several quarters, including the UCSD Academic Senate, and Kraut denied McTigue further access to his lab.

Pelletier and Sawaya speeded up their research and publication efforts, and Kraut presented some preliminary results at a conference in Beijing in an effort to "time-stamp" the work. But it was already too late: in December 1993 Agouron submitted a paper describing the crystal structure of pol ß to *Cell*, one of the most important journals in the field, and the article was accepted. Pelletier's pol ß research was now profoundly devalued in a social world that placed a premium on being first to publish. One year later she filed suit against Agouron for misappropriation of trade secrets, and against McTigue, Davies, and others for breach of confidence.

Here the stories diverge. According to Pelletier and Kraut, Agouron was able to publish ahead of Pelletier because, between 1991 and 1993, Michele McTigue had transferred pol ß data from the Kraut lab to Agouron. Most of that material had been gathered by Pelletier and Sawaya, and it included, Pelletier claimed, photos demonstrating the feasibility of the project, computer files, the recipe for crystallization, and information about some of pol ß's unique properties. McTigue's conference presentation and research article were merely efforts to cover her tracks and justify continuing access to Pelletier's work.

To hear Agouron tell it, Michele McTigue was the victim in this situation. Pelletier had wrested the pol ß project from McTigue just as the latter was starting to make real progress with it, seeking to appropriate from McTigue all the credit as well as the federal funding attached to the study. Pelletier was able to take over the project, and indeed the whole lab, because she was involved in a sexual relationship with Kraut. McTigue had attempted to retain some control over her work by presenting it publicly, and Pelletier had sabotaged that effort by persuading Kraut to withdraw his name from McTigue's paper (thereby preventing its publication). As for sharing some research with Agouron, McTigue saw nothing wrong in making her own insights available to a company that was interested in developing a lifesaving drug rather than merely glory. After all, McTigue's former mentors worked for Agouron, and it was only natural she might go to them for advice on her investigation. In short, the entire situation was a "nasty, vicious, personal battle" between two students at a university and hardly a matter for the courts (Court Transcript [henceforth CT], Defendant's Opening Statement, 48).

I do not intend to evaluate the relative merits of these accounts, and indeed a jury and an appellate court have already decided the matter in

Pelletier's favor. Instead, I want to focus on the property tale Pelletier's case constructed, a story which took the form of a play in two acts. In the first act, Pelletier had to demonstrate her standing as a protagonist, that is, as an owner with a property interest in pol ß. This demonstration placed her in a decidedly uncomfortable position with respect to the norms of academic science, for it depended on a representation of the scientist as an author of data and a representation of scientific findings as artifacts. In the second act, a series of spatial and temporal boundaries around that production had to be specified and "gift" norms mobilized to tell a persuasive story of property. These specifications worked both to partially restabilize scientific data as such and to secure its propertization.

THE STATUS OF THE SCIENTIFIC FACT

Stephen Hilgartner observes that "data" is an inherently problematic category because it continuously escapes compartmentalization. Though commonly envisioned as a discrete set of "neatly packaged and clearly bounded" objects, Hilgartner and his collaborator Sherry Brandt-Rauf suggest, data can be more accurately described as highly contingent, ever evolving "streams" (Hilgartner, 1998, 204; Hilgartner and Brandt-Rauf, 1994). Data streams are composed of groups of products—film, software, written materials, tacit knowledge—that can be combined and recombined to become evidence for some conclusion. A data stream might be represented as and include a set of tables, for example, and then upon further analysis be reconstructed as a bar graph and text. Data might even be rebuilt as a physical model: one of the most popular technologies of the Center for Computing Excellence (CCE) is a large machine that transforms images into three-dimensional objects. Scientists use the machine to construct computer models of their research data, and this information is reprocessed according to an algorithm that tells another machine where and how to deposit thousands of layers of compressed cardboard. The models that result are used, in turn, to produce new knowledge about the material world, because researchers frequently develop fresh conclusions about the data once they have a three-dimensional representation. These models also become data about the CCE itself: they are used to impress tour groups visiting the CCE, including the public officials who help decide whether the CCE will continue to be funded, and one model has even made its way to a major museum.

Thinking of data as a stream highlights the fluidity of both information and sources. Varying entities may contribute to the stream, and the questions and expertise these entities bring to it may alter the stream's content and direction. That very fluidity is in turn a condition of possibility for the production of data as a boundary object. To see how, I want to return to the problem of data ownership.

Entities standing at different "bends" of a data stream may perceive—and try to enforce—conflicting ownership claims. When I asked the researcher who runs the CCE modeling machine about ownership of the models, he admitted he had no ready answer: "We certainly haven't figured out ownership now, particularly when we're not charging [scientists who submit data] anything for these models. I'm footing the bill for the machine, the maintenance and the paper, the supplies, and the labor for doing all this. They're paying me absolutely nothing. So they would be very hard-pressed to say, 'We completely own this.' On the other hand it's absolutely their data so I would be hard-pressed to say, 'I completely own this.' We just punt the issue and hope nothing bad happens." This researcher points to various components of one "bend" in the data stream (money, supplies, know-how, labor, and digitized research results), all of which may come from different sources, and all of which may legitimate—intuitively if not always legally—an ownership claim. Note too that financial support for the machine's operation primarily comes from the National Science Foundation; the research being modeled may also be funded by the NSF. If financial investment is understood to secure ownership, the taxpayers own the data. Yet, as we have seen, if scientific data are understood to be simply factual results, legally no one "owns" them at all. We will return to this point shortly; for now it will suffice to say that a given data stream will be subject to different meanings and related ownership claims in varying social worlds.

That variation helps explain why ownership is an uncomfortable and often unspoken issue in academic science—which is not to say that ownership language is absent. In fact, property-rights language offers a kind of common principle, a way of organizing claims to data even where parties agree the data do not fit easily into property categories. Consider Hilgartner's (1998) description of access practices in the European Community's Yeast Sequencing Program. Different groups of scientists were allotted specific regions of the genome of the yeast *Saccharomyces cerevisiae* to analyze, and the scientists involved in the program referred to these allotments as "ownership rights" and "property rights." These "property rights" were sharply circumscribed, limited in duration, and subject to revocation if data of acceptable quality were not produced. Yet these assignments also underwrote actual legal property rights: scientists were entitled to publish, patent, and distribute data from "their" region.

While Hilgartner describes a particularly overt example of property talk in science, scientists in many fields appear to construct themselves as owners, or possessors, of data (Stevens, 1997). A report on "computational ecology" notes that some scientists and agencies tend to "equate data with power, thereby attempting to hold and protect data, as opposed to sharing data" (Helly et al., 1995, 6). Some scientists do not even want to share data with their "investors": legislation amending the Freedom of Information Act to require federally funded scientists to release all data produced with those funds upon request was roundly criticized by the research community (Hilts, 1999). No wonder Pelletier felt Kraut had "given" her the pol ß project, and no wonder Kraut felt it was his to give.

Except that it wasn't. Pelletier's initial complaint was rejected by Superior Court Judge Ronald Johnson on the grounds that she did not own the research and therefore had no legitimate property interest to defend. Why? Because, argued Agouron, the University of California had already staked a preemptive and legally enforceable claim to the data stream in question. Regulation 4 of the UC Academic Personnel manual stated that records of research conducted under contract with non-university organizations (including federal agencies such as the National Institutes of Health) were the property of the institution, and that the university retained the right to publish that research.[7] The research in question was sponsored by federal grants, so it seemed to fall squarely under this rule. Because UC was, for most legal purposes, a "branch of the state itself," its policies carried the force of law.[8] Opting for the simplest reading of the regulation, Agouron argued that "only the University owns and controls its research and has standing to protect its research" (Respondent's Brief, 6). Agouron also noted that California Labor Code § 2860 assigns ownership to the employer of anything an employee acquires during her employment unless otherwise specified. Since the university had declined to become involved in the case (about which more later), there simply was no case to be made.

Pelletier was surprised to discover she did not own the pol ß data stream, as were members of the UCSD Academic Senate to whom she appealed in 1994. Asked by said members to comment, then-President

Jack Peltason hastened to reassure the Senate that while the university did indeed own research results and underlying data, the intention of the regulation was to make sure no outside organization could prevent an individual researcher from publishing her work.[9] Another objective was simply to promote the long-term availability of the data. Several researchers collaborating on a project might have a falling out, or one might decide to move to another campus and take results produced within the collaboration with her (Stevens, 1997; Mishkin, 1995). A UC attorney with whom I spoke suggested that graduating students were particularly prone to taking laboratory notebooks with them. However, two contract and grant officers at UW told me that faculty members moving to new institutions had also attempted to abscond with research results and had been prevented from doing so by a similar regulation. By claiming ownership, universities could assert a kind of jurisdiction to ensure that no individual researcher was allowed to unreasonably deny access to collaborators. They could use property claims to prevent a form of private appropriation, just as the federal government once patented inventions to keep them public (see Chapter 4).

UC was not alone in this approach. The General Counsel for Johns Hopkins University once declared: "There is no legal issue as to the ownership of data underlying research" (Fishbein, 1991, 133; see also Meyer, 1998). She was substantially correct. In most major universities, data are simply owned by the institution. The Dana Farber Cancer Institute offers one of the strongest statements of ownership, declaring its "ownership and stewardship" of scientific records to be "uncontestable." The University of California San Francisco Brain Tumor Research Center extends the basic UC ownership claim to encompass not only data but also methodology. The policies of other universities and institutes are less definite: the University of Houston, for example, states that while "generators of data (faculty, staff, and students) often believe they own the data produced in their laboratories," the university has a "legal responsibility with regard to access to and retention of data" (quoted in Stevens, 1997, 14). In general, however, the principle of institutional ownership of data holds across the United States and is supported by federal funding agencies like the Public Health Service, which require grantee institutions to retain ownership of data produced with federal funding (Stevens, 1997).

Faced with this apparently insurmountable barrier to her own property claims, Pelletier chose to burrow under a rather different border, the one between fact and artifact. Challenging Johnson's decision before the California Court of Appeal, Pelletier argued that the data stream in question was susceptible to multiple property interests. She herself held three: "(1) a possessory interest in the data accumulated to satisfy the fruits of her creative vision; (2) an interest in the integrity of her own work; and (3) a reputation interest which is dependent upon when and how the data and research results are presented to the scientific community" (Appellant's Opening Brief, 15).

As the language of her claims suggests, Pelletier's argument evoked copyright principles; indeed, the description of Pelletier's property interests reproduced, almost verbatim, portions of Rochelle Cooper Dreyfuss's (1987) influential legal analysis of faculty copyrights. Citing *Caird v. Sime* and *Williams v. Weisser*, Pelletier insisted that, by law and university policy, unpatentable scholarly works were the property of the researcher. In addition, she pointed to a series of disputes over efforts to subpoena confidential research records in which the principal investigator (not the university) was treated as the owner of the research. In this case the principal investigator was Kraut, but he had assigned his "property interest" in pol ß to Pelletier when he made her the lead researcher on the project. Finally, Pelletier reminded the court that the intention behind Regulation 4 was to leave the faculty right to publish "unfettered." As proof of this intention, she quoted Peltason's letter to the UCSD Academic Senate and the University of California Contract and Grant Manual: "Whereas the freedom of a scholar to disseminate the results of his research is a vital part of academic freedom, and is a traditional right of all scholars, Be it resolved that the Academic Senate affirms the right of all persons with academic appointments, except registered students, to make public the results of their research, whether orally or in writing, free from direct or indirect restraint of censorship by any representative of this university" (Opening Brief, 26, citing UC Contract and Grant Manual § 1–430). In other words, the university assigned its "right to publish"—asserted under Regulation 4—to researchers themselves, and that right to publish had been infringed by Agouron's misappropriation. Taking her cue from B. J. Williams (see Chapter 3), Pelletier portrayed Agouron as an unsavory commercial interloper in the university-faculty relationship.

In an unpublished opinion, the California Court of Appeal conceded Pelletier had a legitimate cause of action. Pelletier's interest in the data, the court stated, was "analogous to that of an inventor or a producer of copyrightable material who has not contracted away her rights to her intellectual property."[10] In short, a kind of "academic exception" existed for data as well as for research articles and lectures.

The logic of this analogy, and especially its emphasis on "creativity," rested on the production of the pol ß data stream as a boundary object, the boundary in question being the line between fact and artifact. The "teacher exception" that *Caird* and *Weisser* support is a creation of copyright law. No equivalent exists for trade secrets, in large part because university research is not usually understood to fall under the purview of trade secret law. Thus Pelletier's location of data within the penumbra of the teacher exception depended upon her ability to explain how the production and dissemination of data (a set of facts) was like the production and dissemination of a research article or lecture (an artifact). As Agouron itself later argued, copyright law protects only original works of authorship—creative expression—and not facts such as research data. The relevant precedent is *Miller v. University Studios* (1981), in which the Fifth Circuit held: "The valuable distinction in copyright law between fact and expression cannot be maintained if research is held to be copyrightable . . . to hold that research is copyrightable is no more or no less than to hold that the facts discovered as a result of research are entitled to copyright protection."[11] While Pelletier's reasoning did not define scientific data as specifically copyrightable, it did indicate the arbitrary quality of the "valuable distinction between fact and expression."[12] Pelletier argued that the research was a scholarly work, the product of "years of sustained creative effort" and "creative inspiration," and therefore equivalent to a publication or a lecture (Appellant's Opening Brief, 1, 35). Rejecting Agouron's interpretation of the California Labor Code, Pelletier cited *Weisser* again to insist that the code applied only to "things which an employee 'acquires,' not matter which he creates." In sum, facts discovered in the course of research were not simply preexisting objects waiting to be discovered but products, even expressions, of individual creative genius.

Pelletier's portrayal of data as creations was, in itself, neither new nor exceptional. What was stunning, however, was that such a portrayal came from a working scientist. Despite a scientific tradition of objectivity, for the past three decades a body of historians, philosophers, sociologists, ethnographers—and even a few scientists—have maintained that scientific data are thoroughly "infected with interpretation," as Stanley Fish might put it. Thus scientific data are artifactual, constructed in response to social, economic, and political pressures from many sides.[13] Critical legal theorists have offered similar arguments with regard to other kinds of data, responding in particular to a 1991 case, *Feist Publications Inc. v. Rural Telephone Directory*, in which the U.S. Supreme Court held that an alphabetical compilation of names, addresses, and phone numbers was not copyrightable, despite its compiler's investment of labor, because the compilation did not contain a minimal element of creativity.[14] Writing for the majority, Justice Sandra Day O'Connor insisted that copyrights apply only to original works. O'Connor offered the following analogy: "Census takers, for example, do not 'create' the population figures that emerge from their efforts, in a sense, they copy these figures from the world around them. Census data therefore . . . are not 'original' in the constitutional sense. The same is true of all facts—scientific, historical, biographical and news of the day" (347, citations omitted). The reasoning of the decision has been sharply condemned by the critical legal community, though the opinion's practical effect—limitation of the reach of copyright—has been applauded. Peter Jaszi speaks for several of these critics when he observes that the real problem with the data *Feist* put in question was the data's "embarrassment of very human sources" (1994, 39). Mundane as it may have been, directory information nevertheless comprised "a complex amalgam of choices to which the subject of a given entry, as well as her parents, friends, teachers and others . . . made contributions over time"—selections that were surely imbued with some minimal degree of creativity (ibid.; see also Litman, 1992). O'Connor's "census" analogy did not advance her cause, Jaszi adds: the designers of the census form also made multiple creative decisions about what forms of data were important, and those decisions were instrumental in creating the information produced.

Reconsidering the *Feist* reasoning with regard to scientific facts, the physician and lawyer Mark Meyer argues that scientific research also involves a "*de minimus* quantum of creativity": "The facts are there for all to claim, but the process of doing so, from the choice of what and how to study, to the decision to exclude certain facts and vigorously investigate others, represents creative expression which should be protected by copyright . . . There are many forks in the road leading to the final discovery; nature provides the forks, but the scientist through creativity and ingenuity chooses the path. And if astute, the scientist makes novel observations and innovative conclusions and records these as research, which is entitled to protection" (1998, 23–24). In Meyer's view, scientific data are as thoroughly produced as ideas and literary expression, and therefore copyrightable.

This kind of talk often makes scientists nervous, for it implies that they are writers as well as readers of the Book of Nature. In the past few years, studies of the social and historical contingency of scientific findings have sparked a rash of books and articles accusing social scientists of failing to get their own facts straight (see, for example, Gross and Levitt, 1994; Sokal, 1996). It is therefore surprising that one of the most vulnerable members of the scientific community—an untenured postdoctoral researcher—would publicly suggest that data are artifactual. Certainly few would deny that scientists invest labor in unearthing information about nature, or even that creative inspiration goes into study design, grant writing, analysis, and so on. But Pelletier attempted to argue something more: that the data were a product of her personal, original, and creative investment, "her sweat," and "her scholarship." Echoing comments on *Weissmann v. Freeman*, Pelletier called the notion that the university might exclusively own that product "feudal."

Less surprising in light of *Weissmann* (and *Williams*) was Pelletier's claim to economic rights in her reputation. A trade secret must have economic value to its owner. Pelletier argued that knowledge of how to crystallize pol ß would, released properly, enhance her reputation and make *her* valuable in the academic market. Specifically, she argued that her ability to move "from professional dependency to the status of principal investigator" through publishing had been impaired (Appellant's Opening Brief, 13). This reasoning echoed Judge Cardamone's construction, in *Weissmann*, of the academic system of exchange as both a gift and a market economy and his concomitant treatment of academic reputation as a form of intellectual property. Here, it seemed, the appropriation of research data was equivalent to appropriation of a scholar's investment in her academic persona. To establish herself as victim of such an appropriation, Pelletier not only had to represent herself as primarily motivated in her work by the desire to gain fame, independence, and status in the scientific community but also had to conflate the data and her own persona. Theft of one, in this property story, meant theft of the other. Her narrative leaves far behind a world where one might believe, as did some seventeenth-century writers, that it is "better to have scientific goods stolen and circulated than to have them lost entirely" (Merton, 1957/1973, 317). But that world could not protect a young and relatively unknown scientist from commercial poachers any better than did its present-day academic remnant.

Yet Pelletier's argument also demonstrates the limits of property claims to the academic persona and to data. Despite the proliferation of ownership rhetoric in scientific discourse, scientific norms still reject the portrayal of data as an individual's creation. Pelletier could hardly expect to receive much praise from the scientific community if she claimed in that arena that the crystallization procedure for pol ß was an artifact. Thus the realization of the economic value of her reputational interest would presumably rest on Pelletier's ability to subsequently reconstruct the data as a fact, a reconstruction that would demand that she substantially abandon the claims to originality and creativity that underlay her initial ownership claim.

There is an even larger point of confusion. Assuming the data were artifacts, it was not at all clear that they were *Pelletier's* artifacts. Joseph Kraut, Samuel Wilson, Janet Grimsley, Michael Sawaya, and Michele McTigue, among others, were all arguably "joint authors" of this work. Both parties to the dispute discussed at length one of the claimed "major findings" of the pol ß project: the discovery that the protein splits into two pieces prior to crystallization, a process called proteolytic cleavage. Pelletier argued that this "dramatic result" was her discovery. Agouron counterargued that proteolytic cleavage was common in proteins, that pol ß's tendency to split had been reported by Dr. Wilson at a 1992 conference, that several published articles had indicated it was likely to occur, and that Agouron itself had realized proteolytic cleavage was occurring a month before the Kraut lab's "discovery." What part of the discovery was legitimately Pelletier's? Pelletier's "discovery" of proteolytic cleavage was confirmed in follow-up tests by Sawaya (CT, Plaintiff's Closing Argument, 8). Did that verification contribute to the discovery's ultimate value and by extension the value of Pelletier's reputation in the academic market? If so, did Sawaya have an ownership interest in that trade secret and that reputation?

In his summation, Pelletier's attorney attempted to sidestep some of these questions by noting that Pelletier and Sawaya worked on the project together. "There is nothing different in joint ownership of an intellectual idea than there is between joint ownership of a house or any other kind of property" he argued (ibid., 26). Well and good, but Sawaya was not, as joint owner, bringing the lawsuit. And as Agouron noted in its appeal, much of the information the jury ultimately declared to be Pelletier's trade secret was published under Michael Sawaya's name.[15]

The unresolved questions raised in the case indicate the complexity of the intersection that Pelletier's representation of data occasioned and traversed. In court, the pol ß data stream was produced as both property and nonproperty, the product of natural and unnatural interventions, a fact and an artifact. The data stream was represented as a highly contingent boundary object, subject to multiple jurisdictions yet finally controlled by one individual.

So ended Act I, in which Pelletier claimed, and won, standing to pursue her trade secret claim. The second act of this play, as we shall see, necessitated a similarly complex effort to stabilize and conceal the fluidity of the pol ß data stream. Pelletier had to show how scientific norms of data access paralleled industrial confidentiality practices, and then use that showing to defend both her property rights and her position in the gift economy. Put simply, Pelletier had to mobilize the specter of the gift to defend a private property claim.

TRUST AND POSSESSION

Social and cultural studies of the academy have drawn attention to the appearance of a "market" rhetoric in academic research communities. *Pelletier v. Agouron,* in contrast, imported "gift" rhetoric into a market-oriented body of law. Pelletier had some proof—and strong circumstantial evidence—that McTigue had given Agouron specific details of Pelletier and Sawaya's research. The task, then, was to show why that research, the production of which was supported by public funds and carried out in a public university laboratory, was actually a trade secret, and why McTigue's transmission of some portion of the research constituted a breach of a confidential relationship.

Commercial entities asserting violation of trade secrets must describe the precautions they have taken to keep their data secret, precautions which can range from locked doors to encryption programs. Employment contracts and non-disclosure agreements are used to demonstrate the existence of a confidential relationship. Looking to demonstrate parallel efforts in the academic sciences, Pelletier began by outlining similar precautions in the Kraut lab. The crux of her case, however, was the suggestion that gift relations of obligation and sociality, the very social relations that supposedly made written contracts between members of a lab unnecessary, were confidential by definition. Secrecy, on this account, was as much a part of academic science as the test tube.

This was not an easy argument to make to a jury, for secrecy and academic science commonly are construed to be opposed. Scientists are supposed to share their data and materials to facilitate replication and validation of results and to make new work possible (Burk, 1994; Eisenberg, 1987; Meyer, 1998). Asked why they had chosen academic science, several researchers with whom I spoke identified secrecy as the major difference between academic and industrial investigation. One stressed, for example, that industrial science is "compromised by secrecy." Professors who had recently left the private sector told me that one of the benefits of coming to the university was a new ability to "talk to everybody."

Indeed, that ability to "talk to everybody" is one of the hallmarks of modern science. Openness was the point at which science *(theoria)* and technology *(techne)* historically diverged. While the craft guilds closely guarded their technological secrets, their system of protection forming one of the antecedents of modern trade secret law, the gentleman philosophers of scientific societies forged a different tradition, objecting less to secrecy as such than to what Steven Shapin calls "intellectual individualism," or the belief in individuals' ability to determine truth for themselves. Sir Francis Bacon, among others, argued that privacy and individualism threatened state order, while disciplined, collectively determined, public knowledge could be mobilized on behalf of state and society. Worried about how to make their experiments "public," natural scientists designed modes of writing and publication that would allow others to bear "witness" to the work by replicating it (Shapin, 1996). Echoing that concern several centuries later, an attorney for the University of California told me that the university chose not to get involved in Pelletier's case precisely because the university does not treat data as confidential and proprietary. Recall that UC president Peltason took pains to emphasize to the UCSD Academic Senate that the university's limited ownership claims to research data produced under its auspices would be invoked only where a scientist failed to live up to her professional obligation to share.

Ironically enough, both parties to the pol ß dispute sought to align themselves with that tradition. Agouron's opening statement noted that Michele McTigue had declined to sue Pelletier because she did not "believe the courts [were] the place to resolve academic squabbles" (CT, Appellant's Opening Statement, 50). Agouron also noted that McTigue had published her own early research on pol ß in fulfillment of her obligation to the taxpayers. "Dr. McTigue believed you are supposed to publish what the federal government pays you to do . . . You are not supposed to hide it and then sue somebody to get money for it" (50). Pelletier was equally invested in cloaking herself in scientific norms of openness, for much of the moral force of her argument depended on her ability to represent herself as an academic scientist against profit-driven Agouron Pharmaceuticals. In his closing statement, Pelletier's attorney used the fact that Pelletier had deposited 106 crystal structures with the Protein Data Bank—thereby making them available to other scientists—to establish Pelletier's scientific authenticity and simultaneously undermine Agouron's suggestion that Pelletier had exploited an improper personal relationship with Kraut. "Is that [the deposits] the work of a harlot or is that the work of a real scientist, who is able to make a contribution to society?" he asked (CT, Plaintiff's Closing Argument, 26). Thus Pelletier and Agouron were just as interested as the university in constructing a public domain of facts and locating themselves in that domain.

Seeking to reconcile her private property claim with her public domain location, Pelletier reminded the court that openness has hardly been an unqualified scientific value. To garner publications for its *Philosophical Transactions,* the Royal Society had to assure seventeenth-century scientists that their findings and works in progress would be kept secret until publication (Hull, 1985). More contemporary forms of assurance have been characterized as a "scholars' privilege" of protection from "premature disclosure of their research," one that helps create a "breathing space" for "creative expression" (Meyer, 1998, 18). Describing the mechanisms his lab used to create that breathing space, Joseph Kraut observed that confidentiality prior to publication was the rule and not the exception in academic science. The mechanisms enforcing that rule at the Kraut lab included locks, passwords, rules limiting discussion of the project to members of the lab, the maintenance of notebooks in the lab at all times, and a requirement that all pol ß publications be authorized by Kraut, Wilson, or Pelletier (Declaration of J. Kraut). Looking to IP law to supplement those mechanisms, Pelletier's attorney theorized that "allowing the individual scholar to maintain her work as a trade secret permits the scholar to time the publication of her work to obtain the optimal personal or professional benefit [and] to control the quality of the work published" (Appellant's Opening Brief, 32). Free inquiry, he continued, also meant freedom to investigate without fear that one's peers might appropriate one's findings.

The policing mechanisms that Kraut described are replicated by scientists in a variety of contexts. Indeed, the viability of some electronic forums has depended on their ability to develop such mechanisms. The SenseLab databases discussed earlier, for example, allow anyone to peruse published materials, but access to unpublished data is carefully policed.[16] Laboratories using the Olfactory Receptor Database, for example, are permitted to compare their own findings with those of other labs, but in the case of a potential match the inquiring lab is given only contact information for the matching lab—not a view of the matching findings themselves. The only person with access to unpublished data is the database administrator, who is not involved in neurobiological research.

The contradictions these limits on scientific openness embody are partially resolved by a crucial distinction between scientific and legal discourses of ownership. Legal discourse conflates "data" and "fact." In scientific discourse, however, data do not fully attain the status of "scientific fact" until they are published—incorporated into artifacts—and reproduced by peers (Latour and Woolgar, 1979; Latour, 1987). The data should not even be submitted to peers, moreover, until the researcher herself is perfectly satisfied of their validity. This is why, according to one senior researcher I interviewed, secrecy is part of scientific responsibility: "Science, the validation of it comes with reproducibility . . . All the findings that go on in the lab have to be thought about, reproduced, worked over . . . it takes a long time before you're ready. Furthermore, when you go about disclosing it, you can't just put the first thing that comes into your mind down on paper. Revise, revise, revise, help the reader . . . There are all the responsibilities about explaining what came before it, to [acknowledge] other labs that contributed and so forth . . . [The research] has to be put out responsibly, and that may take time." This researcher coded secrecy as a form of service to, rather than a contradiction of, what Merton called the "communist" elements of the "scientific ethos" (1942/1973, 272–275). The above comments were echoed in many conversations I had with researchers about data access. Professors and students stressed their willingness to share ideas and data—just as soon as those ideas and results were published.[17] As Pelletier herself put it during the trial, even revealing research results to fellow lab members involved "exposing your underbelly." To scientists, then, secrecy is a filter, rather than a dam, in a given data stream.

Yet this kind of confidentiality is difficult to maintain, even if one is not competing with a private pharmaceutical company, because data have a way of escaping. Grant-review processes, for example, have been subject to intense criticism for compromising scientific secrecy. Applicants often present preliminary research in funding requests, and they must trust that their reviewers will not use or circulate the findings. Honest scientists are supposed to ignore results encountered in review processes, visits to labs, and so on, and sometimes even to stop work on their own projects if they have been "contaminated" by contact with another lab's results. But even honest scientists may slip: as one senior researcher conceded, "It's hard to read something and forget it." In practice, not everyone tries to forget—recall the experiences with plagiarism described in Chapter 2—else there would be no need for the formal and informal mechanisms that enforce the "ethos" of science. According to a student with whom I spoke, anxiety about data exchange can be so high that professional conferences are painful: "[I was talking] with this guy who's doing something similar, and there were times when obviously he's probing. He's trying to get me to give him some information that I could give or not. And when I would ask a question . . . he kind of would give these guarded responses like 'Well, we haven't really looked at that.' I hate that." Again, part of the reason for this anxiety is that the findings do not "count" as facts until they have been incorporated into an artifact—a gift—and their value confirmed through peer review.

Scientific secrecy thus is not really a matter of withholding knowledge from a community; scientific data do not count as factual knowledge until they are reproduced. As Bruno Latour and Steve Woolgar observe, scientific *facts* are public by definition, for "a fact only becomes such when it loses all temporal qualifications and becomes incorporated into a large body of knowledge drawn upon by others" (1979, 106). Because unpublished data occupy a strange position as not-yet-facts, scientific secrecy only limits the circulation of a kind of "pre-fact." By the same token, Pelletier did not violate scientific norms of openness in bringing the case, for she was only claiming that "pre-facts" were private trade secrets—the facts, presumably, would be public.

To give legal force to the space of privacy in the public domain she sought to create, however, Pelletier had to do more than expose the secretive procedures of academic science. She also had to portray membership in a lab as premised on a kind of mutual non-disclosure agreement. One of the crucial components of a trade secret tort is that the information be obtained by improper means, such as through a breach of a confidential relationship. Collaborations within and between labs, Pelletier argued, establish a web of trust relationships, and it is understood by collaborators that results are not to be released to the disciplinary community without the permission of the principal investigator and "primary author" of the research. This boundary between laboratory and disciplinary communities was drawn by many of the scientists with whom I spoke as well. As one put it: "I would say there are few secrets in this group . . . What you say in these walls is everybody's business but we make everybody aware this is not something you want to share." Pelletier's lawyers drew a detailed and hierarchical picture of the Kraut group, from the principal investigator to students and technicians, and argued that McTigue had abused her "position of trust" within that hierarchy to advance her husband's career. That abuse included telling her husband (with whom she was presumably involved in another kind of trust relationship) about Pelletier's progress and not telling Kraut and Pelletier of Agouron's interest in pol ß.

Testifying at trial, Pelletier drew a sports analogy to explain McTigue's violation: "[By discussing your research results] you are exposing yourself and you want to do this in front of people you trust . . . I played on a lot of teams and the coach would come in with a playbook and the coach didn't put out a play in the basketball game and say, 'Now keep it to yourself.' We all knew" (CT, Testimony of H. Pelletier, 37). But who, exactly, played on the team in question? Pelletier claimed thirteen trade secrets and argued that, taken together, these made up the crystallization conditions of pol ß. Agouron counterargued that many of the "secrets" were in fact already "public." The most contentious example was the use of a salt (ammonium sulfate) in the crystal-growing process. Agouron argued that the salt was commonly used by crystallographers as part of the regular "trial and error process." Pelletier insisted that it was one of many possible substances, and that it was she who had discovered it would work to form pol ß. Agouron might have made this discovery eventually, but her work saved them the trouble.

As this dispute suggests, pol ß's status as a trade secret depended on the creation and management of a border not only between the known and the newly discovered but also between the lab and the crystallographic community. As Agouron argued, the use of salt to grow crystals was known to the community—but until the results were officially released, the use of the substance to grow pol ß was known only to persons in the Kraut laboratory. Those persons were, unless and until the secret was released, enmeshed in a web of obligations that left them partially cut off from the community of science.

Yet the trade secret claim required that Pelletier herself simultaneously rip that web apart by separating her interests from those of her colleagues. Because neither the lab nor the university, as a community, chose to bring the lawsuit, Pelletier had no choice but to litigate her own individual ownership interest and, in the process, obscure any communal claim the lab might have wished to assert. Pelletier argued that the economic value of the research—and therefore the damages to which she was entitled—took the form of the economic benefits she personally would realize when the data were published. To sustain that argument, she had to show why she had an individual economic interest in the data. Part of that showing was made in her initial effort to establish standing. Another part was accomplished by reference to the initial agreement between Pelletier, Sawaya, and McTigue, which carefully parsed the research itself into different scientific and temporal components. Pelletier's interest was confined to those specific facts "discovered" by Pelletier and Sawaya once they took over the project. (Agouron itself indirectly reinforced Pelletier's interest when it tried to argue that much of what Pelletier claimed as "hers" had been discovered by McTigue in the early stages of the project. Agouron thus was backed into the very quarrel it sought to avoid: over the ownership claims of respective lab members rather than whether the data could be owned by university scientists at all.)

As the reader may already suspect, the key to Pelletier's individual claim lay in academic hierarchy. Kraut's final decisionmaking authority on publications and project assignments was emphasized in testimony and briefs filed by Pelletier. That very authority, the reasoning went, gave Kraut the power to transfer ownership of the project to Pelletier. As

Kraut put it, "I understood, agreed, and expected she would, in consultation with me as the laboratory director, control and direct the course and scope of the research, determine when and what would be published and in what journal, and who, other than herself, would work on the project and be included as authors . . . In short, I gave her the project" (Declaration of J. Kraut, 13–14). Pelletier, in other words, became the principal investigator on the project and, as such, its "owner." Authority was the true source of ownership of data as of other academic artifacts, and, once transmogrified into an ownership interest, it was transferable from one individual to another.

Pelletier's arguments reproduced a dynamic we have encountered before: the production of a boundary object—in this case, data as trade secret—that serves as a vehicle for the deployment of norms usually associated with gift economies in the service of private property claims. IP rights are not neutral instruments, for they carry with them a set of assumptions that shape and limit the articulation of other rights and duties. That underlying set included, in this case, the presumption that Michael Sawaya's research was, in a sense, a "work for hire." As we saw in Chapter 3, one defense of the teacher exception to work-for-hire copyright rules is based on the idea that universities do not, and should not, direct or control the course and scope of the research and teaching activities of their faculty. Presumably, then, the university could not direct Michael Sawaya's research and publication. But as principal investigator, Pelletier apparently controlled not only her own investigations but also those of her nominal subordinate, Sawaya. McTigue had been prevented from publishing without Pelletier and Kraut's approval. Like McTigue, Sawaya lacked a "right to publish." Only Pelletier had the right to decide when and under what circumstances the pol ß results would be made available to the scientific community.

This property story, told through a particularly contentious trial, culminated in victory for Pelletier. After deliberating for nearly two weeks, the jury awarded Pelletier $200,000 in damages. Not surprisingly, both sides appealed—Pelletier asking for more damages and attorneys' fees, Agouron demanding a reconsideration of the verdict and the prior ruling that Pelletier owned the data. In September 2000 the California Court of Appeal confirmed the jury's decision that Agouron had misappropriated trade secrets from Pelletier and had been unjustly enriched thereby.[18] The story would properly end there, but for the court's surprising other ruling: that while Pelletier had proved a violation, and while she had suffered actual loss through that violation, she had failed to provide objective evidence of the monetary value of her loss. Her damage award was therefore reduced to one dollar. Further, the court found, she had failed to comply with the statutory requirements necessary to get attorneys' fees.[19] I will take up each of these rulings in turn.

In an unpublished opinion, Judge Work found that Pelletier's inability to publish constituted an actual loss, specifically the loss of "a competitive advantage for future collaboration and funding."[20] However, he continued, Pelletier failed to introduce sufficient evidence to establish the value of that loss, such as compensation she would have received if she had published first. She was therefore entitled only to nominal damages. In other words, she had failed to put a price on the really important property: her reputation.

In making this decision, the Court of Appeal brought the case full circle, redrawing the gift/market boundary its main decision necessarily blurred. The problem with the academic market, at least for those who wish to use property rhetoric to defend their market position, is that it retains gift-oriented structures. Heidi Weissmann and B. J. Williams also received minimal damages: Weissmann was denied damages for copyright infringement (though she was awarded a major sum for the sexual discrimination claims), and Williams won only $1,500. Damages, under copyright law, are measured either as the amount of lost sales (where the infringer competes directly with the infringee) or by "market value": what a willing buyer would have paid for the work. Some market value could be determined for Williams's lecture notes, on the basis of Weisser's previous sales. That determination was much more difficult in Weissmann's case, for neither she nor Freeman would have been compensated specifically for the syllabus—which is one reason Judge Pollack insisted Freeman's use was necessarily noncommercial.

Trade secret law allows a victim to receive compensation for actual loss, unjust enrichment of the thief, and, if willful and malicious conduct is shown, "exemplary damages."[21] As a rule, damages for loss and unjust enrichment cannot be speculative, meaning that specific harm must be shown and supported by substantial evidence. Pelletier, unlike most entities bringing trade secret claims, could not ask for compensation for her investment of time and equipment in identifying the trade secrets, as the research was funded by a federal grant. The competitive advantage

Pelletier would have received had she published first is difficult to quantify in monetary terms, for she would not have been guaranteed future grant money, salary, honoraria, and so on. As holder of a tenure-track position in a major medical school by the time the case went to trial, Pelletier was hard-pressed to demonstrate concrete immediate harm to her career. Though she subsequently faced considerable difficulty obtaining grants to continue her research—perhaps because she had been identified as a "troublemaker" as well as a "second publisher"—that difficulty was not evident at the time of the jury's verdict. Nor, more important, would a connection between second publication and a competitive disadvantage in grant approval have been easy to delineate. Grant awards are supposed to be based on the quality of the preliminary research and the value of the project to progress in the field as well as the reputation of the scientist. Agouron could easily argue that the former criteria were more important than the latter. That argument, despite the odd source, should remind us that multiple entities invest in academic reputation, including colleagues, mentors, students, and funding agencies. In this case, the only clear financial victim of the misappropriation was the federal government, to the extent that it expected first publication as a return on its original investment in the research.[22] On these facts, the appellate court concluded, the jury's award could only have been speculative.

Pelletier might have been able to claim exemplary damages and attorneys' fees if she had shown willful and malicious misappropriation. In fact, considerable evidence of animosity between McTigue and Pelletier, as well as willful use by Agouron of the purloined data, was presented at trial. Pelletier did request that the jury be instructed to rule on the issue, but the trial judge refused to do so, and also refused to find such conduct on his own. Still, the statutory language and the case law did not firmly establish that willfulness and maliciousness had to be determined by the jury. Faced with this ambiguity, the appellate court ruled that willfulness and maliciousness were "matters of fact" rather than "matters of law." The jury, in this case, was the "trier of fact" and thus the only body authorized to decide whether the conduct existed (19–21).

This ruling, taken in conjunction with the fact that the judge refused to publish his opinion (virtually eliminating it as useful precedent), can be read as an effort to discourage future suits of this type. As the court itself noted, the law is not settled on the issue of whether "willful and malicious appropriation" must be found by the jury rather than a judge. The court's refusal to find such conduct as a matter of law allowed apportionment of minimal damages and no attorneys' fees. In concrete terms, the decision sent a message to attorneys and future potential plaintiffs that the courts are not the place to hear this kind of dispute. Echoing opinions of the Seventh Circuit Court of Appeals *(Weinstein v. University of Illinois),* and the District Court for the Southern District of New York *(Weissmann v. Freeman),* the Fourth Appellate District signaled that the academy is the site of principles, rather than commerce, and it would do well to handle its disputes itself.

The court's refusal to publish the appellate rulings in the *Pelletier* case considerably lessened their impact. Unpublished opinions cannot, ordinarily, be cited as precedent for future property stories. Nevertheless, the case was a landmark on the knowledge frontier. At a minimum, the reasoning advanced by both sides of this "academic squabble" confirmed what cultural critics of law and science have been arguing for some time: data streams have multiple sources; they do not simply "sit" waiting to be discovered but are rather constructed in social and political activity. The production of data as a boundary object in the *Pelletier* case—the property story told about the results, the difficulty of determining who did and did not count as a protagonist in that story, the use of gift rules to manage that difficulty—brought into sharp relief the multivalence of scientific data and the instability of the borderline between public and private knowledge upon which academic science and IP law rely.

The *Pelletier* case set another precedent, one to which future participants in legal and extralegal contests for the meaning of data and data ownership should pay equal attention. Pelletier's victory could add a new weapon to the arsenal of scientists looking to prevent appropriation of their data, and we can expect to see it used against fellow academics as well as commercial entities. That weapon will, in turn, make it more difficult to conceive of the university as the anchor of the commons. Consider, for example, the legislation concerning database ownership discussed earlier. Database publishers might use *Pelletier* to argue that data collection involves creative labor and should therefore be treated as a unique form of intellectual property or, alternatively, be protected by copyright law. Counterarguments from librarians and public interest groups that statutory protection for databases would impoverish science will be harder to mount when scientists themselves are looking to assert property rights in data, using legal and contractual mechanisms to police access to data and community membership, and arguing that scientific and trade secrecy are essentially indistinguishable. Database publishers should take note, however, that despite the nominal damages awarded to Huguette Pelletier, her technical success might still prompt academics of all persuasions to demand that publishers using scholarly data compensate the "originators" of those data for their time and creative effort.

PROPERTY STORIES AND ETHICAL PRACTICES

I began this inquiry by observing that intellectual property law and the academy comprise a bipolar epistemic regime, with the former policing the realm of property and the latter policing the commons. I have tried to unpack some of the contradictions, paradoxes, and shared assumptions upon which that regime relies and to delineate how the foundational paradox of the modern research university—the idea that to be useful it must be useless—is forged and navigated by interested subjects. Throughout, I have sought to offer an intimate experience of boundaries and boundary work.

The *Pelletier* case encapsulates many of the problems and negotiations I have suggested are characteristic of the production of academic intellectual property. This particular contest also brings into sharp relief the need for political strategies and definitions that engage a "necessarily messy world" (Traweek, 1996, 50). One of the messiest issues in *Pelletier*—academic freedom—raises broader questions about the definitions currently advanced in the borderland of knowledge production.

Running through the briefs and testimony in *Pelletier* was an only partially articulated but nevertheless persistent argument about academic freedom, one that we have encountered before in debates over lecture ownership and that provides the subtext of many arguments about rights in academic articles and inventions. Both the University of California's policy and Pelletier's own reading of that policy assumed that the best way to protect academic freedom was through the assertion and exercise of property rights. The university asserted corporate ownership of the data in the name of defending the faculty's academic freedom, and Pelletier claimed individual ownership of the data on the same principle. Both claims demand a further reconsideration of what academic freedom means in "revolutionary" times. How did freedom of inquiry become bound up in freedom of property, and what are the consequences of that binding? Students of contemporary rights discourse suggest that struggles to realize "ideals of freedom" frequently reinstall, rather than transform, the discursive formations in opposition to which those ideals emerge (Brown, 1995). Do current rearticulations of academic freedom similarly reinscribe old foundational claims and thereby foreclose new interpretive possibilities?

Given that the perennial "crisis" of the academy is often represented as a problem of academic freedom, we might also ask whether property-based defenses of academic freedom participate in a crisis-driven strategy of social control. In the 1920s the academy required protection from the concerns of businessmen; in the 1950s anticommunist witch hunts were the threat; in the 1960s government and university administrators assumed the role of enemies of freedom. The 1980s and 1990s saw the emergence of an especially complex argument, with some members of the academy insisting that "political correctness"—which seemed to include critical work of all stripes—was a threat to freedom, and other members arguing that academic freedom was itself in need of redefinition. Participants in each of these controversies shared the fear that scholars might permit commercial and political interests to impinge on what Ronald Dworkin calls scholars' right and duty to "discover and teach what they find to be important and true" (1996, 189).

Defending this right and duty in 1967, the Supreme Court declared: "Our Nation is deeply committed to safeguarding academic freedom, which is of transcendent value to all of us."[23] But the Court's language was misleading. Academic freedom is not of transcendent value; academic freedom as a value is specific, contextual, and contested. Among other things, academic freedom has historically been tied to specific political freedoms, and especially freedom of speech. Indeed, academic freedom has been characterized as a "special concern of the First Amendment," on the theory that the academy itself was one of the most socially important arenas of free speech.[24] As Peter Byrne observes, "academic freedom is the only First Amendment right enjoyed solely by members of a particular profession" (1989, 264). This "special concern" has not been clearly articulated by the courts, however, and in light of *Pelletier* and *Williams* it is telling that parsing the respective rights of professors and universities has turned out to be especially difficult.[25]

Even as interested parties struggle to reconcile academic freedom and free speech, however, the former term is being reframed as the stuff of property rights rather than civil rights. Huguette Pelletier turned to trade secret law to defend not only her reputation but also her right to publish and thus to control her own work—her academic freedom. We saw in Chapters 2 and 3 that Heidi Weissmann and B. J. Williams called on copyright law to defend their claims to their work, their reputations, and, by extension, their ability to engage in free and open inquiry. The dynamic works somewhat differently in the realm of technology transfer described in Chapter 4, but there, too, inventors, attorneys, and technology transfer managers rework legal concepts of novelty, conception, and utility to produce and maintain academic science's claim to being a space of free, open, and disinterested study.

In short, the contest for the meaning of academic freedom is taking place on shifting ground according to novel rules. But previous contests have produced some useful tools for thinking about this uncertain terrain, such as Joan Scott's characterization of academic freedom as an ethical practice. Scott quotes Michel de Certeau as follows: "Ethics . . . defines a distance between what is and what ought to be. The distance designates a space where we have something to do" (de Certeau, 1986, 199). In a collection of essays, Scott and other scholars from a variety of disciplines (among them Richard Rorty, Evelyn Fox Keller, and Edward Said) consider what it means to practice academic freedom and how that practice can be justified (Menand, ed., 1996). Contributors to this collection take a variety of analytic perspectives, but the authors share—though not perhaps intentionally—a vision of academic freedom as a complex of informal and formal activities in which communal and individual self-governance are inextricably linked. This linkage derives from the basic distinction between academic freedom and freedom of speech: both protect expression and inquiry, but academic freedom also demands financial and institutional support for that inquiry.

Such claims—and support—are justified and regulated by professional mechanisms. Thomas Haskell argues, for example, that academic freedom "came into being as a defense of the disciplinary community (or, more exactly, the university conceived as an ensemble of such communities)" (1996, 54). Scott puts it another way, observing that "disciplinary communities . . . share a common commitment to the autonomous pursuit of understanding, which they both limit and make possible by articulating, contesting, and revising the rules of such pursuits and the standards by which outcomes will be judged" (1996, 175). Once an individual gains some status in the community, her right to pursue whatever she finds important—and to be financially supported in that endeavor—is protected by that community. She may need to find additional funding for that pursuit, but here too a disciplinary community operates: funding decisions generally depend on some form of peer review, and those peers are supposed to ensure that support is given to projects that contribute to the common understanding. Thus academic freedom mandates not that all work will be valorized and supported by a given disciplinary community but rather that "decisions about what counts as good work in sociology shall be made by sociologists" (Menand, 1996, 17).

Academic freedom, then, has never been "unconstrained" in the modern university. Indeed, there is a sense in which knowledge management comes almost full circle in the modern practice of academic freedom. Trade secret law and the university share roots in the craft guilds of medieval Europe. The production of the research university did not completely dissolve the tradition of the masters' guild, but rather, as we saw in Chapter 3, extended and reconfigured craft ideals to legitimate new strategies of cognitive exclusiveness. Academic freedom was one such strategy, articulated in terms of, rather than in opposition to, elements of traditional knowledge monopolies (Hofstadter and Metzger, 1955).

All of which helps explain why intellectual property rights, despite their individualist premises, have become appealing defensive tactics. It has never been the case—nor is it now—that the multi-layered production of academic work as intellectual property is solely motivated by desire for profit. Rather, intellectual property claims of all stripes are often tactics for protecting cognitive property by locating academicians as knowledge owners rather than knowledge workers. IP rights seem to offer a ready-made strategy of self-governance, a certificatory system, a way of protecting one's credit, and even, curiously enough, a method for affirming and maintaining community boundaries. Above all, they seem to offer a strategy for survival, especially for subordinate members of the community, like Heidi Weissmann and Huguette Pelletier, who feel they cannot count on a disciplinary community for protection.

This kind of protection depends, however, on the continuing ability of both the academy and IP law to simultaneously engage, deny, and affirm transgression, to produce boundary objects but pretend that what sits on either side of any given border remains intact and distinct. Not coincidentally, basic foundational categories in IP law and academia—authorship, propriety, inventorship, facts and artifacts—are all available to be produced as objects that create and bridge common boundaries between legal and academic discursive fields. The cases and practices I have discussed, however, indicate just how difficult the rescue operation is becoming. As in other arenas, property rights discourse offers to preserve and protect a depoliticized "balance" between intellectual property and the commons, even as the invocation of that discourse assists in the ongoing reconfiguration of that balance. Intellectual property is not a neutral category but a lens shaped by a set of assumptions about the nature of cultural production that brings particular aspects of cultural work into focus while blurring or obscuring other facets. In particular, IP law carries with it the assumption that knowledge is the product of the efforts and inspirations of individuals or groups of individuals who may be identified by specific characteristics. IP law also embodies the notion that the only forms of cultural work that can be "protected" are those that can be owned.

Viewed through this lens, academic research looks like a matter of individual inspiration and labor; pedagogy like an equally individualized one-way activity; the university like a fully autonomous corporation; and professors like Hollywood actors. More generally, the conflation of property rights and "academic rights" participates in a set of discourses which offer to replace the hierarchies of the academy with the inequalities of the free market, discourses in which freedom can only be understood to mean "individual free enterprise." In this emergent property story, academic freedom is simply the "right of self-interest," and the "self" in question is an individual, rather than a disciplinary community.[26] In retelling this tale academics risk losing a language for talking about knowledge as other than private property and the university as other than economically "useful."

In other words, the contents of the domains boundary objects are supposed to bridge are fundamentally changed by the production of those objects. It is crucial to remember, in this regard, that boundary objects are not simply vehicles by which one world imposes its vision on another—to succeed as such, objects must intermediate conflicts and are themselves changed in the process. Vigorously argued, formed and reformed, boundary objects "contain at every stage the traces of multiple viewpoints, translations, and incomplete battles" (Star and Griesemer, 1989, 413). Those battles and translations are ongoing and the battle lines do not remain stable.

The productive activities I have traced herein pose problems for IP law as well, for they demonstrate the contingency of the foundational assumptions of IP discourse, among them the human inventive genius; the dualisms of fact/artifact, gift/market, public/private; and even the Romantic author. The massive effort of boundary marking required to reestablish those assumptions seems to demand a fundamental reconsideration of current law. If data are works of authorship, for example, they should be as susceptible to copyright protection as other artifacts. But we might put the same observation another way: if no meaningful distinction can be established between data and works of authorship, perhaps property rights cannot be justified for either category.

The conflation of freedom of inquiry and freedom of property points as well to the conceptual poverty of calls to put the IP system back "in balance" by shoring up the public domain. James Boyle (1997) among many others, has argued that IP law does a poor job of nurturing and supporting the commons, and that the public domain is treated as a kind of empty discursive field (see also Lange, 1981; Litman, 1990). What is left of that space is ever harder to discern, argues Boyle, in a legal regime organized around the economic interests of entities that can perform original authorship. The public domain must therefore be reinvented, he concludes, in the context of a new "politics of intellectual property." If so, the guiding inquiry of that politics should not be (borrowing from Thomas Streeter) "how can we protect public [gift, nonproperty] interests from private [market, property] interests?" (1996, 323). That question signals an attempt to reinstall the very dualisms that the rhetorics and processes I have discussed expose as unstable and often illusory.

In this book I have tried to lay the groundwork for a different investigation. The difficulty of producing a "public domain" in the very institution that has been imagined as its bulwark is an invitation to consider not only the limits of IP law but also the definition of academic freedom, the uses of the university, and what it means to live in what Bill Readings calls a "ruined institution." To respond to that invitation—to decide whether and how we will choose to "dwell in the ruins," as Readings advises, or rebuild the institution, or find another dwelling place—we must think creatively and strategically about the languages we choose to define intellectual work. We might take Litman's observation, that the concept of public domain allows us to sidestep disquieting questions about origination, as a starting point and find ways to put those irritating questions front and center. The contests for meaning—of originality, of factuality, of the line between fact and expression—that interrogation would engender could lead us to ask, in turn, a version of what Streeter calls the Realist question: What kinds of property relations are most appropriate to supporting what kinds of academic inquiry and expression?

Left unproblematized, however, current academic intellectual property stories may obscure those questions. The political theorist Wendy Brown observes that when social hurt is answered by legal remedies, "political ground is ceded to moral and juridical ground." In the process, "injury is . . . rendered intentional and individual [and] politics is reduced to punishment" (1995, 27). A variety of injuries to academic freedom have been conveyed to one branch of law for resolution, and protection by the courts may come at the cost of redefining knowledge work according to a limiting set of legal categories. If so, potentially fruitful and necessary discussions may be limited or foreclosed. This operation indicates the final irony of academic intellectual property: its deployment undermines strategic interventions in the very constellation of activities and assumptions that make that deployment seem both necessary and desirable. That constellation of activities designates the space between what is and what ought to be, a space in which we still have much to do.

Introduction

1. *Restatement of Torts* § 757, comment (b).
2. Traditionally categorized into copyright ("original, expressive information"), patent ("technological information"), and trademark ("symbolic information"), intellectual property is most easily defined as ideas fixed in a tangible means of expression or reduced to practice. These property rights are guaranteed primarily by the Copyright Law of 1976, the Patent Act of 1952, and the Lanham Act of 1946, respectively, and fall under federal jurisdiction. Other forms of IP include trade secrets, common law copyright, unfair competition, and rights of publicity. These are usually regulated by state law and may be preempted by federal statutes.
3. Bruno Latour (1987) claims to have "forged" the term "technoscience" to avoid having to endlessly write "science and technology" (29). He and other practitioners of science studies have demonstrated how thoroughly technologies—social, mechanical, political—penetrate and are penetrated by what is formally dubbed "science," suggesting that "science" and "technology" are effectively interwoven.
4. John Locke (1694) and William Blackstone (1766) both offer pseudohistorical descriptions of human evolution from a state of plenty, to the gradual accumulation of goods by individuals, to the creation of a trading money economy, and finally to the creation of government (see C. Rose, 1994). There are many fairytale qualities to this pseudohistory: money, for example, is rather suddenly "invented" in Locke's account.
5. Thus, for example, Native American rights of first possession in much of the American continent could be ignored by white settlers on the American "frontier" because the Native Americans did not use the same codes—fences, title documents, and so on—as the whites (C. Rose, 1994).
6. Mark Lemley (1997) uses "propertization" to describe the increasing use of moralist, "real property" rhetoric in debates about information. Infringements, for example, are referred to as "thefts." I use the term in a more general sense of "(re)producing information as property" to distinguish that process from one of "commodification." Commodities are goods produced for sale in a market; a property may or may not be a commodity (see generally Schiller, 1994).

Propertization may be the first step toward commodification, but the two terms are not commensurate and I will endeavor to distinguish them. I focus primarily on propertization, such as the processes through which an invention comes to be treated as property. Full understanding of that invention's commodification would require an analysis of licensing, development, and marketing activities that I do not attempt here.

7. Frug's approach draws on a tradition of legal scholarship that dates to the Realist movement of the 1920s. The Realists sought to show how legal struggles are, at root, political struggles, with political as well as legal consequences. Critical legal studies binds this insight to political economic analysis in order to expose the incoherence of basic legal principles (such as formal equality and legal neutrality) and to show how the law's promise of equal justice serves to justify inequality (Kairys, 1982; Horwitz, 1992; Mensch, 1989; Gordon, 1989). Law, in this frame, is constructed in and through hegemonic processes that are nevertheless sites of struggle, conflict, and opportunity. Law will "mask nothing, legitimize nothing, contribute nothing to any class's hegemony" if it does not occasionally uphold its own logics of equity (Thompson, 1975). For law to operate as ideology, in other words, it must not only appear to be just but, on occasion, actually *be* just. This obligation means legal principles can be appropriated to resist hegemony.

8. The treatment of law as pre-political does not originate with liberal theory. Hannah Arendt (1958) has noted that the ancient Greeks allowed noncitizens to serve as lawmakers, while reserving participation in the *polis* to citizens. "Laws" she argues, "were made by craftsmen before the political work began" (194).

9. Peter Gabel and Jay Feinman (1982) argue that contract law is "an elaborate attempt to conceal what is going on in the world" (183). In the nineteenth century, socioeconomic relations were organized through a free market, and contract law accordingly treated individuals as free and equal competitors. In the mid-twentieth century, the "social order" was organized around regulated monopolies, and contract law traded the principle of free competition for a model of competition regulated by trade custom. According to Gabel and Feinman, in both historical moments the law faced the same problem: how to transform itself to match the "actual organization of daily life" (179). Absent from their account, however, is the role of law in shaping, or helping produce, that "actual organization."

10. For example, in France, the producer of a film is assigned ownership in it, although directors can claim a moral right in the work. The property right is distributed in this way, Edelman notes, because the courts have found that the producer has responsibility for all the elements in a film. Responsibility, he suggests, means *financial* responsibility. In French legal discourses, financial direction becomes creative direction and the influence of capital becomes "the creative influence" (1979, 58).

11. "Community of Science" has been trademarked by a Web-based consortium founded by Johns Hopkins University to "accelerate the creation of knowledge." Community of Science, Inc., uses its large and growing database to put academic scientists in contact with one another, funding agencies, and, not incidentally, venture capitalists and technology companies (see www.cos.com/).

12. A few works have been especially helpful on this subject: Veysey (1965), Hofstadter and Metzger (1955), Rothblatt and Wittrock, eds. (1993), Ridder-Symoens (1996), Wittrock, (1993), Kimball (1986).

13. I do not intend to suggest, however, that those interrogations alone are responsible for the erosion of belief.

14. These institutional names are pseudonyms, as are the names ascribed to the research centers discussed below. Any similarity to the names of actual universities and research institutions is purely coincidental.

15. The two sites were chosen for their conceptual proximity to the university-industry borderland. The first site, which I shall call the Institute for Research in Computational Engineering (IRCE), is a relatively young, small, but flourishing research unit. It is housed in Collingwood's Engineering School. IRCE receives substantial funding from a consortium of industrial "partners" who are encouraged to work with IRCE scientists to develop a "strong, relevant, program" through biannual "research reviews," less formal brainstorming sessions, research exchange programs (partners can send employees to work at IRCE), and informal visits. The partners help fund IRCE, and these monies are primarily used to support graduate students and summer faculty research. Potential inventions arising from research partially funded by the member companies are covered by an exceptional policy that had to be specifically approved by the president of the university. As a rule, the university's primary negotiating stance is that it owns all rights to any inventions arising on its campus (though there are exceptions). Under this policy, the director of IRCE reviews research articles for patentable inventions prior to their submission to any journal, and any identified invention is jointly owned by IRCE and all the member companies that contribute to the development of the invention. As of this writing, however, the fourteen faculty (and one postdoc) affiliated with IRCE have yet to patent an invention produced with IRCE funding, in part because this funding forms a relatively small portion of their total research money. Two of the eleven students with whom I spoke thought they might have developed a patentable invention, but neither had raised the issue with anyone else. Some professors (I interviewed ten) emphasized that their research, because it was "theoretical," was unlikely to generate patentable inventions.

The second site, a large computing research facility I shall call the Center for Computational Excellence (CCE), was populated by electrical engineers as well as biologists, neuroscientists, computer scientists, and physical scientists who use advanced computing technologies in their research. In part, I chose the latter site because my conversations there gave me a chance to compare practices in engineering with those in other fields. In addition to interviewing fourteen scientists, three doctoral students, and five senior and mid-level staff members, I spent four months working in the CCE external relations department, which gave me access to a wide range of information about the activities of CCE scientists and the history of the center. I also chose CCE because of its unique location with respect to Collingwood as a whole. Until just a few months prior to my research, CCE was not formally part of the university structure, although many of its researchers were affiliated with that structure as professors. Formally it was a subsidiary of a private corporation, which I will call General Industries (GI), but its funding actually came from the National Science Foundation. CCE had developed a distinctive culture, which, according to my respondents, combined the best of the academic and private sectors. CCE staff (from senior researchers to security administrators), felt more closely connected to the campus on which the center was located than to the private corporation that administered it from afar, partly because GI's senior executives had little experience with scientific research, but mostly because many people at CCE were engaged in basic research projects of their own choosing. They were happy to be exempt from the "publish or perish" rules of academic life, however, and they found academic bureaucracy hopelessly inefficient. In short, CCE presented a fascinating "borderline case" that highlighted the distinctions and blurred boundaries between academia and industry.

1. Building an Epistemic Regime

1. Treichler usefully distinguishes between "meaning" and "definition." "Meaning" signifies "what is meant"—what is intended and also what is understood. Thus the term implies a degree of interpretive work and potential resignifications. "Definition," however, is a limiting term that implies a claim to describe "how things are" (1990, 123)

2. Two examples should establish the point. First, there is the question of whether universities, as internet service providers, should be obligated to police web sites developed under their auspices for copyright infringement. In debates over the Digital Millennium Copyright Act of 1998, universities argued that such policing activities would not only tax their resources but require excessive interference with teaching and research and thereby undermine open inquiry and intellectual engagement. The educators and librarians won special protection for nonprofit institutions by reminding legislators that the information economy needs the products of that "open inquiry."

A second point of tension, the subject of legislative efforts in 1999 and 2000, involves electronic databases. Database providers such as LEXIS-

NEXIS™ and Melvyl™ give discounts to university subscribers on the condition that the subscriber ensure that only students, faculty, and librarians will use the database. That assurance is provided by a system of passwords and, sometimes, informal questioning of users. The librarian at the database center at UW questioned visitors to make sure they were really students and not, say, lawyers or staff. These barriers protected the commercial value of access to the database, but also circumscribed the librarians' ethical commitment to public education.

3. Other limits include the doctrine of fair use, which permits some forms of intellectual property to be used for educational or critical purposes, and restraints on the length of the monopoly. No clear limits on the common law right of publicity have been established, although the statutory right in several states is set at fifty years after the death of the property owner. Trademarks are theoretically perpetual, so long as the owner does not abandon them or permit them to become common currency.

4. In the past five decades alone, the American research university has gone through at least three distinct "crises." In the 1950s the university was thrown into "crisis" by McCarthyite threats to academic freedom and specifically efforts by many administrators to require faculty to sign loyalty oaths. In the 1960s the "crisis" was ostensibly provoked by student protests against pedagogical and disciplinary practices, university involvement in military research, and the Vietnam war. These protests fueled intense antagonism between university administrators and faculty and government entities as well. In the 1980s the "crisis of the university" was pictured as a moral problem, with universities attacked from within and without as bastions of "cultural relativism" rather than reason.

5. The first academic revolution, which I will discuss later, involved the rationalization of the academy and the concomitant prioritization of research over teaching as the university's primary mission (Hofstadter and Metzger, 1955; Jencks and Reisman, 1968)

6. This argument was cited, for example, by Arizona State vice-provost Jonathan Fink in defense of a faculty member, Robert Balling, who received funding from the fossil-fuel industries for several years but did not acknowledge that support in his publications on climate change. Fink admitted that the support looked "a little funny" but insisted any university interference in that relationship would constitute a violation of Balling's academic freedom (Blumenstyk, 1998a).

7. Which raises another problem: How is time to be defined? At one major research university, policy requires that professors devote four-fifths of their working week to the university—the one-day-a-week rule. It is not clear, however, whether the "working week" lasts five or seven days.

8. In a 1992 University of South Florida case, a student was sent to a work camp for patenting in his own name research conducted under industrial contract. Petr Taborsky, an undergraduate in biology and chemistry, worked as a lab as-

sistant for Professor Robert P. Carnahan on a research contract for a utility holding company, Florida Progress, Inc. Taborsky allegedly "disappeared" with several research notebooks and used information in them to file and win two patents on a sewage cleanser. But the university had long since ceded IP rights in any research arising from the contract to the utility company. Taborsky himself did not sign an agreement to this effect until months after the discovery, and he insists the invention was the product of independent research unrelated to the contract itself. Thus far he has retained the patent rights, but USF was able to have him sentenced to three and a half years of work camp for his "theft" of the notebooks.

9. Kerr (1963/1995) insists that the term was actually coined by the student activist Mario Savio.

10. However, the booksellers remained the "master manufacturers," according to Daniel Defoe, while writers were "workmen" (in Bettig, 1992, 140).

11. The first exclusive monopoly patent was granted to the architect Filippo Brunelleschi by Florence for a barge with hoisting gear (Shulman, 1999).

12. MacLeod points, for example, to the British Crown's repeated denial of patents for techniques to improve the efficiency of salt production.

13. *Hornblower and Maberley v. Boulton and Watt* (1799), cited in Dutton, 1984, 72.

14. The invocation of Locke in this context is doubly provocative. According to Kirstie McClure (1996), Locke was fundamentally concerned with how individuals could think rationally about the common good. The answer, McClure suggests, was provided by early economic theories which identified individual prosperity with the prosperity of the nation. This literature helped build a bridge between the politics of individualism and the politics of management and supported the gradual suppression of the theistic dimensions of the language of natural rights. It was also perfectly consonant with prevailing justifications for patent rights. The discourse of inventorship, like the discourse of authorship, was thus firmly positioned within what McClure calls the eighteenth-century "fusion of the language of law, right, liberty, equality, and property with emerging scientific constructions of social processes" (286).

15. It may also help explain the explicit requirement in U.S. law that patents only be granted to human persons (copyrights, in contrast, can be owned by corporate persons). See Chapter 4.

16. This case was not reported in any law record series. Historians have relied on newspaper accounts and pamphlets published by the litigants and other interested parties (Dutton, 1984; Adams and Averley, 1986)

17. I am thinking here of Latour's (1993) distinction between mediation and intermediation. The discourse of modernity, Latour suggests, is organized around dichotomies and the operation of intermediaries between the poles of these dichotomies. Mediation implies compromise and thus slippage from the pure forms of these poles, while intermediation implies instead a negotiation between these poles—but they, in their pure form, are left intact.

18. U.S. Patent no. 6,004,230.

19. *San Francisco Arts and Athletics, Inc., v. United States Olympic Committee,* 107 S. Ct. 2971 (1987).

20. This public domain was not unbounded. Proprietary practices common in the Renaissance, for example, were replicated in the seventeenth century. Galileo Galilei used codes and anagrams to keep his discoveries secret until publication and to establish priority for them. In the seventeenth century the Royal Society secretary Henry Oldenburg persuaded scientists to write up their discoveries and deposit them in a sealed box at the Royal Society until they could be published. Thus the publicness of scientific findings was temporally bounded. It was determined by the community as well: the members of Francis Bacon's mythical House of Salomon, which provided the model for modern scientific societies, were required to share discoveries among themselves but to keep secret the ones members chose not to publish. In other words, scientists were obligated to be open with one another but were not yet under a special obligation to the general public.

21. Indeed, many inventors received little more than that prior to the eighteenth century, for patent law was highly volatile, and the strength of the patent depended primarily on the financial resources available to defend it. MacLeod has suggested that in many cases patents were pursued as marks of recognition: as the text confirmed the author, in other words, so patents confirmed inventors.

22. See, e.g., Hofstadter and Metzger (1955), Young (1992), Veysey (1965), and Wittrock (1993).

23. Some less privileged persons had a chance to develop this mastery as well. Even in the thirteenth century a university education was seen as a ticket to upward mobility—some means were required, but students might be the sons of artisans or sponsored by an entire village in need of a scribe (Rudy, 1984).

24. Well into the seventeenth century, academic debates were less concerned with the production of new truth than with the exercise of rhetorical forms. According to Shapin (1996), the linkage of traditional natural philosophy to the "disputatiousness" of university scholarship led to its rejection by moderns. The logical and rhetorical tools of the university were seen as "litigious," "verbose," and divisive. In contrast, modern natural philosophy offered a systematic method for producing effects rather than more words.

25. Scientific and university discourses were not fully dissociated. As Wilhelm Schmidt-Biggeman (1996) has observed, universities provided training and financial support for many early modern natural and social scientists, even if clear intellectual affinities were lacking. And some universities, notably those of Holland and Scotland, were crucial to the spread of Enlightenment ideals.

26. Theorists from Aristotle to Nietzsche have embraced this characterization. Derrida observes that Aristotle's *Metaphysics* establishes a theoretico-political hierarchy, wherein the ability to teach is to "know the causes" and therefore to

be able to direct the work of others: "Before anyone else, [the theoretician] answers to the principle of reason which is the first principle . . . And that is why he takes orders from no one." The theoretician is invested with superior science, "with the power it confers by its very lack of utility" (1983, 18). A similar disdain for useful activities (e.g. training lawyers and military men) is found in Heidegger and Nietzsche. Instead the theoretician produces knowledge, and his (I use the masculine pronoun advisedly) ability to do so depends on its autonomy from the demands of practical expediency.

27. And yet this autonomy is always denied, for it depends on the authorization of the state (Derrida, 1983; Weber, 1911/1974). In German universities, even the appointment of professors had to be approved by the state. To understand this as a conflict, however, is to misunderstand the basic dynamic of liberalism, for the liberal subject's autonomy is always, as Marx noted, dependent on the recognition of the state.

28. Adam Smith would soon characterize intellectual work as a surplus, supported by the activity of capital in wealthy societies (1978; Rothblatt, 1985). Yet Smith, too, saw the deployment of reason to produce reasoning subjects as useful, because reasoning subjects were more effective market actors and more inventive producers (Young, 1992).

29. Kant's vision was partially anticipated by the emergence of the social sciences in central and northern Europe (Rudy, 1984). As early as the sixteenth century, universities were training a corps of civil administrators in public law, political economy, and history. The reproduction of this corps would be governed by professors strongly influenced by rationalism and utilitarianism. Thus the first university forays into science were tied to a new regime of surveillance, a relationship that would later be picked up in American social science. But these forays were also relatively scattered and stayed outside of the academic mainstream until the nineteenth century.

30. Kant thus began a tradition of desire for an idea of the university that never was. Consciously drawing a parallel between the market and the university, Kant suggested that the philosophy faculty simply be let alone. But the philosophy faculty could not be let alone where its job was to produce the nation, and in practice German academic independence was sharply circumscribed by state control. As Weber put it eighty years after the founding of the University of Berlin, "the 'freedom of science' exists in Germany within the limits of political and ecclesiastical acceptability" (1908/1974, 17). Thus the autonomy of the university would be constructed as a perennial absence and object of struggle: never complete, always betrayed, always "alleged" (Shils, 1989; Weber, 1908/1974).

31. Excellence, Readings argues, is less a criterion of quality than of administration, a "nonreferential principle that allows the maximum of uninterrupted internal administration" (1996, 120). It might be more precise to say that excellence, like reason, has no reference but itself.

32. As several historians have noted, the liberal arts college was no more empty of modern scientific thought than the modern research university is empty of humanist study. Scientific study was part of the liberal education curriculum even early in the nineteenth century (Guralnick, 1996; Kimball, 1986). What changed with the modern research university was that ideals of rationality, specialization, and investigative research more thoroughly associated with the natural and applied sciences than the liberal arts became the foundational principles of the university.

33. For a twentieth-century articulation of this ideal, see Walter Lippmann's (1922) embrace of political science.

34. These monopolies were never complete, however. For example, David Noble (1977) has delineated some of the limits of the monopoly held by the engineering profession. Nineteenth-century shop-men were highly entrepreneurial and relatively autonomous, while the professional engineer of the early twentieth century was usually an employee in a corporate hierarchy. Standards of professional competency and training, moreover, were strongly influenced by the expressed needs of industrial corporations.

35. As Veysey notes, Thorstein Veblen's famous 1918 attack on "the conduct of the universities by business men" was addressed to both "scientists" and "scholars."

36. For example, long-distance power transmission and petroleum cracking (problems with direct commercial use) became central occupations of electrical engineers and chemical engineers, respectively (Leslie, 1993).

37. *Weinstein v. University of Illinois*, 811 F. 2d 1091, 1092 (1987).

2. An Uncommon Controversy

1. Bourdieu notes that academic capital does not accrue through publication alone. He identifies several other types of capital that successful French academics must accumulate, many of which are necessary to the American academic as well, including a reputation for academic worthiness (earned through service on committees, organizing conferences, and so on) and also authority in the sense of occupying positions, such as that of laboratory director, that allow the control of other positions. These kinds of capital are founded on the investment of time in the reproduction of the professions and academe itself and, by extension, the reproduction of a broader academic market within which scientific capital (founded primarily on research and publication) can operate and accumulate.

2. This account is based on court documents and newspaper coverage of the case.

3. 684 F. Supp. 1248 (1988).

4. 868 F. 2d 1313 (1989).

5. *Childress v. Taylor*, 945 F. 2d 500 (1991). See Jaszi, 1994.

6. Unless otherwise noted, page numbers refer to the judicial opinion as reproduced in the cited case report.

7. I do not intend to suggest here that markets are any more purely instrumental forms of exchange than gift economies are purely social. Personal bonds of trust existed between suppliers, producers, and consumers participating in local markets in the nineteenth century, and these bonds of trust helped discourage excessive profit-making (Blau, 1993). Social ties are still crucial to the operation of some markets, for example the job market, wherein personal links partially constrain where and in what capacity persons sell their labor (Granovetter, 1973). I am interested in contrasting rhetorics of exchange—such as what Blau summarizes as the marketplace rhetoric of "individualism, self-interest, competition, autonomy and efficiency"—and the assumptions on which those rhetorics rest (29).

8. Mario Biagioli has argued that the gift economy of scientific authorship contains its own dualism: credit/responsibility. Credit for new discovery attaches to a scientist's name, but that named scientist is also, theoretically, responsible for the truth of that claim. The practice of granting "courtesy" authorship to individuals only loosely associated with the project undermines this form of responsibility, as cases of scientific fraud in biomedicine have illustrated (Biagioli, 1998; see also LaFollette, 1992).

9. Recent legal history suggests the truth of this perception for many kinds of scientific fraud. For example, Carolyn Phinney, a graduate student who sued her mentor for appropriating her thesis data, has been unable to find work in her field despite having won the case. Phinney also referred to that appropriation as "intellectual rape." *Phinney v. Verbrugge,* 222 Mich. App. 513 (1997); Hilts, 1997, A13.

10. That enforcement network does not seem to be very effective: several victims of plagiarism noted that their plagiarizers were still prominent in their fields.

11. These norms, and their informal enforcement, are not confined to technoscience. Thomas Mallon describes the case of a history professor at Texas Tech, who was exposed as a dedicated plagiarist. Several of his writings, including a book manuscript, were revealed to have been plagiarized. The professor was denied tenure, but little further action was taken. The book was published, with few revisions. Some years later, after leaving the university, the professor was evaluating other people's research as a grant monitor for the National Endowment for the Humanities (NEH). His plagiarism did at last become "public" when reviews of the published book called attention to it (one of the people asked to review the book was the historian whose work he had copied). Despite the scandal and a subsequent accusation of plagiarizing yet another work in his next book, the professor kept his job at the NEH for several years (Mallon, 1989).

12. This practice is not universal. In experimental physics, for example, authors' names are commonly listed in alphabetical order.

13. A notable exception was a student who had changed his dissertation topic and completed most of the research without consulting his nominal advisor—because consultation would have obligated him to list the advisor as an author. That, he felt, would have betrayed others who had assisted in the research. This student felt justified in excluding his advisor from authorship credit but admitted a degree of uneasiness in doing so, noting that "it's basically unheard of."

14. *Edward B. Marks Music Corp. v. Jerry Vogel Music Co.*, 140 F. 2d 266 (1944), at 267.

15. See, e.g., *Feist Publications Inc. v. Rural Telephone Directory*, 111 S. Ct. 1282 (1991) (ownership of collections of information); *International News Service v. Associated Press*, 248 U.S. 215 (1918) (ownership of news).

16. 17 U.S.C. § 107.

17. See, e.g., *Princeton Univ. Press v. Michigan Document Servs.*, 99 F. 3d 1381 (1996).

18. The broadening of scope has accelerated in the past two decades. In 1974 the Ninth Circuit declared that an ad showing a race car with distinctive markings was sufficient to evoke the identity of the race car driver Ray Motschenbacher: 498 F. 2d 821, 9th Cir. The decision in *John W. Carson v. Here's Johnny Portable Toilets*, 698 F. 2d 831 (1983), affirmed Johnny Carson's right of publicity claim in the phrase "Here's Johnny" (used nightly by Ed McMahon to introduce Carson). A few years ago the courts accepted arguments from Bette Midler and Tom Waits that commercials which used "sound-alikes" had infringed on their right of publicity: *Midler v. Ford Motor Co.* 849 F. 2d 460 (1988) cert. denied; *Waits v. Frito-Lay, Inc. and Tracy Locke Inc*, 978 F. 2d 1093 (1992). In the latter case, a Waits song was not even used: Waits's attorneys won simply on the resemblance to Waits's singing style and "gravelly" voice. Opposing counsel's suggestion that the "sound" might owe at least as much to Louis Armstrong was not persuasive (Kent, 1992).

19. Indeed, academic authors might do well to take lessons from Vanna White, for the ability to claim ownership in reputation has enabled some celebrities to gain firmer control over the circulation of their performances. Professors, like stars, might seek to limit uses of their reputations through the assertion of intellectual property rights. To take just one well-publicized example, U.S. academics were recently shocked to discover that their dissertations were being made available for sale on the Internet, through a website called "Contentville.com." University Microfilms Incorporated (UMI), which contracts with many major universities to reproduce Ph.D. dissertations on request, has agreed to allow an Internet "content provider" to market those dissertations on the Web (Blumenstyk, 2000). Graduating students are required to give copies of their works, as well as nonexclusive rights to reproduce those works on request, to UMI. Few imagine that those works will be offered for sale on a website backed by major entertainment corporations such as CBS and NBC. Copyright law gives those who object to this use of their work little legal support, but Judge Cardamone's reasoning may offer an alternative strat-

egy. The association of one's work with a site like "Contentville.com" could be portrayed as unauthorized appropriation of academic reputation.

20. *Lombardo v. Doyle* 396 N.Y.S. 2d 661, 664 (1977); *Hirsch v. S.C. Johnson and Co.,* 280 N.W. 2d 129, 134–135 (1979).

21. *Uhlaender v. Henricksen,* 316 F. Supp. 1277, 1282 (1970).

3. *"University Lectures Are Sui Generis"*

1. In meetings I attended, committee members stressed that they did not intend to suggest that faculty members did *not* own lectures and class materials, but only that ownership of some kinds of works was a complicated issue in need of further discussion and evaluation. Depending on the circumstances of production, multiple entities might have reasonable claims to a given set of materials.

2. There are exceptions. I spoke with a few faculty who were very concerned about the copyright transfer issue, and librarians and other staff at UW stressed that once faculty are "educated" they tend to support copyright retention efforts. The education process is delicate, however, and often takes the form of targeted, one-on-one discussions. Librarians and administrators, said one university librarian, "have to make sure that the raising of the issues that are going to be difficult . . . can't be attributed to us as attacks on the faculty. Because then the faculty will counterattack and that's when all hell breaks loose." That kind of diplomacy takes time, while publishing prices soar.

3. *CCNV v. Reid,* 490 U.S. 730, 751 (1989).

4. *Weinstein v. University of Illinois,* 811 F. 2d 1091 (1987); *Hayes v. Sony Corp,* 847 F. 2d 412 (1988).

5. For example, the U.S. District Court for Colorado found that although a veterinary professor had prepared course materials "on his own time with his own materials," those materials were legally works for hire because their creation was "fairly and reasonably incidental to his employment." *Vanderhurst v. Colorado Mountain College District,* 16 F. Supp. 2d 1297, 1307 (1998).

6. 2 Atk 342, 26 ER 608.

7. 4 Burr 2303, 98 ER 201.

8. 13 Court Sess. Cas. 4th Series 23, 25 (1885).

9. L.R. 12 App. Cas. 326 (H.L.) (1887).

10. Note the characterization here of university corporations as distinctly subject to public supervision, in contrast to the U.S. Supreme Court holding that corporations were legal persons in *Santa Clara v. Southern Pacific,* 118 U.S. 394 (1886), one year earlier.

11. 3 L.J. [Ch.] 209 (1825).

12. The Lords may have been influenced by Blackstone's own statement, in the preface to the 1765 edition of his *Commentaries,* that the publication was intended to put an end to the "clandestine sale" of flawed transcriptions of

his lectures. He would "rather . . . submit his own errors to the world," he wrote, "than to seem answerable to those of other men" (quoted in *Caird*, 330n2).

13. This argument, too, had been specifically rejected by four justices in the Court of Session, one of whom observed that, absent an *explicit* contract, a professor could hardly prevent a student from using his own notes as he pleased.

14. Two cases came closest to directly raising the problem of professorial copyright. The first, *Sherrill v. Grieves*, 57 Wash. L.R. 286 (1929), involved a U.S. military instructor's copyright in course materials prepared for classes at Fort Leavenworth. (Grieves argued, unsuccessfully, that the material was owned by the U.S. government.) The second, *Public Affairs Associates v. Rickover*, 177 F. Supp. 601 (1959), addressed a U.S. admiral's copyright in speeches made in the course of his official duties. An appellate court found that the admiral could claim copyright in the speeches, but because he had distributed them widely prior to registering his claim to copyright, they were effectively dedicated to the public.

15. *Brown v. Molle Co.*, 20 F. Supp. 135 (1937).

16. *Fairfield v. American Photocopy Co.*, 138 Cal. App. 2d 82 (1955). The attorney argued that the advertisement had caused friends and colleagues to suppose he had endorsed the product for money.

17. According to Sheila Slaughter (1980), the decade 1965–1975 saw a distinct rise in firings for political reasons. Activist scholars—including Michael Parenti, George Murray, Angela Davis, and Staughton Lynd—faced termination or were not hired despite substantial, even unanimous, support from faculty and department administrators.

18. The relevant sections of the California Constitution state: "The University of California shall constitute a public trust, to be administered by the existing corporation known as the Regents of the University of California," with full powers of organization and government, subject only to such legislative control as may be necessary to insure the security of its funds and compliance with the terms of the endowments of the university . . . Said corporation shall also have all the powers necessary or convenient for the effective administration of its trust, including the power to sue and be sued, to use a seal, and to delegate to its committees or to the faculty of the university, or to others, such authority or functions as it may deem wise . . . The university shall be entirely independent of all political or sectarian influence and kept free therefrom in the appointment of its regents and in the administration of its affairs": Art IX, § 9(a) (f). See Scully (1987) and Horowitz (1978) for arguments for and against (respectively) allowing greater judicial and legislative interference in the University of California's activities.

19. 38 Cal. App. 2d 698, 699 (1940).

20. *Tolman v. Underhill*, 39 Cal. 2d 708, 712 (1952).

21. *Red Lion Broadcasting Co. v. FCC*, 395 U.S. 367 (1969).

22. On this point Judge Kaus could not resist conceding that some benefits might come from university ownership of lectures. He quoted Lord Fitzgerald's comment in *Caird:* "Again it was urged that the professorial practice of repeating the same lecture session after session, in like manner as a minister repeats his sermon, would be interfered with [if professors were denied copyright in their lectures]. If this was so, it would seem to be a desirable result." L.R. 12 App. Cas. 326, 354 (1887).

23. Though Judge Kaus may not have known of it, such a custom is solidly present in the history of the modern U.S. university. According to the historian Julie Reuben (1996), early twentieth-century university presidents sought to protect freedom of intellectual inquiry while maintaining institutional dignity— both of which were necessary to the reproduction of the "useful uselessness" of the American university—by drawing a line between ideas and conduct. The content of professorial speech, the argument ran, was immune to regulation, but inappropriate manner of expression was not. Politically dangerous speech was characterized as "exaggerated," "immodest," "sensationalist," and/ or "provocative." Framed in this way, the speech could be treated as a sign of incompetence and moral indiscretion. The principle of reason was invoked in support of this argument by the brand-new AAUP. "The liberty of a scholar to set forth his conclusions, be they what they may" the AAUP contended in 1915, "is conditioned by there being conclusions gained by a scholar's method and held in a scholar's spirit . . . they should be set forth with courtesy and temperateness of language" (quoted in Reuben, 1996, 199). With improper expression linked to improper behavior, the liberal public/private binary was reproduced as well. Political speech was treated as "free" so long as it could be linked to an abstracted, autonomous, rational person. Persons who had demonstrated their irrationality, however, were instantly subject to the disciplinary mechanisms of the private sphere, namely termination for moral turpitude.

24. Kaus's phrasing is telling. Whenever a professor works, he argues, are his "working hours": "Since it is not customary for a college to prescribe the hours of the day when a teacher is to prepare for class, it follows that the time when he does so automatically ceases to be leisure time" (739). One of the characteristics of a profession is the ability of its members—rather than employers or clients—to determine how long a given task will take (Larson, 1977).

25. See, e.g., *Lin-Brook Builders Hardware v. Gertler,* 352 F. 2d 298, 300 (1965); *Brattleboro Publ'g Co. v. Winmill Publ'g Corp.,* 369 F. 2d 565, 567–68 (1966) (which expanded the definition of "employer," for purposes of work-for-hire doctrine, to include those who hire independent contractors where the work was created at the "instance and expense" of the hiring party); *Siegel v. National Periodical Publications,* 508 F. 2d 909, 914 (1974) (which defined an employer as one who had been "the motivating factor in producing the work"); *Picture Music, Inc., v. Bourne, Inc.,* 457 F. 2d 1213, 1216 (1972); *Scherr v. Universal Match Corp.,* 417 F. 2d 497, 500 (1969) (which defined an employer as one who had

the rights "to direct and supervise the manner in which the writer performed his work"). See Hughes (1998) for an analysis of these decisions as challenges to the "personhood interests" of the creative worker.

26. *Weinstein v. University of Illinois,* 811 F. 2d 1091, 1094 (1987).

27. See *Motschenbacher v. R. J. Reynolds Tobacco Co.,* 498 F. 2d 821 (1974); *Eastwood v. Superior Court,* 149 Cal. App. 3d 409 (1983); *Lugosi v. Universal Pictures,* 25 Cal. 3d 813 (1979).

28. Note that the common law right of privacy is distinct from the constitutional right of privacy. The latter generally refers to the right of citizens to be protected from some kinds of governmental intrusion. The former covers the right to be free from commercial intrusion and to control the circulation of information about oneself (McCarthy, 1987).

29. *Haelan Laboratories v. Topps Chewing Gum,* 202 F. 2d 866 (1954).

30. This "full circle" would be drawn rather differently in many Western countries. In a civil law country, such as France, Williams's argument would be coded as an assertion of a *droit d'auteur,* also called a moral right. French authors can claim the right to control the disclosure of the work and, once the work has been sold, a right to withdraw or disavow the work; a right of "paternity," or attribution; and a right of integrity, to ensure that the work is neither abridged nor distorted. Under a moral rights regime, Weisser's reproduction of the lectures could have violated Williams's rights of disclosure and integrity. It would not, however, have been seen to violate his *property* rights.

31. Responding to criticisms of the deal, Associate Dean of Operations John Sandbrook said Dean William Pierskalla, who had negotiated the contract, "believes very, very strongly in the Judeo-Christian ethic that our society is largely based on, and that is forgiveness" (Mecoy, 1994).

32. Indeed, the existence of a kind of star system in the academy is manifest in the almost desperate competition for a short list of "hot" scholars. The English professor Stanley Fish, for example, has parlayed his reputation into a pair of Jaguars and a $230,000 salary at the University of Illinois at Chicago. Defending his compensation package, Fish stated that "academics are like any other commodity" (Levy, 1999).

33. In the end, however, the market may have been as effective as the law: by late 2000, several online providers of lecture notes had gone under, and the remaining few faced serious financial woes (Ridge, 2000).

4. Metes and Bounds

1. I interviewed senior and junior researchers, senior and junior technology transfer associates (TTAs), research and conflict-of-interest administrators, and attorneys involved in patent prosecution and associated litigation for Collingwood and UW (including both in-house and outside counsel). Because

the interviews with patent-holding researchers at my initial research sites were biased toward engineers, I used a combination of random and snowball sampling techniques to develop a list of inventors from other disciplines. Eight people in biological, ocean, and earth sciences agreed to be interviewed, for a total inventor sample of twenty. Most of the total sample held at least one patent (several held many more). A few were involved in discussions with the university about pursuing a patent on some aspect of their research, but had not yet completed the formal process. While these researchers work in very different contexts, I found substantial commonalities in their experiences with invention and inventorship. Where necessary, details of inventions have been changed or omitted to protect confidentiality.

Background and historical materials are drawn from policy documents, government documents and secondary sources, one of which deserves special mention. Gary Matkin's *Technology Transfer and the University* (1990) offers an excellent historical survey of technology transfer in U.S. universities, based on an extensive review of policy documents, legislative committee hearings and reports, newspaper and magazine accounts, and interviews with some of the central actors in technology transfer in the 1980s. Equally useful were the minutes of UW's Patent Board, a body that has existed in various guises from 1943. Much expanded today, in both membership and mission, this group is now understood to govern "technology transfer" rather than simply patent policy, and worries about "transfer in" (the use of commercially patented materials in university research) as much as "transfer out."

2. These programs were often portrayed as necessary to prevent the unethical exploitation of research. The Yale University professor Yandell Henderson, writing in *Science* in 1933, put the argument as follows: "It is properly the business of the creative scholar to see to it that, if possible, his ideas serve mankind in his own generation . . . he should [also] see to it that his invention is not misused. He should control it. He should find one or more high-grade concerns to develop it. He should afford them at least such little protection as a patent gives against cut-throat competition [and thereby] so far as possible prevent the sale of inferior or harmful imitations" (quoted in Palmer, 1947, 682).

3. At UW as elsewhere, that ambivalence was reflected in policies that required faculty to report inventions to the university but disallowed university claims to those inventions. In 1931 UW abandoned even this requirement in favor of a voluntary disclosure policy. As late as 1942, UW's Committee on Privilege and Tenure recognized "no distinction between the rights of a professor to his royalties from his patents . . . [and] the income from copyrights." After all, the committee added, "No one has yet had the temerity to suggest that a professor who publishes a 'best seller' should turn his financial gains over to the university" (Response to Recommended Patent Policy, April 1942). At that point, a professor was as likely to publish a bestseller as to patent a really profitable invention—it happened, but not often.

4. The Board of Regents had rejected Steenbock's offer to donate the patents directly to the university, in part because of these same criticisms of university ownership of the products of publicly funded research (Matkin, 1990). Between 1925 and 1988 WARF granted over $150 million to the University of Wisconsin. The bulk of this money was derived from investment of royalties generated by patents on research by Wisconsin scientists and scholars (Erickson and Baldwin, 1988).

5. It should not be supposed that the Carter administration as a whole was opposed to the privatization of government-sponsored research. In October 1979 President Carter advocated new provisions to give small businesses and universities patent ownership in government-sponsored inventions (Eisenberg, 1996).

6. Much of this argument was based on a poor record of commercialization of "public" patent inventions, although it was matched by an almost equally poor record for inventions patented by contractors, including universities. Less than 13 percent of inventions licensed to contractors had made it to market by 1979 (Graham, 1979).

7. 447 U.S. 303 (1980); 450 U.S. 175 (1981). Strictly interpreted, *Diamond v. Diehr* only established that inclusion of a software program in a patent application should not result in an automatic rejection by the Patent Office. The decision nevertheless opened the door to patentability for software, and subsequent decisions would open it further. By the early 1990s the number of software patents issued had skyrocketed (Shulman, 1999).

8. This starting point is admittedly somewhat arbitrary. The TTA may be aware of the invention prior to the submission of the disclosure form. A professor might, for example, have contacted the TTA to describe a piece of research she is about to publish and ask whether it should be disclosed. Depending on the situation, the TTA may seek a quick submission or, alternatively, suggest that the research is not an invention "yet" and ask the professor to get back in touch later.

9. UW Guidelines on University–Industry Relations, Office of the President (1989).

10. An attorney may also get involved at this point, if the TTA decides to contract for a patentability search. If so, an outside counsel may do a search of prior literature and evaluate the proposed invention according to criteria discussed below. This process is expensive, however, and most TTAs prefer to determine patentability themselves.

11. Under U.S. law, once an inventor has "published" her invention (in written or oral form), she has one year to file a patent application on it. This is because our law gives priority to the "first to invent." But most countries have "first to file" systems, and the inventor will lose major foreign patent rights if she publishes the invention before filing a patent application. When an invention has been disclosed just prior to a publication date, TTAs often choose to file a pro-

visional patent application. Provisional applications are inexpensive, skeletal versions of a standard patent application, and they effectively hold priority for the invention. The inventor then has one year to file a full application for a patent or let the matter drop.

12. When a patent application is rejected but new research will strengthen some portion of the claim, the inventor may also file a "continuation in part" that builds on the previous application rather than starting the whole process anew.

13. Several respondents reported intense irritation at the university IP policing mechanisms. An engineering professor with several years of experience in private industry gave a typical response: "I inform them I have this funding . . . and the company would like me to review their technology, not a whole lot of time involved . . . And boy, it took so long to get the situation resolved that the terms of the consulting agreement, the dates, had long expired by the time I was officially told I could go ahead and do this . . . [The review] was clearly related to my line of research. But on the other hand the companies were saying, 'Wait a minute, we're paying this guy as a consultant, and if in the course of his helping us we come up with this terrific idea, we want to be able to take advantage of it' . . . There's got to be a better way to make these things work." Conflict of interest officers and TTAs, for their part, are full of stories of faculty sneaking software out the back door. As one senior administrator put it: "Look at the total number of faculty members in [UW] . . . and the very distinguished nature of the faculty, and the total research support . . . and then look at the total number of inventions coming out of the base . . . They're still producing technology [so] where's it going? They're either publishing it or they are just reporting the activity to their funding sources."

14. Licensing agreements often include "due diligence" requirements such as a timeline for development of the technology into a marketable product, testing, and so on. Failure to meet these requirements can be grounds for breaking the agreement.

15. This observation may hold particularly true for transfer of life science technologies because they are, overall, higher-risk, higher-profit ventures. Biotechnologies are more likely to involve dramatic innovations and require lengthy and costly product development, and patents on them are stronger because they cannot be "reverse-engineered." Physical science and engineering inventions tend to be more incremental, cheaper to develop, with lower profit margins (Young, 1999).

16. My study did not focus on the fourth social world of the licensees, but many aspects of this side of technology transfer have been explored elsewhere. See e.g., Saxenian (1994); Jones (forthcoming).

17. Assuming it is to be considered for a utility patent. Design patents may be obtained for "new, original and ornamental" designs for "an article of manufacture," and asexually reproduced "distinct and new" plant varieties may also be

patented. Utility patents are the most common form of patent, but plant patents have also been lucrative for UW.

18. 35 U.S.C. 101; 35 U.S.C. 102.

19. *New Idea Farm Equipment v. Sperry Corporation,* 916 F. 2d 1561 (1990).

20. In tech transfer parlance, an inventor or TTA might be asked about her "patent position" on an invention. This can be taken as an inquiry about the patentability of an invention, her legal claim to the invention, whether a patent application has been filed on it or, more generally, where the invention stands in the patent-prosecution process. The term emphasizes the performative dimensions of patent claims: one takes a "position" on an invention long before one actually owns it.

21. A patent story may also be recoded as a scientific tale simply by virtue of the inventor's knowledge base. As Norbert Wiener observed, "A piece of work which is patchy and incomplete may seem to be an invention, whereas more thorough study of it might reveal its essence to be a law of nature" (1993, 138). Thus it may not serve an inventor to understand his invention too well, and he may even lose rights in it as a limited invention by being fully aware of a larger law of nature of which it is a part.

22. Utility has historically rested as well on a sense of materiality. Until 1970 the U.S. Patent Office required physical models of all inventions submitted for patents. These models were a popular tourist attraction in Washington, drawing up to 10,000 visitors per month (Shulman, 1999). Again, under patent law the public domain is defined as the space of principles and laws of nature: the realm of the abstract. The utility requirement pulls the idea in question into the realm of the concrete. This conceptual link may explain the difficulty the U.S. courts have had in identifying patentable subject matter in more "abstract" inventions in fields such as computer science (Wagner, 1998). The courts have dealt with this difficulty by withdrawing from the fray. The "tangibility" or "physicality" dimensions of the patentability inquiry, in particular, have been largely abandoned in the past decade, leaving novelty, obviousness, and useful applicability as the primary requirements.

23. *American Cyanamid Co. v. Gentex Corp.,* 641 F. Supp. 88, 91 (1986): "The truth is [invention] cannot be defined in such a manner as to afford any substantial aid in determining whether a particular device involves an exercise of the inventive faculty or not." *McClain v. Ortmayer,* 141 U.S. 419, 427.

24. For example (from U.S. Patent no. 5,832,656): "I claim: 1. A mouse trap comprising: a housing; a cover for closing an opening of the housing and defining a cell there between, said cover having an entrance opening providing access to the cell; a door, disposed in said housing for closing the entrance opening; biasing means for biasing the door toward a closed position wherein the door closes the entrance opening and egress from the cell is prevented; a first post structure integral with and projecting from the door, having a recessed portion; a second post structure integral with the housing; tape means lapped

about the first and second post structures for maintaining the door in an open position wherein the entrance is open and access to the cell is permitted, until the tape is rent; and a bait disposed in the recessed portion of the first post structure so as to be covered by the tape. 2. A mouse trap as set forth in claim 1, wherein said first post structure is shaped in a manner which reduces the amount of surface area in contact with said tape to minimize interface between the tape and the first post structure and resistance to separation of said first post structure from said second post structure when the tape is broken by a creature gnawing through the tape in an attempt to gain free access to said bait."

25. *Towne v. Eisner,* 245 U.S. 418, 425 (1918).

26. *Dolbear v. American Bell Tel. Co.,* 126 U.S. 1 (1887).

27. A recent biotechnology patent case has sharply limited the reach of the attorneys' imagination. In the early years of biotechnology, the law governing its patentability was unclear, and patent examiners' decisions were inconsistent. Attorneys responded by "reaching" as far as possible. In *Regents of the University of California v. Eli Lilly,* 119 F. 3d 1559, the Court of Appeals for the Federal Circuit found the UC's description of rat insulin DNA insufficient to allow a claim to human insulin DNA. In deciding against UC, the CAFC signaled its desire to prevent future overly broad patents. See Plimier (1998).

28. This is particularly true for biotechnologies, in part because the financial investment required to bring them to market can only be justified by the potential profits attendant on a dramatic "breakthrough."

29. Packer and Webster (1996) observed a similar tension among British scientists. Scientists saw patent criteria of novelty and nonobviousness as relatively lax and ill-defined compared with academic standards. Their scientific work was responsive to the expectations of specific communities, while their inventions would be evaluated according to an abstract "universal" community of persons conversant in a wide range of relevant literatures but of "ordinary skill in the art."

30. This point was underscored for one senior researcher by her involvement in patent litigation. She gave the following account of her trial testimony: "At the end of the last day, he had the last word, he was questioning me and he [asked], 'So when you had done this assay, what did you really think?' And I was supposed to say, he was hoping or expecting me to say, 'Eureka!' And what I did say [is] it looked really promising. And I thought he was going to kill me. Because that doesn't mean a thing! Because that doesn't count, it was like admitting failure, to them."

31. 35 U.S.C. § 115.

32. 35 U.S.C § 102(f). This obsession with "true inventorship" is practically unique on the international scene—the Philippines is the only other country in which priority is given to the "first to invent" rather than the "first to file" an application—and it responds to and reinforces the American ideology of invention.

According to the historian Paul Israel, the 1836 Patent Act, which continues to provide the basic structure of patent law, was influenced by the belief that invention was an "intermittent and discontinuous activity undertaken by inspired individuals" (1992, 14). The statute was written as craft models of production were being rapidly replaced by small and large manufacturing businesses and individual entrepreneurs. Such icons as Benjamin Franklin, Robert Fulton, and Eli Whitney provided models for the new generation of entrepreneurial craftsmen and manufacturers. Then as now, the figure of the individual inventor represented as well the "American pioneering spirit" and the doctrine of "first possession" that backed those pioneering claims. The doctrine of first possession, Carol Rose notes, "gives the earth and its creatures over to those who mark them so clearly as to transform them, so that no one will mistake them for unsubdued nature" (1994, 20). In patent discourse, persons who can subdue the laws of nature, marking their metes and bounds so clearly as to transform them, can claim a right of first possession in the "marking" if not the laws themselves. It is not surprising, then, that the Patent Act rewarded "pioneering" individuals—the first and original inventors.

33. *Edison & Foote v. Randall*, 1871 C.D. 80 (1871).

34. *Mergenthaler v. Scudder*, 11 App. D.C. 264; *Hybritech v. Monoclonal Antibodies*, 802 F. 2d, 1367.

35. *Sewall v. Walters*, 21 F. 3d 411 (1994); *Cameron & Everett v. Brick*, 1871 C.D. 89, 90 (1871).

36. An odd remnant of the seventeenth-century image of invention as the work of Providence rather than of an individual does run through patent discourse. In *Cameron & Everett v. Brick*, Patent Commissioner Leggett added that conception is complete "when the 'embryo' has taken definite form and seeks deliverance" (90). It is as if the invention itself, rather than the human inventor, directs the inventive action.

37. *American Cyanamid Co. v. Gentex Corp.*, 641 F. Supp. 88, 91 (1986).

38. 687 F. 2d 450.

39. The irony is that neither of these individuals actually owned the patent they were fighting about: it had already been assigned to the university, under the provisions of the patent assignment every employee signs along with a loyalty oath and an employment contract. The student tried to withhold his signature from the patent application when his advisor was listed as an inventor over his protests. He was advised that the university did not need his signature to go ahead, only a copy of the patent assignment. They did need his signature, however, to release any royalties to him. He signed.

5. Telling Tales Out of School

1. It is possible, however, to be issued a temporary visa. At Collingwood, members of the general public are excluded from using many of the electronic data-

bases. However, according to a senior librarian, librarians have chosen to treat people who come to the library as "students." Thus members of the general public willing to visit the university's physical space can claim a status unavailable to those who seek to connect with the institution's cyberspace.

2. Uniform Trade Secrets Act, § 1(4).

3. I use the term "norm" here to refer to a standard which may or may not be attained but is a central value of scientific life (Merton, 1942/1973; Biagioli, 1998; Shapin, 1996; Rothblatt, 1985).

4. For example, the occupational health researcher Dr. David Kern of Brown University was fired when he reported his discovery of a new and deadly lung disease in a nylon-flocking plant to the U.S. Centers for Disease Control and spoke about it at a conference. The plant owners had tried to use a trade secrecy agreement with Brown to prevent release of the findings. Kern's employer could not prevent him from speaking about the disease, but it could, and did, let his contract lapse (Hotz, 1999).

5. Agouron was not completely insensitive to its reputation; throughout the trial it expressed the fear that Pelletier would damage its standing with the scientific community.

6. This account is derived from court documents filed by plaintiffs and defendants and personal communications from Pelletier and Pelletier's attorneys. Agouron representatives and attorneys declined to be interviewed.

7. The relevant section of Regulation 4 states: "All such research shall be conducted so as to be as generally useful as possible. To this end, the right of publication is reserved by the University. The University may itself publish the material or may authorize, in any specific case, a member or members of the faculty to publish it through some recognized scientific or professional medium of publication. A report detailing the essential data and presenting the final results must be filed with the University. Notebooks and other original records of the research are the property of the University."

8. *Ishimatsu v. Regents of the University of California,* 266 Cal. App. 2d 854 (1968); *Regents of the University of California v. Superior Court of Los Angeles,* 3 Cal. 3d 529 (1970).

9. Letter from Jack Peltason to Elizabeth Ziegler, June 1, 1995.

10. Super. Ct. No. 677772, Slip op., 9 (Cal. Ct. App., 4th Dist., Div. 1, Feb. 14, 1997).

11. 650 F. 2d 1365, 1372.

12. Parallel reasoning is present in patent law, as Pelletier herself noted in her explanation of the inapplicability of the UC patent policy to the question of ownership. Even if Regulation 4 were ignored, Agouron argued, UC's requirement of assignment of rights in all patentable and potentially patentable work meant UC still owned the work. Trying to have it both ways, Pelletier responded by emphasizing the factuality of the work for patent purposes—"No one has sug-

gested that the research data . . . are or ever have been (or even could be transmogrified into) an invention"—even as she emphasized that the data were the product of her creative inspiration (Appellant's Opening Brief, 17).

13. See, e.g., Latour and Woolgar's (1979) discussion of the social construction of Thyroid Release Factor (TRF) as fact. The authors note that a 1962 representation of TRF, although later proved correct, was challenged and rejected because the researcher could not prove his claim. Because the 1962 work was based primarily on deduction and could not be replicated, it "became regarded as an artifact" (120). Seven years later two other researchers, following a new definition of proof, offered the same conclusion. At that point, TRF began to take on the status of a fact, and that status was secured when samples of TRF began to be circulated and used by researchers less interested in TRF as such than in its usefulness for other research areas. The point, as Latour and Woolgar stress, is not to deny the solidity of scientific fact but to demonstrate that data streams are produced in and through human agency and that production involves at least a minimal spark of creativity.

14. 499 U.S. 340.

15. According to Pelletier, Sawaya was named as first author on the final publication because, once the Kraut lab learned of Agouron's research, Sawaya was assigned the task of completing a paper Pelletier had started. Pelletier felt it was her duty, as a mentor, not to claim first authorship even though she had led the research upon which the paper was based (personal communication, Oct. 25, 2000).

16. See ycmi.med.yale.edu/senselab/ordb.

17. In a survey conducted by Stephen J. Ceci (1988), 87 percent of scientists questioned reported that they routinely share prepublished data with colleagues, but 59 percent said their colleagues were reluctant to reciprocate.

18. The court's discussion of the trade secret and unjust enrichment claims reiterated and approved the reasoning behind its earlier ruling (that Pelletier had an ownership interest in the data) and noted that the jury had sufficient evidence to find that Agouron had violated that interest.

19. The breach-of-confidential-relationship claim against McTigue was also thrown out for procedural reasons.

20. Super. Ct. No. 677772, Slip op., 9 (Cal. Ct. App., 4th Dist., Div. 1, Sept. 11, 2000).

21. California Civil Code § 3426.3 (codifying the Uniform Trade Secrets Act).

22. Pelletier was prevented from claiming much in the way of unjust enrichment damages because Agouron had actually lost money on the research. She had hoped to show that Agouron's publication had produced economic benefit for the company, in the form of positive publicity, but the judge refused to permit the argument (personal communication from Huguette Pelletier, Daniel MacLeod, and Andria Catalano, Oct. 25, 2000).

23. *Keyishian v. Board of Regents,* 385 U.S. 589, 603.
24. *Regents of the University of California v. Bakke,* 438 U.S. 265, 312 (1978). See also Byrne, 1989.
25. The courts themselves acknowledge this difficulty. In 1985 the Supreme Court observed that "academic freedom thrives not only on the independent and uninhibited exchange of ideas among teachers and students, but also, and somewhat inconsistently, on autonomous decision-making by the academy itself." *Regents of the University of Michigan v. Ewing,* 474 U.S. 214, 226n12 (citations omitted).
26. Discussing technology transfer in his discipline, one senior researcher put the issue rather starkly: "In the community it [has] worked in two ways: either professors start a small business on the side, which is a very traditional way, and another is to align yourself with a group who want to market the idea. Never done that, again because when you align yourself with one group you are enemies with everyone else."

Adams, J., and Averly, G. 1986. The patent specification: the role of Liardet v. Johnson. *Journal of Legal History* 7, 156–177.

Altbach, P. 1980. The crisis of the professorate. In P. Altbach and S. Slaughter, eds., *The academic profession.* Philadelphia: Annals of the American Academy of Political and Social Science.

American Association of University Professors (AAUP). 1999. Statement on copyright. Retrieved June 2, 1999, from www.aaup.org/spccopyr.htm.

——— 1915. General Report of the Committee on Academic Freedom and Academic Tenure. *AAUP Bulletin* 17.

American Intellectual Property Law Association. 1999. *Report of Economic Survey 1999.* Arlington, VA: AIPLA.

Arnold, M. 1869/1993. *Culture and anarchy and other writings.* Ed. S. Collins. Cambridge: Cambridge University Press.

Arendt, H. 1958. *The human condition.* Chicago: University of Chicago Press.

Aronowitz, S., Martinson, B., and Menser, M., eds. 1996. *Technoscience and cyberculture.* New York: Routledge.

Atkinson, R. C. 1996a. Universities and the knowledge-based economy. California State Fiscal Retreat, Berkeley, Feb. 3. Retrieved May 10, 1998, from www.ucop/ucophome/pres/comments/senate/html.

——— 1996b. The California solution. California Coalition for Science and Technology Summit, Sacramento, May 26. Retrieved May 10, 1998, from www.ucop/ucophome/pres/comments/science/html.

Bachrach, S., Berry, R. B., Blume, M., von Foerster, T., Fowler, A., Ginsparg, P., Heller, S., Kestner, N., Odlysko, A., Okerson, A., Wigington, R., and Moffat, A. 1998. Who should own scientific papers? *Science* 281 (Sept. 4), 1459–61.

Barber, B. 1997. The market as censor: Freedom of expression in a world of consumer totalism. *Arizona State Law Journal* 29, 501–517.

Barzun, J. 1968. *The American university.* New York: Harper and Row.

Bettig, R. 1996. *Copyrighting culture: The political economy of intellectual property.* New York: Westview.

——— 1992. Critical perspectives on the history and philosophy of copyright. *Critical Studies in Mass Communication* 9, 131–155.

Biagioli, M. 1998. The instability of authorship: Credit and responsibility in contemporary biomedicine. *FASEB Journal* 12, 3–16.

Blau, J. 1993. *Social contracts and economic markets.* New York: Plenum.

Bloom, A. 1987. *The closing of the American mind.* New York: Simon and Schuster.

Blumenstyk, G. 2000. Sale of theses on Contentville.com raises hackles in U.S. and Canada. *Chronicle of Higher Education* (Sept. 15), A37.

—— 1999. Putting class notes on the Web: Are companies stealing lectures? *Chronicle of Higher Education* (Oct. 1), A31.

—— 1998a. Conflict of interest fears rise as universities chase industry support. *Chronicle of Higher Education* (May 22), A41.

—— 1998b. Royalties on inventions bring $336 million to top research universities. *Chronicle of Higher Education* (Feb. 27), A44.

Born, G. 1996. Immateriality and sociality: The dynamics of intellectual property in a computer software research culture. *Social Anthropology* 4, no. 2, 101–116.

Bourdieu, P. 1988. *Homo academicus.* Trans. P. Collier. London: Polity.

Bowker, G., and Star, S. 1999. *Sorting things out: Classification and its consequences.* Cambridge, MA: MIT Press.

Boyle, J. 1997. A politics of intellectual property: Environmentalism for the net. In *Duke Law Journal* 47, 87–116.

—— 1996. *Shamans, software, and spleens: Law and the construction of the information society.* Cambridge, MA: Harvard University Press.

Brown, W. 1995. *States of injury: Studies in power and freedom in late modernity.* Princeton: Princeton University Press.

Burchfiel, K. 1989. Revising the "original" patent clause: Pseudohistory in constitutional construction. *Harvard Journal of Law and Technology* 2, no. 2, 155–218.

Burk, D. 1997. Ownership of electronic course materials in higher education. *Cause/Effect* 20, no. 3, 13–18.

—— 1995. Research misconduct: Deviance, due process and the disestablishment of science. *George Mason Law Review* 3, 305–355.

—— 1994. Misappropriation of trade secrets in biotechnology licensing. *Albany Law Journal of Science and Technology* 4, 121.

Bush, V. 1945/1960. Science: The endless frontier; a report to the President on a program for postwar academic research. Washington: National Science Foundation.

Butler, J. 1991. Contingent foundations: Feminism and the question of "postmodernism." In J. Butler and J. Scott, eds., *Feminists theorize the political.* New York: Routledge.

Byrne, J. P. 1989. Academic freedom: A "special concern of the First Amendment." *Yale Law Journal* 99, 251–340.

Cambrosio, A., and Keating, P. 1995. *Exquisite specificity: The monoclonal antibody revolution.* New York: Oxford University Press.

Carlson, W. B. 1988/1991. Academic entrepreneurship. In Reynolds, ed., 1991.

Castells, M. 1998. *End of millennium.* Malden, MA: Blackwell.

—— 1997. *The power of identity.* Malden, MA: Blackwell.

————— 1996. *The rise of the network society.* Malden, MA: Blackwell.

Ceci, S. 1988. Scientists' attitudes to data sharing. *Science, Technology, and Human Values* 13, nos. 1–2, 45–52.

Chew, P. 1992. Faculty-generated inventions: Who owns the golden egg? *Wisconsin Law Review* 259–312.

Chodorow, S. 1997. The faculty, the university and intellectual property. Faxon Institute's Second Annual Colloquium on Scholarly Communication, New Orleans, Jan. 7, 1997. *Journal of Electronic Publishing* 3, no. 3. Downloaded Sept. 1998 from www.press.umich.edu/jep/03–03/chodorow.html

Chronicle of Higher Education. 1980. Patent bill should pass, supporters say. (March 24), A14.

Cimons, M., and Jacobs, P. 1999. Biotech battlefield: Profits vs. public. *Los Angeles Times* (Feb. 21), A1.

Clark, B., ed. 1987. *The academic profession: National, disciplinary, and institutional settings.* Berkeley: University of California Press.

Cleveland, H. 1989. How can "intellectual property" be protected? *Change* (May/June), 10–11.

Collins, T., and Tillman, S. 1988. Global technology diffusion and the American research university. In J. T. Kenny, ed., *Research administration and technology transfer.* San Francisco: Jossey Bass.

Commission on Life Sciences. 1999. *Finding the path: Issues of access to research resources.* Washington: National Academy Press.

Cook, W. 1996. Deputizing the ISPs. *Intellectual Property Magazine* (Spring). Retrieved May 1997 from www.ipmag.com/acook.html.

Coombe, R. 1998. *The cultural life of intellectual properties: Authorship, appropriation, and the law.* Durham: Duke University Press.

————— 1996. Embodied trademarks: Mimesis and alterity on American commercial frontiers. *Cultural Anthropology* 11, no. 2, 202–224.

————— 1994. Author/izing the celebrity: Publicity rights, postmodern politics, and unauthorized genders. In Woodmansee and Jaszi, eds., 1994.

————— 1993. Tactics of appropriation and the politics of recognition in late modern democracies. *Political Theory* 21, no. 3, 411–433.

Cooper Dreyfuss, R. 1987. The creative employee and the Copyright Act of 1976. *University of Chicago Law Review* 54, 590–647.

Crews, K. 1993. *Copyright, fair use, and the challenge for universities: Promoting the progress of higher education.* Chicago: University of Chicago Press.

Davis, Natalie. 1983. *The return of Martin Guerre.* Cambridge, MA: Harvard University Press.

De Certeau, M. 1986. *History: Science and fiction. Heterologies: Discourse on the other.* Trans. B. Massumi. Minneapolis: University of Minnesota Press.

Declet, R. 1997. Protecting American intellectual property in China: The persistent problem of software piracy. *New York International Law Review* 10, 57–85.

Deleuze, G., and Guattari, F. 1987. *A thousand plateaus: Capitalism and schizophrenia,* vol 2. Minneapolis: University of Minnesota Press.

Delong, S. 1997. The shroud of lecturing. *First Monday.* Retrieved June 2, 1999, from www.firstmonday.org/issues/issue2_5/delong/index.html.

Derrida, J. 1999. The future of the profession or, the unconditional university. Presidential Lectures and Symposia in the Humanities and the Arts, Stanford University, Palo Alto, April 15, 1999.

——— 1992. Mochlos; or, the conflict of the faculties. In Rand, ed., 1992.

——— 1983. The principle of reason: The university in the eyes of its pupils. *Diacritics* (Fall), 3–20.

——— 1980. Mochlos, or the conflict of the faculties. Paper delivered at the Centenary of the Columbia University Graduate School, New York, April 17.

DuBoff, L. 1984. An academic's copyright: Publish and perish. *Journal of the Copyright Society* 32, 17–37.

Dutton, H. I. 1984. *The patent system and inventive activity during the industrial revolution, 1750–1852.* Manchester: Manchester University Press.

Dworkin, R. 1996. We need a new interpretation of academic freedom. In Menand, ed., 1996.

Dyer, R. 1986. *Heavenly bodies: Film stars and society.* New York: St. Martin's.

Eagleton, T. 1983. *Literary theory: An introduction.* Minneapolis: University of Minnesota Press.

Edelman, B. 1979. *Ownership of the image: Elements for a Marxist theory of law.* London: Routledge.

Eisenberg, R. 1996. Public research and private development: Patents and technology transfer in government-sponsored research. *Virginia Law Review* 82, 1663–1727.

——— 1987. Proprietary rights and the norms of science in biotechnology research. *Yale Law Journal* 97, 177–231.

Erickson, G., and Baldwin, D. 1988. The new frontier of technology transfer. In J. T. Kenny, ed., *Research administration and technology transfer.* San Francisco: Jossey Bass.

Etzkowitz, H. 1997. The entrepreneurial university and the emergence of democratic corporatism. In Etzkowitz and Leydesdorff, eds., 1997.

Etzkowitz, H., and Leydesdorff, L. 1997. Introduction: Universities in the global knowledge economy. In Etzkowitz and Leydesdorff, eds., 1997.

Etzkowitz, H., and Leydesdorff, L., eds. 1997. *Universities and the global knowledge economy: A triple helix of university-industry-government relations.* London: Pinter.

Fasse, W. F. 1992. The muddy metaphysics of joint inventorship: Cleaning up after the 1984 amendments to 35 U.S.C. § 116. *Harvard Journal of Law and Technology* 5, 153–208.

Faulkner, W., and Senker, J. 1995. *Knowledge frontiers: Public sector research and industrial innovation in biotechnology, engineering ceramics, and parallel computing.* Oxford: Clarendon Press.

Fish, S. 1991. The law wishes to have a formal existence. In A. Sarat and T. R. Kearns, eds., *The fate of law*. Ann Arbor: University of Michigan Press.

Fishbein, E. 1991. Ownership of research data. *Academic Medicine* 66, no. 3, 129–133.

Foucault, M. 1980. *Power/knowledge: Selected interviews and other writings*. Ed. Colin Gordon. New York: Pantheon.

——— 1979. *Discipline and punish: The birth of the prison*. Trans. A. Sheridan. New York: Random House.

——— 1978/1990. *The history of sexuality: An introduction*. New York: Vintage.

——— 1977. What is an author? In *Language, counter-memory, and practice*. Trans. D. Bouchard and S. Simon. Ithaca: Cornell University Press.

Fox Keller, E. 1996. Science and its critics. In Menand, ed., 1996.

——— 1985. *Reflections on gender and science*. New Haven: Yale University Press.

Frammolino, R. 1994. Scientific fraud suit to be settled for $1.6 million. *Los Angeles Times* (July 24), A23.

Frug, G. 1980. The city as a legal concept. *Journal of Legal Studies* 95, 1057–1156.

Fujimura, J. 1992. Crafting science: Standardized packages, boundary objects and translation. In A. Pickering, ed., *Science as practice and culture*. Chicago: University of Chicago Press.

Gabel, P., and Feinman, J. 1982. Contract law as ideology. In D. Kairys, ed., *The politics of law: A progressive critique*. New York: Pantheon.

Gaines, J. 1995. Reincarnation as the ring on Liz Taylor's finger: Andy Warhol and the right of publicity. In A. Sarat and T. Kearns, eds., *Identities, politics and rights*. Ann Arbor: University of Michigan Press.

——— 1993. Bette Midler and the piracy of identity. In S. Frith, ed., *Music and copyright*. Edinburgh: Edinburgh University Press.

——— 1991. *Contested culture: The image, the voice and the law*. Chapel Hill: University of North Carolina Press.

Garascia, C. 1996. Evidence of conception in U.S. patent interference practice: Proving who is the first and true inventor. *University of Detroit Mercy Law Review* 73, 717–751.

Gibbons, M., Limoges, C., Nowotny, H., Schwartzman, S., and Trow, M. 1994. *The new production of knowledge: Dynamics of science and research in contemporary societies*. London: Sage.

Gibbons, M., and Wittrock, B., eds. 1985. *Science as a commodity: Threats to the open community of scholars*. Essex: Longman Group.

Gladwell, M. 1991. Nobel winner quits as university chief. *Washington Post* (Dec. 3), A4.

Gleick, J. 1993. *Genius: The life and science of Richard Feynman*. New York: Vintage.

Goldstein, P. 1992a. *Copyright, patent, trademark and related state doctrines*. Westbury, NY: Foundation Press.

——— 1992b. Copyright. *Law and Contemporary Problems* 55, no. 2, 79–92.

Gordon, R. 1989. Critical legal histories. In A. Hutchinson, ed., *Critical legal studies.* Totowa, NJ: Rowman and Littlefield.

Gordon, W. 1993. A property right in self-expression: Equality and individualism in the natural law of intellectual property. *Yale Law Journal* 102, 1533–1609.

Gould, S. 1968. Testimony before New York Joint Legislative Committee on Higher Education. *Chronicle of Higher Education* (March 11), A4.

Graham, B. 1979. Patent bill seeks shift to bolster innovation. *Washington Post* (April 8).

Granovetter, M. 1973. The strength of weak ties. *American Journal of Sociology* 78, no. 6, 1360–80.

Gross, A. 1996. *The rhetoric of science.* Cambridge, MA: Harvard University Press.

Gross, P., and Levitt, N. 1994. *Higher superstition: The academic left and its quarrels with science.* Baltimore: Johns Hopkins University Press.

Grossman, R. 1997. In academe, the serfs are toppling the lords. *Chicago Tribune* (Aug. 24), C1.

Guernsey, L., and Young, J. 1998. Who owns on-line courses? *Chronicle of Higher Education* (June 5), A21-A23.

Guralnick, S. 1991. Sources of misconception of the role of science in the nineteenth century American college. In Reynolds, ed., 1991.

Hagstrom, W. O. 1965. *The scientific community.* New York: Basic Books.

Harmon, A. 1993. Class, please welcome Mr. Milken. *Los Angeles Times* (Oct. 3), A1.

Haskell, T. 1996. Justifying the rights of academic freedom in an era of "power/ knowledge." In Menand, ed., 1996.

Hearings before the Senate Committee on the Judiciary on S. 414, 96th Cong., May 16, 1979; June 6, 1979.

Helly, J., Case, T., Davis, F., Levin, S., and Michener, W. 1995. *The state of computational ecology.* San Diego: San Diego Supercomputer Center.

Henderson, K. 1991. On line and on paper: Visual representations, visual culture, and computer-graphics in design engineering. Doctoral diss., University of California, San Diego.

Hilgartner, S. 1998. Data access policy in genome research. In A. Thackeray, ed., *Private science: Biotechnology and the rise of the molecular sciences.* Philadelphia: University of Pennsylvania Press.

Hilgartner, S., and Brandt-Rauf, S. 1994. Data access, ownership and control: Toward empirical studies of access practices. *Knowledge: Creation, diffusion, utilization* 15, no. 4, 355–372.

Hilts, P. 1999. Little-noticed amendment stirs hornet's nest in scientific community. *San Francisco Chronicle* (July 31), B1.

———— 1997. University forced to pay $1.6 million to researcher. *New York Times* (Aug. 10), A13.

———— 1993a. Science and law clash over fraud case. *New York Times* (Nov. 8), B10.

—— 1993b. Lab limits plan to give company its discoveries. *New York Times* (July 13), A8.

—— 1993c. U.S. seeks to protect fruits of tax-supported research. *New York Times* (June 17), A12.

Hofstadter, R., and Metzger, W. P. 1955. *The development of the academic profession in the United States.* New York: Columbia University Press.

Horowitz, H. 1978. The autonomy of the University of California. *UCLA Law Review* 25, 23–45.

Horwitz, M. J. 1992. *The transformation of American law, 1870–1960: The crisis of legal orthodoxy.* New York: Oxford University Press.

Hotz, R. L. 1999. Secrecy is often the price of medical research funding; Science: Corporate donors and the academic community increasingly are at odds over release of findings. *Los Angeles Times* (May 18), A1.

Houk, V., and Thacker, S. 1991. The responsibilities of scientific publishing. *Scholarly Publishing* (Oct.), 51–55.

Hughes, J. 1998. The personality interest of authors and inventors in intellectual property. *Cardozo Arts and Entertainment Law Journal* 16, 81–181.

Hull, D. 1985. Openness and secrecy in science: Their origins and limitations. *Science, Technology, and Human Values* 10, no. 2, 4–13.

Hyde, L. 1983. *The gift: Imagination and the erotic life of property.* New York: Vintage.

Israel, P. 1992. *From machine shop to industrial laboratory: Telegraphy and the changing context of American invention, 1830–1920.* Baltimore: Johns Hopkins University Press.

Jasanoff, S. 1995. *Science at the bar: Law, science and technology in America.* Cambridge, MA: Harvard University Press.

Jaszi, P. 1994. On the author effect: Contemporary copyright and collective creativity. In Woodmansee and Jaszi, eds., 1994.

Jencks, C., and Reisman, D. 1968. *The academic revolution.* Garden City, NY: Doubleday.

Jones, M. Forthcoming. The begettings of Hybritech: A study in scientific entrepreneurship. Doctoral diss., University of California, San Diego.

Kairys, D. 1982. Legal reasoning. In D. Kairys, ed., *The politics of law: A progressive critique.* New York: Pantheon.

Kamuf, P. 1992. The university founders: A complete revolution. In Rand, ed., 1992.

Kant, I. 1979. *The conflict of the faculties.* Trans. Mary J. Gregor. New York: Abaris Books.

Kaplan, B. 1967. *An unhurried view of copyright.* New York: Columbia University Press.

Kaplan, C. 1999. Universities warn sites posting class notes. *New York Times on the Web* (Oct. 22). Downloaded Oct. 23, 1999, from www.nytimes.com.

Kennedy, D. 1997. *Academic duty.* Cambridge, MA: Harvard University Press.

Kenrick, W. 1774. An address to the artists and manufacturers of Great Britain.

Kent, F. 1992. California court expands celebrities' rights. *New York Law Journal* (Oct. 30), 3.

Kerr, C. 1963/1995. *The uses of the university.* Cambridge, MA: Harvard University Press.

Kevles, D. 1977/1991. The NSF and the debate over post-war research policy: 1942–1945. In Reynolds, ed., 1991.

Kimball, B. 1986. *Orators and philosophers: A history of the idea of liberal education.* New York: Teachers College, Columbia University.

Kreeger, D. 1947. The control of patent rights resulting from federal research. *Law and Contemporary Problems* 12, no. 4, 714–745.

Kulkarni, S. R. 1995. All professors create equally: Why faculty should have complete control over the intellectual property rights in their creations. *Hastings Law Journal* 47, 221–266.

Ladd, E., and Lipset, S. 1973. *Professors, unions and American higher education.* Berkeley: Carnegie Foundation for the Advancement of Teaching.

LaFollette, M. 1992. *Stealing into print: Fraud, plagiarism and misconduct in scientific publishing.* Berkeley: University of California Press.

Landis, J. 1970. *The mechanics of patent claim drafting.* New York: Practising Law Institute.

Lange, D. 1981. Recognizing the public domain. *Law and Contemporary Problems* 44, no. 4, 147–178.

Larson, M. 1977. *The rise of professionalism: A sociological analysis.* Berkeley: University of California Press.

Latour, B. 1993. *We have never been modern.* Trans. Catherine Porter. Cambridge, MA: Harvard University Press.

——— 1987. *Science in action: How to follow scientists and engineers through society.* Cambridge, MA: Harvard University Press.

Latour, B., and Woolgar, S. 1979. *Laboratory life: The social construction of scientific facts.* Beverly Hills: Sage.

Leatherman, C. 1998. Shared governance under siege: Is it time to revive it or get rid of it? *Chronicle of Higher Education* (Jan. 30), A8.

LeFevre, K. 1987. *Invention as a social act.* Carbondale: Southern Illinois University Press.

Lemley, M. 1997. Romantic authorship and the rhetoric of property. *Texas Law Review* 75, no. 4, 873–906.

Leslie, S. 1993. *The cold war and American science: The military-industrial-academic complex at MIT and Stanford.* New York: Columbia University Press.

Levy, C. 1999. Free agency goes to college and profs cash in. *Wall Street Journal* (Feb 19), W13(E).

Leydesdorff, L., and Etzkowitz, H. 1997. A triple helix of university-industry-government relations. In Etzkowitz and Leydesdorff, eds., 1997.

Lippmann, W. 1922. *Public opinion.* New York: Harcourt, Brace.

Lipset, S., and Wolin, S., eds. 1965. *The Berkeley student revolt: Facts and interpretations.* Garden City, NY: Anchor.

Litman, J. 1992. Copyright and information policy. *Law and Contemporary Problems* 55, 185–210.

—— 1991. Copyright as myth. *University of Pittsburgh Law Review* 53, 235–249.

—— 1990. The public domain. *Emory Law Journal* 39, no. 4, 965–1023.

Locke, J. 1694/1952. *The second treatise of government.* Ed. Thomas Peardon. New York: Bobbs-Merrill.

LoLordo, A. 2000. Colleges take note of paid notetakers. *Baltimore Sun* (May 17), 1A.

Long, P. 1991. Invention, authorship, "intellectual property" and the origin of patents: Notes towards a conceptual history. *Technology and Culture* 32, 847–890.

Lowen, R. 1996. *Creating the cold war university: The transformation of Stanford.* Berkeley: University of California Press.

Lunsford, A., and Ede, L. 1994. Collaborative authorship and the teaching of writing. In Woodmansee and Jaszi, eds., 1994.

Lury, C. 1993. *Cultural rights: Technology, legality and personality.* London: Routledge.

MacLeod, C. 1988. *Inventing the industrial revolution: The English patent system, 1660–1800.* Cambridge: Cambridge University Press.

Madow, M. 1993. Private ownership of public image: Popular culture and publicity rights. *California Law Review* 81, no. 1, 125–240.

Mallon, T. 1989. *Stolen words: Forays into the origins and ravages of plagiarism.* New York: Ticknor and Fields.

Martin, E. 1996. Citadels, rhizomes and string figures. In Aronowitz et al., eds., 1996.

Marx, K. 1843/1972. On the Jewish question. In *The Marx-Engels Reader,* ed. R. C. Tucker. New York: Norton.

Matkin, G. 1990. *Technology transfer and the university.* New York: Macmillan.

Mauss, M. 1985. A category of the human mind: The notion of person; the notion of self. In M. Carrithers, S. Collins, and S. Lukes, eds., *The category of the person: Anthropology, philosophy, history.* Cambridge: Cambridge University Press.

—— 1967. *The gift: Forms and functions of exchange in archaic societies.* Trans. I. Cunnison. New York: Norton.

McCarthy, J. 1987. *The rights of publicity and privacy.* Deerfield, IL: Clark, Boardman, Callaghan.

McClure, K. 1996. *Judging rights: Lockean politics and the limits of consent.* Ithaca: Cornell University Press.

McMullin, E. 1985. Openness and secrecy in science: Some notes on early history. *Science, Technology, and Human Values* 10, no. 2, 14–23.

Mecoy, L. 1994. UCLA deal with Milken source of satire, outrage. *Sacramento Bee* (March 14), A1.

Menand, L. 1996. The limits of academic freedom. In Menand, ed., 1996.

————, ed. 1996. *The future of academic freedom.* Chicago: University of Chicago Press.

Mensch, E. 1989. Contract law as ideology. In A. Hutchinson, ed., *Critical legal studies.* Totowa, NJ: Rowman and Littlefield.

Menser, M., and Aronowitz, S. 1996. On cultural studies, science and technology. In Aronowitz et al., eds., 1996.

Merry, S. E. 1990. *Getting justice and getting even: Legal consciousness among working-class Americans.* Chicago: University of Chicago Press.

Merton, R. 1957/1973. Priorities in scientific discovery. In Merton, *The sociology of science: Theoretical and empirical investigations.* Chicago: University of Chicago Press.

———— 1942/1973. The narrative structure of science. In Merton, *The sociology of science.*

Metzger, W. P. 1987. The academic profession in the United States. In B. Clark, ed., *The academic profession: National, disciplinary, and institutional settings.* Berkeley: University of California Press.

Meyer, M. 1998. To promote the progress of science and the useful arts: The protection of and rights in scientific research. *IDEA: The Journal of Law and Technology* 39, 1–34.

Miller, A., and Davis, M. 2000. *Intellectual property: Patents, trademarks, and copyright in a nutshell.* 3rd ed. St. Paul: West Group.

Mishkin, B. 1995. Urgently needed: Policies on access to data by erstwhile collaborators. *Science* 270, no. 5238 (Nov. 10), 927.

Mukerji, C. 1989. *A fragile power: Scientists and the state.* Princeton: Princeton University Press.

Navarro, M. 1996. Dispute turns a researcher into an inmate. *New York Times* (June 9), A22.

Nelkin, D. 1984. *Science as intellectual property: Who controls research?* New York: Macmillan.

Nerona, G. 2000. The battle against software piracy: Software copyright protection in the Philippines. *Pacific Rim Law and Policy Journal* 9, 651–689.

Nimmer, M. 1977. The subject matter of copyright under the Act of 1976. *UCLA Law Review* 24, 978–1024.

———— 1954. The right of publicity. *Law and Contemporary Problems* 19, no. 2, 203–223.

Noble, D. 1998. Digital diploma mills, pt. 3: The bloom is off the rose. Retrieved March 2, 2001, from www.vpaa.uillinois.edu/tid/resources/noble.html.

———— 1997. Digital diploma mills: The automation of higher education. *First Monday.* Retrieved June 2, 1999, from www.firstmonday.org/issues/issue3_1/noble/index.html.

———— 1977. *America by design: Science, technology, and the rise of corporate capitalism.* New York: Knopf.

Norris, D., and Dolence, M. 1995. *Transforming higher education: A vision for learning in the 21st century*. Ann Arbor: Society for College and University Planning.

Okerson, A. 1996. University libraries and scholarly communication. In Peek and Newby, eds., 1996.

O'Neil, R. 1974. Law and higher education in California. In N. Smelser and G. Almond, eds., *Public higher education in California*. Berkeley: University of California Press.

O'Shaughnessy, B. 1996. The false inventive genus. *Fordham Intellectual Property, Media, and Entertainment Law Journal* 7, 147–229.

Packer, K., and Webster, A. 1996. Patenting culture: Reinventing the scientific wheel of credibility. *Science, Technology, and Human Values* 21, no. 4, 427–453.

Palmer, A. 1947. Patents and university research. *Law and Contemporary Problems* 12, no. 4, 680–694.

Patel, H. 2000. State bill will prohibit sale of lecture notes on Web. *Daily Bruin Online* (Sept. 29). www.dailybruin.ucla.edu/db/articles.asp?ID?1236.

Pateman, C. 1989. *The disorder of women: Democracy, feminism and political theory*. Stanford: Stanford University Press.

Patterson, L. 1968. *Copyright in historical perspective*. Nashville: Vanderbilt University Press.

Peek, R., and Newby, G., eds. 1996. *Scholarly publishing: The electronic frontier*. Cambridge, MA: MIT Press.

Perkins, J. 1967. The university and due process. Lecture at New England Association of Colleges and Secondary Schools annual meeting, Dec. *Chronicle of Higher Education* (Dec. 21), A5.

Pew Higher Education Roundtable. 1998. To publish and perish. *Policy Perspectives*, special issue (March).

Phillipson, N. 1974. Culture and society in the 18th century province: The case of Edinburgh and the Scottish Enlightenment. In Stone, ed., 1974.

Plimier, M. 1998. Patent: patentability-enablement: Genentech, Inc. v. Novo Nordisk & University of California v. Eli Lilly and Co. *Berkeley Technology Law Journal* 13, no. 1, 149–161.

Pratt, M. L. 1992. *Imperial eyes: Travel writing and transculturation*. London: Routledge.

Rabinow, P. 1996. *Essays on the anthropology of reason*. Princeton: Princeton University Press.

Rand, R., ed. 1992. *Logomachia: The conflict of the faculties*. Lincoln: University of Nebraska Press.

Readings, W. 1996. *The university in ruins*. Cambridge, MA: : Harvard University Press.

Reagan, R. 1967. Higher education: Its role in contemporary America. Lecture, Kansas State University. *Chronicle of Higher Education* (Nov. 8), A12.

Reich, C. 1964/1978. The new property. In C. MacPherson, ed., *Property: Mainstream and critical positions*. Toronto: University of Toronto Press, 1978.

Reichman, J. H. 1989. Computer programs as applied scientific knowhow: Implications of copyright protection for commercialized university research. *Vanderbilt Law Review* 42, 639–723.

Reuben, J. 1996. *The making of the modern university: Intellectual transformations and the marginalization of morality.* Chicago: University of Chicago Press.

Reynolds, T., ed. 1991. *The engineer in America: A historical anthology from technology and culture.* Chicago: University of Chicago Press.

Ridder-Symoens, H. 1996. *A history of the university in Europe,* vol. 2: *Universities in modern Europe.* Cambridge: Cambridge University Press.

Ridge, P. 2000. Background report on trends in industry and finance. *Wall Street Journal* (Oct. 19), A1.

Roark, A. 1979. Senate bill would give universities limited patent rights. *Chronicle of Higher Education* (March 5), 11.

Rorty, R. 1996. Does academic freedom have philosophical presuppositions? In Menand, ed., 1996.

Rose, C. 1994. *Property and persuasion: Essays on the history, theory and rhetoric of ownership.* Boulder: Westview.

Rose, M. 1993. *Authors and owners: The invention of copyright.* Cambridge, MA: Harvard University Press.

Rosenblatt, R. 1993. Government denounces Scripps-Sandoz deal. *Los Angeles Times* (June 18), D2.

Ross, M. 1994. Authority and authenticity: Scribbling authors and the genius of print in eighteenth century England. In Woodmansee and Jaszi, eds., 1994.

Rothblatt, S. 1993. The limbs of Osiris: Liberal education in the English-speaking world. In Rothblatt and Wittrock, eds., 1993.

—— 1985. The notion of a scientific community in historical perspective. In Gibbons and Wittrock, eds., 1985.

Rothblatt, S., and Wittrock, B., eds. 1993. *The European and American university since 1800: Historical and sociological essays.* Cambridge: Cambridge University Press.

Rotstein, R. 1993. Beyond metaphor: Copyright infringement and the fiction of the work. *Chicago-Kent Law Review* 68, 725–804.

Rudy, W. 1984. *The universities of Europe, 1100–1914.* London: Associated University Presses.

Sakaiya, T. 1991. *The knowledge revolution, or, a history of the future.* Trans. G. Fields and W. Marsh. New York: Kodansha International.

Salomon, J.-J. 1985. Science as a commodity: Policy changes, issues, threats. In Gibbons and Wittrock, eds., 1985.

Sanders, A. 2000. URlazy.com. *Forbes* (May 15), 338.

Saxenian, A. 1994. *Regional advantage: Culture and competition in Silicon Valley and Route 128.* Cambridge, MA: Harvard University Press.

Scarry, E. 1988. *The body in pain: The making and unmaking of the world.* New York: Oxford University Press.

Schevitz, T. 1999. UC tries to halt online class notes. *San Francisco Chronicle* (Oct. 2), A31.

Schiller, D. 1999. *Digital capitalism: Networking the global market system.* Cambridge, MA: MIT Press.

——— 1994. From culture to information and back again: Commoditization as a route to knowledge. *Critical Studies in Mass Communication* 4, no. 1, 93–115.

——— 1981. *Objectivity and the news: The public and the rise of commercial journalism.* Philadelphia: University of Pennsylvania Press.

Schmidt, P. 1998. Governors want fundamental changes in colleges, question place of tenure. *Chronicle of Higher Education* (June 19), A38.

Schmidt-Biggeman, W. 1996. New structures of knowledge. In Ridder-Symoens, ed., 1996.

Scott, J. W. 1996. Academic freedom as an ethical practice. In Menand, ed., 1996.

——— 1988. Deconstructing equality-versus-difference: Or, the uses of poststructuralist theory for Feminism. *Feminist Studies* 14, 33–50.

Scully, C. 1987. University autonomy. *Hastings Law Journal* 38, 927–955.

Shapin, S. 1996. *The scientific revolution.* Chicago: University of Chicago Press.

——— 1994. *A social history of truth: Civility and science in seventeenth century England.* Chicago: University of Chicago Press.

Shapiro, D., Wenger, N., and Shapiro, M. 1994. The contributions of authors to multiauthored biomedical research papers. *Journal of the American Medical Association* 271, no. 6, 438–442.

Shils, E. 1989. The modern university and liberal democracy. *Minerva* 27, no. 4, 425–460.

Shulman, S. 1999. *Owning the future.* Boston: Houghton Mifflin.

Simon, T. 1982. Faculty writings: Are they "works made for hire" under the 1976 Copyright Act? *Journal of College and University Law* 9, 485–513.

Siskind, L. 1998. The holy land comes of age. *Intellectual Property Magazine* (June). Retrieved Oct. 1998 from www.ipmag.com/98-jun/siskind.html

Slaughter, S. 1980. The "danger zone": Academic freedom and civil liberties. In P. Altbach and S. Slaughter, eds., *The academic profession.* Philadelphia: Annals of the American Academy of Political and Social Science.

Slaughter, S., and Leslie, L. 1997. *Academic capitalism: Politics, policies, and the entrepreneurial university.* Baltimore: Johns Hopkins University Press.

Smith, A. 1978. *Lectures on jurisprudence.* Ed. R. L. Meek, D. D. Raphael, and P. G. Stein. New York: Oxford University Press.

Sokal, A. 1996. A physicist experiments with cultural studies. *Lingua Franca* (May/June), 62–64.

Spector, B. 1994. Unusual settlement caps sex-discrimination case. *Scientist* (April 18), 1.

Stadtman, V. 1970. *The University of California, 1868–1968.* New York: McGraw-Hill.

Star, S. L., and Griesemer, J. R. 1989. Institutional ecology, "translations," and boundary objects: Amateurs and professionals in Berkeley's Museum of Vertebrate Technology, 1907–39. *Social Studies of Science* 19, 387–420.

Stearns, L. 1992. Copy wrongs: Plagiarism, process, property, and the law. *California Law Review* 80, 513–553.

Stevens, A. 1997. *Ownership and retention of data.* Washington: National Association of College and University Attorneys Publication Series.

Stone, L., ed., 1974. *The university in society,* vol. 2. Princeton: Princeton University Press.

St. Onge, K. R. 1988. *The melancholy anatomy of plagiarism.* Boston: University Press of America.

Strathern, M. 1997. Multiple perspectives in intellectual property. *Intellectual, biological and cultural property rights.* Port Moresby, Papua New Guinea, Aug.

———— 1996. Potential property: Intellectual rights and property in persons. *Social Anthropology* 4, no. 1, 17–32.

Streeter, T. 1994. Broadcast copyright and the bureaucratization of property. In Woodmansee and Jaszi, eds., 1994.

———— 1996. *Selling the air: A critique of the policy of commercial broadcasting in the United States.* Chicago: University of Chicago Press.

Sutz, J. 1997. The new role of the university in the productive sector. In Etzkowitz and Leydesdorff, eds., 1997.

Swan, J. 1994. Touching words: Helen Keller, plagiarism, authorship. In Woodmansee and Jaszi, eds., 1994.

Tarnow, E. 1999. The authorship list in science: Junior physicists' perceptions of who appears and why. *Science and Engineering Ethics* 5, no. 1, 73–88.

Thomas, J. 1998. Of text, technique, and the tangible: Drafting patent claims around patent rules. *John Marshall Journal of Computer and Information Law* 17, 219–276.

Thompson, E. P. 1975. *Whigs and hunters: The origin of the Black act.* New York: Pantheon.

Torstendahl, R. 1993. The transformation of professional education in the nineteenth century. In Rothblatt and Wittrock, eds., 1993.

Traweek, S. 1996. When Eliza Doolittle meets 'enry 'iggins. In Aronowitz et al., eds., 1996.

Treichler, P. 1990. Feminism, medicine and the meaning of childbirth. In M. Jacobus, E. Fox Keller, and S. Shuttleworth, eds., *Body/politics: Women and the discourses of science.* New York: Routledge.

Tresansky, J. 1974. Inventorship determination. *Journal of the Patent Office Society* 56, 551–573.

Turpin, T., and Garrett-Jones, S. 1997. Innovation networks in Australia and China. In Etzkowitz and Leydesdorff, eds., 1997.

U.S. Congress, Senate Committee on the Judiciary. 1979. *The university and small business patent procedures act: Hearings before the Committee on the Judiciary, United*

States Senate, 96th Cong., 1st sess., on S. 414 . . . May 16, and June 6. Washington: U.S. GPO.

Veblen, T. 1918/1965. *The higher learning in America: A memorandum on the conduct of universities by businessmen.* New York: A. M. Keller.

Veysey, L. 1965. *The emergence of the American university.* Chicago: University of Chicago Press.

Wagner, A. 1998. Patenting computer science: Are computer instruction writings patentable? *John Marshall Journal of Computer and Information Law* 17 (Fall), 5–40.

Waldron, J. 1993. From authors to copiers: Individual rights and social values in intellectual property. *Chicago-Kent Law Review* 68, 841–887.

Walshok, M. 1995. *Knowledge without boundaries: What America's research universities can do for the economy, the workplace, and the community.* Foreword Daniel Yankelovich. San Francisco: Jossey-Bass.

Warren, S., and Brandeis, L. 1890. The right to privacy. *Harvard Law Review* 4, 193–220.

Weber, M. 1946/1966. Class, status and party. In R. Bendix and S. Lipset, eds., *Class, status and power,* New York: Macmillan.

———— 1919/1974. Science as a vocation. In E. Shils, ed., *Max Weber on universities.* Chicago: University of Chicago Press.

———— 1908/1974. The alleged "academic freedom" of the German universities. In Shils, ed., *Max Weber on universities.*

Webster, A., and Packer, K. 1997. When worlds collide: Patents in public sector research. In Etzkowitz and Leydesdorff, eds., 1997.

———— 1996. *Innovation and the intellectual property system.* London: Kluwer Law International.

Weiss, K. 1998. A wary academia on the edge of cyberspace. *Los Angeles Times* (March 31), A1.

West, R. 1991. Disciplines, subjectivity and law. In A. Sarat and T. R. Kearns, eds., *The fate of law.* Ann Arbor: University of Michigan Press.

Wiener, N. 1993. *Invention: The care and feeding of ideas.* Cambridge, MA: MIT Press.

Wilson, R. 1998. Provosts push radical plan to change the way research is evaluated. *Chronicle of Higher Education* (June 26), A12.

Wittrock, B. 1993. The modern university: The three transformations. In Rothblatt and Wittrock, eds., 1993.

Wolin, S. 1981. Theme note. *Democracy* 1, no. 1, 6–8.

———— 1978. *Politics and vision.* London: Allen and Unwin.

Wolin, S., and Schaar, J. 1970. *The Berkeley rebellion and beyond.* New York: New York Review.

———— 1965. The abuses of the multiversity. In Lipset and Wolin, eds., 1965.

Woodmansee, M. 1994a. *The author, art and the market: Rereading the history of aesthetics.* New York: Columbia University Press.

——— 1994b. On the author effect: Recovering collectivity. In Woodmansee and Jaszi, eds., 1994.

Woodmansee, M., and Jaszi, P., eds. 1994. *The construction of authorship: Textual appropriation in law and literature.* Durham: Duke University Press.

Work Group on Commercialization of Lecture Materials. 1995. Commercialization of University of California lecture materials: An interim report to President Peltason. (memorandum).

Young, R. 1992. The idea of a chrestomathic university. In Rand, ed., 1992.

Young, T. 1999. University relations with the electronics and telecommunications industries: IP rights in contract research. Association of University Technology Managers Annual Meeting, San Diego.

ACKNOWLEDGMENTS

I incurred many debts in the completion of this work, and I am pleased to acknowledge them here. Heartfelt thanks first of all to the researchers, students, staff members, technology transfer associates, and attorneys who invested in this work that most precious form of academic capital, time. I am equally indebted to Valerie Hartouni and Robert Horwitz, who sparked my interest in property stories and asked critical questions that forced me to clarify my own narratives. Special thanks also to Mark Rose, whose advice and encouragement at crucial moments kept me inspired to complete the work. Chandra Mukerji and the Critical Studies Writing Group at the University of California, San Diego, taught me about science and science studies and helped me work out my methodology. The comments of Mario Biagioli, Peter Galison, Harry Hirsch, Dan Schiller, and the anonymous readers for Harvard University Press on drafts of the work much improved its final incarnation. The remaining faults are my own responsibility. Finally, thanks to Lindsay Waters of Harvard University Press for his support and enthusiasm. All of these people give me reason to believe that there is a vibrant and engaging culture in the ruins of the university.

I owe many debts as well to family and friends near and far. The support and patience of Terence McSherry, Dolores DeFrancesco, Lisa McSherry, and Christopher Breyer have sustained me throughout the preparation of this work. Nic Sammond, Suzanne Thomas, Maribel Castañeda Paredes, Anthony Freitas, and Tamara Falicov were loyal and inspiring fellow travelers. Kelly Coyne, Amy Greenstadt, Erik Knutzen, Yvette MacDonald, Serena Rivera, and Phillip Suh pulled me away from my desk and kept me well acquainted with the twin sisters of irony and ambiguity.

Kathleen McGill taught me most of what I know about rhetoric. She read and commented on several chapters, and lent me her ears, her books, and her dog when I most needed them. It's on the tab.

And then there is Mr. Kelly, without whom this work truly would not have been written. For listening to and critiquing tentative ideas, for editorial commentary, for knowing the place of science and of business, and for general care and feeding, my deepest thanks.